DATE DUE

SIX ARMIES IN TENNESSEE

GREAT CAMPAIGNS OF THE CIVIL WAR

SERIES EDITORS

Anne J. Bailey
Georgia College &
State University

Brooks D. Simpson
Arizona State University

STEVEN E. WOODWORTH

Six Armies in Tennessee

The Chickamauga and Chattanooga Campaigns

University of Nebraska Press
Lincoln and London

1998 by
the University of
Nebraska Press
All rights reserved
Manufactured in the
United States of America
⊗ The paper in this book
meets the minimum requirements
of American National Standard
for Information Sciences—
Permanence of Paper for
Printed Library Materials,
ANSI Z39.48-1984.
Library of Congress
Cataloging-in-Publication Data
Woodworth, Steven E.
Six armies in Tennessee : the Chickamauga
and Chattanooga campaigns / Steven E. Woodworth.
p.   cm.—(Great campaigns of the Civil War)
Includes bibliographical references (p.   ) and index.
ISBN 0-8032-4778-8 (cloth : alk. paper)
1. Tennessee–History–Civil War,
1861-1865–Campaigns.
2. Chickamauga (Ga.), Battle of, 1863.
3. Chattanooga (Tenn.), Battle of, 1863.
4. United States–History–Civil War,
1861-1865–Campaigns.   I. Title.   II. Series.
E470.4.W66   1998
973.7′359–dc21
97-29435
CIP

For Nathan,
firstborn son
and companion on battlefield explorations
from Hoover's Gap to Horseshoe Ridge

To God alone be the glory

Contents

Illustrations

Maps

Series Editors' Introduction

Americans remain fascinated by the Civil War. Movies, television, and video—even computer software—have augmented the ever-expanding list of books on the war. Although it stands to reason that a large portion of recent work concentrates on military aspects of the conflict, historians have expanded our scope of inquiry to include civilians, especially women; the destruction of slavery and the evolving understanding of what freedom meant to millions of former slaves; and an even greater emphasis on the experiences of the common soldier on both sides. Other studies have demonstrated the interrelationships of war, politics, and policy and how civilians' concerns back home influenced both soldiers and politicians. Although one cannot fully comprehend this central event in American history without understanding that military operations were fundamental in determining the course and outcome of the war, it is time for students of battles and campaigns to incorporate nonmilitary themes in their accounts. The most pressing challenge facing Civil War scholarship today is the integration of various perspectives and emphases into a new narrative that explains not only what happened, why, and how, but also why it mattered.

The series Great Campaigns of the Civil War offers readers concise syntheses of the major campaigns of the war, reflecting the findings of recent scholarship. The series points to new ways of viewing military campaigns by looking beyond the battlefield and the headquarters tent to the wider political and social context within which these campaigns unfolded; it also shows how campaigns and battles left their imprint on many Americans, from presidents and generals down to privates and civilians. The ends and means of waging war reflect larger political objectives and priorities as well as social values. Historians may continue to debate among themselves as to which of these campaigns constituted true turning points, but each of the campaigns treated in this series contributed to shaping the course of the conflict, opening opportunities, and eliminating alternatives.

Steven E. Woodworth's inaugural volume in the series offers a fresh, perceptive overview of military operations in Middle and Eastern Tennessee during the summer and fall of 1863. These operations culminated in the battle of Chattanooga in November, but rather than treat each battle separately, Woodworth discusses the Tullahoma and Knoxville campaigns as integral parts of the larger Chickamauga and Chattanooga campaigns. He looks at how political pressures in both Washington and Richmond influenced military decisions in the Western Theater. He shows how subsequent events affected the outcome of the fighting in Tennessee and how these battles influenced the larger course of the war. Although numerous books cover one or more of these battles and campaigns, no other single volume brings them together and analyzes them as a whole. Woodworth gives us a unified synthesis that draws on the full body of existing secondary literature but also tests accepted conclusions against pertinent primary sources. He focuses on features that bear most significantly on the world beyond the battlefield and also examines how personalities helped to determine military results. His work is destined to set the standard for future research on the Western Theater in late 1863.

Preface

The series of campaigns that resulted in Union forces extinguishing the Confederacy's control of its remaining portions of Tennessee in the last half of 1863 are both important and fascinating. The struggle for Tennessee greatly influenced the outcome of the war. Coming on top of the better-known victories at Gettysburg and Vicksburg, the Union's successful culmination of these operations left the Confederacy in desperate condition and set the stage for the final Northern drive toward victory in 1864 and 1865. The conquest/liberation of Middle and East Tennessee raised Union morale, lowered Confederate morale, and cost the Confederacy thousands of fighting men it could not afford to lose, as well as thousands of square miles of productive territory. It established Federal control of Chattanooga, a key transportation nexus and the gateway of the southern Appalachians, and exposed the Deep South to Union invasion. The road to Atlanta—and to Durham Station—began at Chattanooga.

Another measure of the campaigns' importance, and an ingredient in their fascination, is the amount each side was willing to invest in the struggle. In hopes of reversing a year and a half of defeat in the West, Confederate president Jefferson Davis detached two divisions of Robert E. Lee's hitherto all but sacrosanct Army of Northern Virginia and sent them to the aid of Braxton Bragg's hard-pressed Army of Tennessee. With those two divisions went one of the Army of Northern Virginia's most renowned generals, Lee's "Old War Horse," Lt. Gen. James Longstreet. The Union already had two armies in the western theater of operations, the Army of the Cumberland, second largest of the republic's armies, and the smaller Army of the Ohio, advancing into East Tennessee. The Union responded to the Confederate moves to raise the stakes in Tennessee by sending substantial elements of its other two major armies. From Mississippi came the victors of Vicksburg, the tough, irrepressible veterans of the Army of the Tennessee (not to be confused with the Confederate Army of Tennessee), and from Virginia came two corps of the Army of the Potomac, veterans of Gettysburg and many another eastern battlefield. To command this gathering of armies, the North had some of the finest generals of the war, as well as others of moderate talent. George H. Thomas replaced the stunned and defeated William S. Rosecrans in command of the Army of the Cumberland. William T. Sherman commanded the Army of the Tennessee. Joseph Hooker, who had once commanded the entire Army of the Potomac against Lee, now led the two-corps contingent that came west. True, another former Army of the Potomac commander, the unfortunate Ambrose Burnside, commanded the Army of the Ohio, but most important, the overall command of the four Union armies in Tennessee would be in the hands of the North's foremost general, Ulysses S. Grant.

The contest that was eventually to draw six armies to Tennessee was played out over a vast area of rugged and mountainous terrain. It involved use of railroads on a scale hitherto unknown to warfare. It featured complicated maneuvering and furious fighting and saw the introduction of new techniques and the continued use of some old ones. It made and broke the reputations of generals and helped set the course for the remainder of the Civil War.

An event this important and with so many elements of interest has of course not been ignored by historians. The two major battles, Chickamauga and Chattanooga, have each drawn several books (though the Tullahoma and Knoxville campaigns have not). The struggle for Tennessee also figures prominently in the biographies of some of the Civil War's most important participants and in other works ranging from Thomas L. Connelly's two-volume history of the Army of Tennessee to Edward Carr Franks's excellent groundbreaking article on the significance of Longstreet's November 1863 transfer to East Tennessee.[1] Even the dramatic rail transfer of the Army of the Potomac's XI and XII Corps is now the subject of a study of its own, an excellent forthcoming book by Roger Pickenpaugh.

The purpose of this book is to provide a narrative synthesis of the entire campaign and a new and thoroughgoing analysis based both on the mountains of information that other historians have turned up and on the original sources. It may not present readers with any particular detail that could not be found somewhere in the voluminous and sometimes contradictory published literature pertaining to these events, but it should give them a better overall grasp of the broad sweep of the action in these momentous campaigns. It is not a bullet-by-bullet account of any battle. Very high quality works of that sort already exist and others are in progress. Rather, its goal is to sift and compare all the evidence for a large series of campaigns, analyze that evidence carefully, and present a coherent narrative so that the readers will come away with a better understanding of the events and their significance. That should make them better able to understand why history took the course it did.

Acknowledgments

It is a pleasure to extend grateful recognition to those who have aided in the preparation of this book. Dana Camp provided useful resources from his personal library. Eugene Youngblood recovered large segments of text from the hard drive of a computer toasted by a lightning-induced power surge. Dorothy Kelly of the Knoxville Civil War Round Table took me on a guided tour of Knoxville's battlefields, which was more helpful to me than she probably realizes. Jim Ogden, of Chickamauga National Military Park, took me on a very informative tour of that battlefield.

The editors of this series, Anne J. Bailey and Brooks D. Simpson, have been helpful in giving direction and refining the concept and scope of the book and have given useful feedback on the text. Edward Carr Franks and Philip L. Shiman also read and commented on the manuscript. They all have helped greatly to improve the book, though naturally they can hardly be held responsible for any errors it may contain.

Last and greatest, I could not forbear to mention once again my loyal and supportive wife, Leah, who helps and facilitates my work in more ways than I could count.

SIX ARMIES IN TENNESSEE

CHAPTER ONE

The Army Begins to Move

Gray-clad pickets gazed northward through the dim early morning light, made dimmer by the overcast that had come up the night before and the steady drizzle that had started just after dawn. It was June 24, 1863. The sun rose early these midsummer days, and behind the sentries' right shoulders it was already well up, visible now only as a lighter patch in the overcast sky. Below it, the hills of the Highland Rim loomed faintly and intermittently through the shifting curtain of rain, making a lumpy horizon of darker gray against the pale gray sky behind the Southern soldiers' backs. In front of them the cedar-dotted Middle Tennessee landscape rolled gently northwestward, hill and dale, into an indefinite murk toward which these Confederates, men of the First Kentucky Cavalry, strained their eyes. As the foremost outposts of Braxton Bragg's Army of Tennessee, their business was to see and to report what they saw.

One of the Kentuckians must have made out moving shapes emerging from the mist, a vague line of figures a couple of hundred yards off and more or less evenly spaced. He would have recognized them almost immediately as Federal skirmishers. Moments later the cavalrymen were peering over the sights of their carbines and squeezing off the first shots of what was to become a five-month struggle for control of half the state of Tennessee and the momentum of the war. Several hundred yards away, men of the Seventy-second Indiana Mounted Infantry raised their Spencer Repeating Rifles and hammered back half a dozen shots for every one of the Rebels'. The Kentuckians were soon mounting up and galloping back toward their prepared position in the hills, with the Hoosiers—and a full army corps of their comrades—in hot pursuit. The Kentucky cavalrymen would be the first to carry the news to the rest of Bragg's army that William S. Rosecrans's

Federal Army of the Cumberland was finally moving out from its base at Murfreesboro.[1]

If Bragg and his men had waited with apprehension for this day, others had waited with considerably more eagerness and less patience. During the six months since the armies last clashed in Middle Tennessee, the Federal authorities in Washington, President Abraham Lincoln, Secretary of War Edwin M. Stanton, and General in Chief Henry W. Halleck, had chafed at the inactivity of Union forces in Tennessee, but Rosecrans was not to be hurried.

William Starke Rosecrans was a forty-three-year-old Ohioan who had graduated fifth in the fifty-six-man West Point class of 1842. That brilliant record earned him a place in the elite Corps of Engineers, but his subsequent army career had been disappointing. He missed service in the Mexican War and by 1854 had only just made first lieutenant. Like many a bright officer in that decade, he resigned his commission and turned to civilian pursuits. The outbreak of the Civil War found him in Cincinnati, trying to make a go of a kerosene refining business. The country needed trained soldiers in the spring of 1861, and Rosecrans was soon back in uniform and on the fast track to high rank, first under George B. McClellan in the area that was to become West Virginia and later under West Point classmate Ulysses S. Grant in Mississippi. There, on October 3 and 4, 1862, he experienced his greatest success up to that point, commanding the garrison of Corinth, Mississippi, when it repulsed a determined assault by a small Confederate army under Earl Van Dorn.

Rosecrans came into the limelight at an opportune moment, for the authorities in Washington were just then thoroughly disgusted with Maj. Gen. Don Carlos Buell, who with his Army of the Ohio had, in the campaign then coming to a close, performed so feebly as to allow a Confederate army under Braxton Bragg to go all the way to central Kentucky and then back to Tennessee more or less unscathed. Buell's situation had been difficult. The nature of the war had been changing even as he endeavored to wage it by the old rules, but from Washington he had appeared sadly lacking both in enterprise and in aggressiveness. So before the month was out, Buell was packed off into retirement, and Rosecrans had command of his army, now christened the Army of the Cumberland and operating with Nashville as its base.[2]

Lincoln wanted fighting, and he soon got it from his new army commander. Two months later, having heard that Confederate president Jefferson Davis had weakened Bragg to reinforce Confederate troops in Mississippi, Rosecrans advanced against the Southern army at Murfreesboro, some thirty-five miles to the southeast. There, however, at the battle of Stones River, Bragg had introduced himself to the new Federal army commander, seizing the initiative, overrunning a good bit of the Army of the Cumberland, and coming within a whisker of sending Rosecrans back to Nashville in disgrace. Several factors combined to make it otherwise. For one thing, Bragg had problems of his own because all was not well in the high command of the Rebel army. For another, Rosecrans rose to the occasion, fearlessly riding his lines under deadly fire, even after his chief of staff and close personal friend Maj. Julius Garesché was decapitated by a cannonball only a few feet away, splattering Rosecrans with gore. The commanding general's inspiring leadership steadied the troops in the face of the Confederate attacks.[3]

A third reason for Federal victory at the battle of Stones River was the presence of Maj. Gen. George H. Thomas, Rosecrans's top lieutenant. Three years older than Rosecrans and two years ahead of him at West Point, Thomas was a Union-loyal Virginian who had served with distinction in every battle of what was now the Army of the Cumberland. Indeed, he could have had the command of it that fall when Bragg was moving north and Washington was disgusted with Buell, but he had declined to avoid a change of commanders in the midst of a campaign. When the campaign was over, for whatever reason, the command went to Rosecrans instead. At Stones River, Thomas was a tower of strength. His crucial section of the line held firm and became the key to stopping the Confederate assault. His sturdy influence steadied Rosecrans through the ordeal. After Stones River, his continued presence in the army, commanding the XIV Corps, was one of its greatest strengths.[4]

Rosecrans had prevailed at Stones River simply by avoiding defeat and thus had received the accolades of victory for what was really a very indecisive battle. The praise Rosecrans received had as much to do with politics as it did with anything that happened on the fields outside of Murfreesboro. Lincoln needed a victory. Less than three weeks before the armies met on the banks of Stones River, Maj. Gen. Ambrose Burnside had led the Army of the Potomac to one of the war's most humiliating and lopsided defeats at Fredericksburg. Lincoln had just given Burnside command in place of McClellan, who, like Buell, had shown a reluctance to advance. That Burnside had now advanced and butchered his army was not exactly a recommendation of Lincoln's policy. The Congressional Committee on the Conduct of the War redoubled its carping, the cabinet was bitterly divided, and the generals—and perhaps the soldiers—of the Army of the Potomac were in a well-nigh mutinous humor. The president had remarked grimly, "If there is a worse place than hell, I am in it."

Then, less than a week before Stones River, Grant's campaign against Vicksburg had come to grief when Confederate cavalry under Earl Van Dorn cut his supply lines, forcing the retreat of his overland expedition and leaving his river-based drive under William T. Sherman to suffer at Chickasaw Bayou a small-scale repetition of the slaughter of Fredericksburg. Union morale needed a victory, and in the absence of evidence to the contrary, Stones River would do well enough. Months later Lincoln wrote to Rosecrans, "I can never forget, whilst I remember anything, that about the end of last year, and beginning of this, you gave us a hard-earned victory which, had there been a defeat instead, the nation could scarcely have lived over."[5]

And so Rosecrans, for a time, was in very good favor with the authorities at Washington, and Stanton wrote him, "There is nothing within my power to grant to yourself or your heroic command that will not be cheerfully given." Whether because of this extravagant assurance or the shock of his hairbreadth escape from disaster at Stones River or what he had seen of the face of battle there, Rosecrans soon made it clear that he and his command would need a great deal more of everything before they were ready for another such encounter. He would have to move through rough country and would need plenty of scouting. Then, too, he would have long supply lines to guard. That meant he needed more cavalry—and more horses and carbines to mount and equip them. Also, he might have to maneuver a good distance from the railroad and perhaps be out of touch with it for some time. That meant he would need to accumulate mountains of supplies, which would require many more wagons to haul them and, in turn, would require still more horses and mules. Nor was that all. As weeks passed, Rosecrans's list of needs grew to include all manner of supplies, equipment, and reinforcements. Remarkably, the demands were generally met, but as fast as they were, Rosecrans drew attention to additional wants. His plaintive requests went on at such length and with such frequency that Halleck was moved to remonstrate with him at "the enormous expense to the Government of your telegrams; more than that of all the other generals in the field."[6]

Such demands would have gone far, all by themselves, toward wearing out Rosecrans's popularity in the capital, but they were the least of his problems with the Lincoln administration. For nearly a year, Lincoln had been trying to get his generals to implement his strategy of applying constant, relentless pressure on the Confederacy on all fronts at once. His problem had been finding generals who would do so. The only one that had surfaced thus far—and the one who would eventually apply that strategy to achieving Union victory—was Grant. Buell had been among the worst offenders as a general seemingly wedded to the old, scientific, methodical school of warfare in which campaigns were merely giant equations to be solved in the most mathematically arcane manner possible. What Lincoln wanted—and Stanton and Halleck wanted on his behalf—was the kind of hard-driving, pit-bull style of warfare that Grant later characterized with the prescription: "Get at the enemy as quick as you can. Hit him as hard as you can; and keep moving on."[7]

The trouble with Rosecrans, as far as Lincoln was concerned, was that he was not Grant. As weeks stretched into months after the battle of Stones River and Rosecrans made no offensive movement, the Washington authorities became increasingly impatient. Halleck and Stanton tried bluster and blandishment and even old-fashioned nagging but could get no results. Rosecrans responded with excuses and requests for more of everything. On March 1 Halleck telegraphed, "There is a vacant major generalcy in the Regular Army, and I am authorized to say that it will be given to the general in the field who first wins an important and decisive victory." Rosecrans professed to "feel degraded" at the idea of "such an auctioneering of honor." He made it clear that he was far above the quest for battlefield promotion. He was not, however, above requesting of Stanton, presumably pursuant to the secretary's promise to grant anything in his power, that his (Rosecrans's) commission as a major general of volunteers be backdated so that he could outrank Grant. Lincoln himself responded, and though his language was, as always, gentle and soothing, his point was that the matter of relative rank between two generals in different departments was irrelevant, and would Rosecrans please get on with the war?[8]

He would not—at least not for a considerable length of time—though his dispatches occasionally held out hope that the long-sought culmination might be in sight. As spring came and with it the opening of crucial campaigns in both Mississippi and Virginia, Rosecrans's inactivity became still more irksome and the urgings from Washington more insistent though equally futile. When Grant successfully penned John C. Pemberton's Confederate army into the fortifications of Vicksburg, Bragg was able to detach ten thousand infantry to what the Richmond government hoped would be a relieving force under Joseph E. Johnston. Word of the move got back to

Washington, but when Halleck taxed Rosecrans with this obvious ill effect of his idleness, the Army of the Cumberland's commander coolly replied that in fact his delay was good strategy. If he attacked Bragg, he might drive him to join Johnston with his whole army and thus defeat Grant. Besides, since Union armies were engaged in mighty struggles in Mississippi and Virginia, strategy dictated that Rosecrans's army, as the republic's last reserve, await the outcomes of those campaigns.[9]

And so Rosecrans planned and prepared and accumulated the stuff of war, and Lincoln may well have reflected that whereas he had appointed Rosecrans in October 1862 in hopes of finding someone who would make war the way Grant was even now doing, he had in fact gotten merely a better Buell.

If Lincoln had his command problems that spring, so did the Confederates. Facing Rosecrans's Army of the Cumberland was the Confederate Army of Tennessee. Its commander was Braxton Bragg. A forty-six-year-old native of Warrenton, North Carolina, Bragg was a member of the West Point class of 1837, in which he had ranked fifth. He had gone to war in Mexico nine years later as a captain commanding a battery of artillery and at Buena Vista had won nationwide fame when his guns stopped a crucial Mexican attack. His performance had been comparable to the best of those of the many Mexican War junior officers who were destined for larger responsibility in the Civil War. During the 1850s Bragg followed the example of many brother officers and left the army for civilian employment. He married a Louisiana heiress and settled down to take up the life of a planter.[10]

The Civil War brought him back into uniform, this time a gray one. His first post was Pensacola, Florida, during the days when it appeared that the war might begin there instead of at Charleston, South Carolina. He had demonstrated himself a skillful organizer and rigorous trainer. When things went sour for the Confederacy in Tennessee in February 1862, the South could no longer afford to keep able commanders and large garrisons in such places as Pensacola. Bragg was brought to Corinth, Mississippi, to join the army with which Albert Sidney Johnston hoped to turn the tide in the West. Johnston made his bid at Shiloh, and there he died. In that battle Bragg gained further favorable notice, and though his tactics were not especially creative, they were no worse than anyone else's. Within a few months Bragg found himself promoted to full general and elevated to command of the main Confederate army in the West in place of P. G. T. Beauregard, Johnston's successor, who left the army because of sickness. Bragg began his tenure auspiciously, taking advantage of the scientific, methodical, and uninspired campaigning of Federal generals Halleck and Buell to swing his army all the way into Kentucky, threatening Louisville and Cincinnati, affording Kentuckians the opportunity to rally to the Confederate standard, and seemingly reversing the course of the war in the West. Then everything seemed to go wrong. Kirby Smith, an independent commander whom Jefferson Davis had declined to place under Bragg's authority, failed to cooperate with Bragg and thus hamstrung the campaign. Leonidas Polk, a subordinate general who actually was under Bragg's authority, refused to carry out a key order and thus further deranged Bragg's plans.[11]

Polk was an 1827 West Point graduate who had resigned without ever serving as an officer so as to enter the Episcopal priesthood, in which career he had since risen to bishop. In all those years he had not read so much as a single book on military affairs but nevertheless considered himself a competent general and expert on sundry matters. He might have served out the war in his Louisiana diocese as a likable if eccentric bishop who was a bit of a crank on military matters. He did not because he was ambitious, persuasive, and had an old West Point crony named Jefferson Davis. The Confederate president had appointed Polk major general direct from civilian life. Polk's headstrong incompetence had already cost the Confederacy, and before the Kentucky campaign, Bragg had hinted that the bishop-general needed to go. Davis refused. Bragg, unlike Lee, would not be allowed to assemble his own team of lieutenants but would have to work with whomever Davis felt inclined—or politically obliged—to assign him.[12]

Worse than Polk's disobedience—for the outcome of the Kentucky campaign—was the decision of the Kentuckians themselves. Although the exploits of such colorful Confederate cavalry raiders as John Hunt Morgan might excite much admiration in some quarters, the state's populace was predominantly Unionist. Those who did lean toward the Confederacy and were not already in the gray and butternut ranks were reluctant to take their stand until they could see with more certainty which way the wind was blowing. Recruits were few, and Bragg was left with a large consignment of extra weapons, brought to arm men who had not chosen to join the colors. That so few joined Bragg was significant because the entire campaign was based on the premise that large numbers of Kentuckians would rise to help rid their state of Union troops. That was the expectation held out to Bragg by Morgan and other Kentucky officers in the Confederate army, but it was now demonstrated to have been wishful thinking. Bragg recognized as much, and the Kentucky officers—men such as John C. Breckinridge, Simon B. Buckner, and William Preston—never forgave him for it. Despite a

limited tactical success at Perryville, Kentucky, the campaign offered insufficient prospects of long-term success, and so Bragg took his army back to
Tennessee.[13]

If the events of October 1862 marked the end for Buell in Kentucky, they
were merely the beginning of sorrows for Bragg and the Army of Tennessee.
All Southerners were disappointed at the failure of Bragg's fall offensive, as
well as those of Lee in Maryland and Van Dorn in Mississippi. The Kentuckians were bitter and directed their ire at Bragg. In doing so they were
joined by generals whose own roles in the campaign had been less than sterling successes, notably Kirby Smith and Polk. The latter, who was second in
rank to Bragg in what was now coming to be called the Army of Tennessee
and who both resented Bragg's authority and coveted his position, began to
use his ingratiating manners and winning ways to turn the army's other officers against Bragg.[14]

One of Polk's first converts was his fellow corps commander William J.
Hardee. Hardee had a distinguished "Old Army" career behind him, including service in the Mexican War and a stint as commandant of cadets at
West Point. He was also the author of the U.S. Army's standard tactics man-
ual. These qualifications gave him considerable respect and influence with
the junior officers of his corps, for whom he held regular classes of instruc-
tion. Henceforth those classes would subtly be aimed at demonstrating the
incompetence of their commanding general.[15]

Others despised Bragg as well. Though a prewar enemy of Jefferson
Davis when the latter was secretary of war and Bragg an army officer, Bragg
had nevertheless by this time come to be viewed as a Davis protégé. It was
a dubious distinction, for with it came the enmity of all Davis's foes in politics and the press. Of even more importance within the army was Bragg's
strict discipline. One abuse that Bragg was particularly keen on stamping
out was drunkenness among the officer corps. Hard-drinking generals like
B. Franklin Cheatham and John C. Breckinridge rankled under that re-
gimen. Others, such as John P. McCown, were incompetent and knew that
Bragg thought so. The result was a seething unrest among the officer corps
of the Army of Tennessee, a bitter concoction of hatred and mistrust that
poisoned the army's operations.

That dissatisfaction was an ingredient of Confederate failure at Stones
River. McCown blundered, and Breckinridge's performance was open to
question. Cheatham was apparently so drunk he fell off his horse, at least,
that was what one observer reported. In any case, he too turned in a miserable day's work, and on the whole, the army's command system was creaky

and stiff-jointed. Despite these miscues, Bragg nevertheless managed to handle Rosecrans about as roughly on the first day of the battle as Lee and Thomas J. "Stonewall" Jackson would handle Joe Hooker in winning the celebrated victory at Chancellorsville four months hence. The difference was that Hooker would retreat but Rosecrans first held his ground and then took up a position that gave him an advantage over Bragg. Outnumbered and likely to become more so, Bragg had to face the fact that a Civil War army was next to impossible to destroy, and thus the general who had the larger one could keep taking punishment about as long as his nerve lasted and his supply lines remained sound. At Stones River, that general was Rosecrans. So at the urging of his subordinate generals, Bragg reluctantly withdrew another thirty-five miles to the vicinity of Tullahoma.[16]

The bright hopes of victory that had blazed up with word of the first day's success now faded into the cold, dull realization of defeat, and many a Confederate was heartsick. Such bitterness sought a victim, and the natural one was Bragg, who now became the butt of twice as much denunciation as before. Polk, unbeknownst to Bragg, stepped up his lobbying with Davis to have Bragg removed. Also, among the many newspaper articles excoriating him, some had the sound of inside sources and claimed that Bragg had retreated from certain victory and against the advice of all his generals. Stung by the criticism, Bragg did something very foolish. He wrote a circular to his generals mentioning his apprehension that Richmond was about to sack him, asking them if they had advised him to retreat at Stones River, and adding, "I shall retire without regret if I find I have lost the good opinion of my generals, upon whom I have ever relied as upon a foundation of rock." Apparently Bragg had no idea how bad things had gotten in the army. Worse, six of his top supporters among the generals were then absent with wounds or on leave. The result was that most of the generals who replied admitted that they had counseled retreat but urged Bragg to resign anyway. Word of the exchange got back to Richmond, where Davis commented, "Why General Bragg should have selected that tribunal and have invited its judgments upon him, is to me unexplained." He then ordered Bragg's immediate superior, Confederate commander of the western theater Joseph E. Johnston, to go to Tullahoma and look into the matter. Johnston, by his mere presence, would be in immediate command of the army. Then Bragg could be eased out from under him.[17]

That was how Davis planned it, but as on many another occasion in the war, Jefferson Davis had not reckoned with the contrary nature of Joseph E. Johnston. For one thing, Johnston seems not to have read his copy of the script and thus sent back from Tullahoma a glowing report of the army's condition. True, some of the generals, particularly those who had performed poorly, were disgruntled, but morale in the ranks seemed as high as ever. Also, the army's discipline, training, and equipment were good. Thus, Johnston concluded, Bragg should remain. When Davis made himself more plain, Johnston insisted and added that if Bragg were removed, he, Johnston, would not take the job. After griping to all and sundry for several months about how much he hated his present supervisory role and wanted command of an individual army, Johnston was now embarrassed to take one lest it appear he had connived to get it.

The exasperated president now sent a direct order that Bragg be sent to Richmond. Johnston asked that a copy be sent to Bragg. It was, and Johnston asked that its execution be delayed so that Bragg could remain with his wife, then dangerously ill at nearby Winchester. By the time Elise Bragg was better, Johnston himself was too ill to command an army so Bragg could not be spared and the order had to be delayed still further. Before Johnston had fully recovered, disaster had struck in Mississippi in the form of Grant's spring campaign against Vicksburg. Since Mississippi was the other half of Johnston's supervisory command, Davis ordered him to go there and see what he could do. Johnston departed and played no further role in the struggle for Tennessee. By default, and without the confidence of either his top subordinates or his commander in chief, Bragg remained in command of the Army of Tennessee. To him would fall the task of stopping Rosecrans whenever that officer finally felt ready to advance.[18]

At stake in this struggle would be the very stage on which the conflict was to be fought, the eastern half of the state of Tennessee and adjacent parts of Alabama and Georgia. This area was bounded on the east by the long, slanting line of the Blue Ridge. Angling northeast to southwest, this towering rampart formed the eastern boundary of Tennessee and was a solid barrier to military operations and supply. Like the Blue Ridge, many of the other landforms of the region slanted northeast to southwest.

One such was the Great Valley of the Appalachians, which lay at the western foot of the Blue Ridge. In Tennessee, this broad natural trough holds the upper Tennessee River and, farther north, the Holston River, both flowing southwest. The valley, however, continues northward into Virginia, beyond the watershed of the Holston, to become the valley of the Shenandoah. Virginia and the Shenandoah Valley were offstage for this campaign but nevertheless very important. Northeastward up the Great Valley from Chattanooga some two hundred miles to Virginia—and then out onto the piedmont and

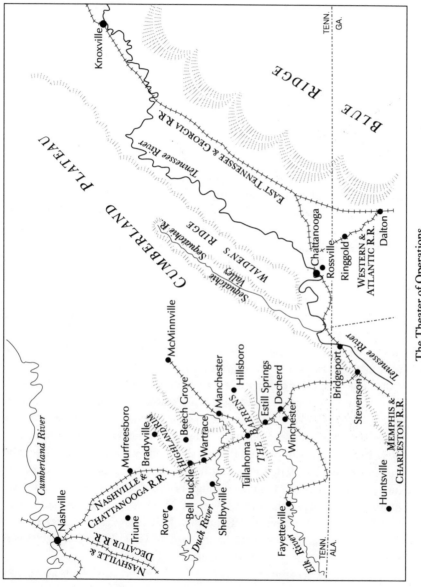

The Theater of Operations

all the way to Richmond—ran the Virginia & Tennessee Railroad, the most important east-west rail link in the Confederacy. About halfway between Chattanooga and the Virginia line on this railroad (and the Holston River) was the city of Knoxville, in the heart of the East Tennessee Unionist country that Lincoln had wanted to liberate for more than two years.

Looming over the Great Valley on the northwest runs the eastern rim of the Cumberland Plateau. Rising nine hundred to a thousand feet above the Tennessee Valley, the Cumberlands are a formidable barrier. Their top is a relatively level but rugged plateau twenty-five to thirty miles wide, and they parallel the Great Valley from Virginia into Alabama. Although the soil of the Great Valley is fairly fertile and supported a scattering of farms, the plateau is barren and offered next to nothing to a foraging army. In southern Tennessee, the Cumberland Plateau is cut into two narrower parallel plateaus by the Sequatchie Valley, a narrow rift that slashes lengthwise down the southern Cumberlands. This geological feature carries the Sequatchie River down to the Tennessee near the place where Georgia, Alabama, and Tennessee join. Thence the larger river itself lays claim to the cleft as it angles southwest into Alabama. The narrower plateau east of the Sequatchie Valley and north of the Tennessee River is called Walden's Ridge.

Chattanooga lies on the south bank of the Tennessee River at the foot of the Cumberlands near the southern boundary of Tennessee, where the river turns from southwest to west, leaves the Great Valley, and breaks halfway through the Cumberlands in a scenic, winding gorge before turning southwest again and flowing well down into Alabama to get clear of the mountains. The Tennessee River gorge, just west of Chattanooga, separates Walden's Ridge on the north from Lookout Mountain on the south. The latter comes to an impressive rocky point towering fourteen hundred feet over the river and town. West of Lookout Mountain lies Lookout Valley and then a huge block of the Cumberland Plateau sliced off by the Tennessee River and known as Sand and Raccoon Mountains. Southeast of Chattanooga the long, straight line of Missionary Ridge bisects the Great Valley, rising six hundred feet above the town. West of Missionary Ridge, Chattanooga Creek flows north to join the Tennessee. East of the ridge, Chickamauga Creek does the same. South of Chattanooga the Great Valley itself gives way to a region of parallel valleys and ridges.

Though a town of only about twenty-five hundred inhabitants at the time of the Civil War, Chattanooga was by 1863 a point of considerable strategic importance. After Richmond and perhaps Atlanta, Chattanooga was the most important rail junction remaining to the Confederacy. Not only was it the southern terminus of the Virginia & Tennessee Railroad, but two other rail lines came together there at the foot of Lookout Mountain. The Western & Atlantic ran from Chattanooga southeastward to Dalton, Georgia, and beyond it to Atlanta and points south. The Nashville & Chattanooga ran westward alongside the river through the gorge to Stevenson, Alabama, before turning northwestward toward Nashville. At Stevenson it was joined by the Memphis & Charleston, running farther east all the way to the Mississippi. The Memphis & Charleston was less important now than it had once been because the Federals controlled its western reaches. It did offer Rosecrans a possible alternative supply line because it connected at Decatur, Alabama, with the Nashville & Decatur, another railroad that ran more or less straight north and south between those two cities.

The main railroads, however, were the three that actually came together at Chattanooga. The Western & Atlantic had the potential to bring Bragg moderate amounts of supplies. The Virginia & Tennessee shared such potential as well as the possibility of reinforcements from the Confederacy's other main army. The Nashville & Chattanooga would be Rosecrans's supply line, and he could be expected to advance southeastward toward Chattanooga somewhere near its line.

After its detour to Stevenson, the Nashville & Chattanooga climbed northward over the Cumberlands and descended onto a lower plateau, rolling and with poor soil. This was known as the Barrens, and it stretched in a belt about thirty miles wide, also angling roughly northeast to southwest. The railroad went straight across it, over the Elk River and then, about halfway across the Barrens, through the town of Tullahoma. North of Tullahoma was the valley of the Duck River, and going north from that stream the trains climbed a long grade to Bell Buckle Gap, a gentle passage through a chain of hills known as the Highland Rim. Once clear of the Highland Rim, the tracks descended into the Nashville Basin, where lay some of the most fertile soil in the state. About ten miles into this rich agricultural region lay Murfreesboro, Rosecrans's base for the coming campaign. His ultimate target, at the other end of well over one hundred miles of track, was Chattanooga.

Bragg had made his headquarters at Tullahoma and had deployed his infantry behind the Highland Rim in a wide-spreading position that was a good fifteen miles from end to end, with the cavalry stretched far beyond on either flank. Two reasons dictated this deployment. The first and more important was a matter of supply. One of the Confederacy's chief handicaps was its inefficient supply system. The fact that a region whose only eco-

nomic strength was its abundant agriculture nevertheless proved unable to
supply its armies with food is powerful evidence that the Confederate commissary department was simply incompetent. Robert E. Lee's Army of
Northern Virginia was the Confederacy's premier army and got the lion's
share of all the region's manpower and resources, though it certainly had no
surplus. In fact, the Virginia army was drawing supplies all the way from
the heartland of the South, the very area that Bragg's army was defending.
The Army of Tennessee was actually prevented by its own government from
drawing supplies from the friendly country directly to its rear. During a period that spring when the Atlanta depot was shipping Lee half a million
pounds of salt meat every week, Bragg received a grand total of sixty thousand pounds—enough to last his army about three days on short rations. If
the Army of Tennessee was to stave off starvation, it would have to shift for
itself, living on what food its own wagons could haul in from the surrounding countryside. It was for this reason that Bragg dispersed his army so
widely, maximizing the territory that could be swept clean of supplies.[19]

That system would work, however, for only a short time. As weeks
passed into months, the army exhausted even its extended neighborhood of
food for man and beast. Then the wagon hauling began in earnest. By mid-
April the army's wagons were making round-trips of over 150 miles westward into the agriculturally somewhat superior region around Pulaski, Columbia, and even Franklin, then back again with the badly needed supplies.
Franklin was just 20 miles from Nashville and squarely in the Federal rear,
and going there involved a long haul around Rosecrans's flank. Confederate
cavalry had to be spread as far as Columbia to afford the wagons what protection it could. Incredibly, Bragg's teamsters drew from even farther out on
the other flank, occasionally hauling meat all the way down from central
Kentucky, several hundred miles inside Federal territory. Confederate cavalry had to be extended far out to Bragg's right to screen such expeditions
around the Federal flank. Bragg even had men out on the north side of the
Highland Rim, reaping the wheat harvest almost under the noses of the
Federals in their entrenchments around Murfreesboro. It was nip and tuck,
but somehow he kept the army at least minimally fed.[20]

Bragg's second reason for spreading his army to cover a wide front was
tactical. If at all possible, he hoped to prevent Rosecrans from doing what
almost any Civil War general could almost always do to his opponent if he
took the initiative: steal a march and turn the opponent's position, forcing
him either to retreat (if he could) or to fight at a disadvantage. The left of
Bragg's infantry, Polk's corps, was anchored in solid fortifications around

the town of Shelbyville, about twenty miles northwest of Tullahoma and twenty-five miles due south of Murfreesboro. Shelbyville covered the southern end of Guy's Gap, the broadest and easiest of four gaps in the Highland Rim, through which passed the turnpike from Murfreesboro to Shelbyville. Further right, Hardee had established the headquarters of Bragg's other infantry corps at the little village of Wartrace, eight miles east of Shelbyville and about fifteen miles north of Tullahoma. Hardee's corps was deployed more or less covering the southern ends of the other three gaps. They were, from west to east, Bell Buckle, Liberty, and Hoover's. Another tolerably good pike passed through Hoover's Gap on its way from Murfreesboro to Manchester, another Barrens town about ten miles northeast of Tullahoma on a branch line of the Nashville & Chattanooga that ran on up the Barrens to McMinnville.

Shelbyville, Hoover's Gap, Manchester, and Tullahoma thus formed the corners of a rough parallelogram, with Bragg's headquarters at Tullahoma and his line running from Shelbyville to Hoover's Gap. Bragg had to cover all four gaps, including the railroad and the two pikes. He also had to be alert to any possible move by Rosecrans to go wide around either flank, where the hills were much easier. That provided an additional reason, besides screening supply operations, for the Confederate general to keep his cavalry spread far on the flanks.

Bragg thought a Federal advance against Hardee the most likely scenario because few generals would be foolish enough to hurl their armies against the defensive works at Shelbyville. In that event, he planned to have Hardee hold Rosecrans in position while Polk swung forward and to the right to strike the Federals in flank. The question was where Hardee should make his stand. He could fall back to the extensive fortifications Bragg had had built around Tullahoma, but though that would make him all but impervious to frontal attack, it would also present the Federals with the opportunity of sliding around the Confederate right and turning the entire position. Holding a line right along the Highland Rim would be safer in that respect but would be difficult. Rosecrans could make the hills work for him, screening his movement until he popped through one of the passes. Hardee would have to react quickly and decisively at that moment to seal off the Union penetration before the whole position gave way. Neither option was attractive, but Bragg, though uncertain, was leaning toward the latter approach by early June and pushed Hardee's troops up closer to the Highland Rim.[21]

If Bragg's task as defender was problematic, that did not mean that Rosecrans faced an easy assignment. Real and serious problems threatened each of the possible ways to get at Bragg. As Bragg suspected, the prospect of a frontal assault on the Shelbyville defenses turned the Union general's stomach. That eliminated Guy's Gap. Sticking close to the railroad and using Bell Buckle or Liberty Gap would bring him into the heart of Hardee's position around Wartrace. That left Hoover's Gap; yet several obstacles seemed to bar the way there as well. If the Confederates reacted in time, they could meet him before the gap widened out on the south side, thus canceling much of his advantage in numbers. Even if they did not, he could push through the gap with only a part of his army because presumably a sizable portion would have to cover the direct route to Murfreesboro lest Bragg react by turning the attackers. True, a good road led from Hoover's Gap to Manchester, where he could threaten Bragg's rear, but that road crossed Garrison's Fork of the Duck River and then climbed out of the river valley through a narrow ravine known locally as Matt's Hollow. In short, the Hoover's Gap route offered plenty of opportunities for an enterprising defender to make Rosecrans's life miserable.

Of course, Rosecrans need not limit himself to the gaps of the Highland Rim. He could swing directly east from Murfreesboro, ascend the plateau of the Barrens, then angle south to McMinnville, on Bragg's flank. The trouble was that this would take him far from the railroad through barren country devoid of food and forage. It was seventy-five miles from Murfreesboro to Tullahoma by way of McMinnville and the roads across the Barrens between the latter two towns were questionable at best. Dragging the army on that roundabout route would thus be a logistical nightmare.[22]

An added worry if this option were chosen was that it would place the fifteen-thousand-man Confederate force in East Tennessee squarely on the Army of the Cumberland's flank. That problem was to have been eliminated by a simultaneous offensive by Ambrose Burnside's newly named Army of the Ohio. If Burnside struck for Knoxville, Rosecrans's right flank would be secure. Here, however, Rosecrans's procrastination was his undoing, for idle troops were seen by Washington as potential reinforcements for the fronts commanded by fighting generals. Early in June half of Burnside's army was transferred to Mississippi to help Grant take Vicksburg. For the indefinite future, the Army of the Cumberland would have to take care of its own flanks.[23]

Going around Bragg's southwestern flank eliminated most of those problems. The hills were lower, and no difficult defiles blocked the way. The country was more bountiful than the Barrens, and a moving army could draw at least some of its supplies off the land. Also, the Nashville & Decatur Railroad, if put back in running order, might serve as an alternate supply line. The trouble with this route was that it would not bring the Federals much closer to Chattanooga and would expose them to a possible counterstroke if Bragg should drive toward Nashville.[24]

The problems might have looked all but insurmountable save for an important advantage that Rosecrans possessed—his knowledge of Bragg's army and its dispositions. Rosecrans was operating an excellent intelligence service. Though shockingly informal by modern standards, this seat-of-the-pants spy operation was nevertheless more efficient than those most Civil War generals enjoyed and certainly a good deal better than anything Bragg had. This, along with an increasingly active, numerous, and efficient cavalry arm, ensured that Rosecrans knew the obstacles he faced, both natural and in the form of enemy troops, and he could turn his considerable intellect to finding a way to deal with them.[25]

While he pondered, Washington fumed. "I would not push you to any rashness," Lincoln wrote on May 28, "but I am very anxious that you do your utmost, short of rashness, to keep Bragg from getting off to help Johnston against Grant." Rosecrans curtly dismissed the president's prodding. "Dispatch received," he wired back. "I will attend to it." Then on June 2 Halleck telegraphed, "If you can do nothing yourself, a portion of your troops must be sent to Grant's relief." Rosecrans blandly promised action at some unspecified future date and polled his corps and division commanders in hopes of finding support for his continued inaction. He was not disappointed. The fifteen generals were virtually unanimous in declaring their belief that Bragg had detached no substantial forces to Johnston, though Rosecrans almost undoubtedly knew better. They also agreed that an advance by the Army of the Cumberland would not likely prevent such a transfer. Most of all, they agreed that an immediate advance was not a good idea. The only dissenter was Rosecrans's new chief of staff, Brig. Gen. James A. Garfield. The thirty-one-year-old Garfield was correct in pointing out the opportunity for an immediate advance, but he usually had a keen eye for politics and may well have been most concerned with the impression his statement would make in Washington.[26]

If the near-unanimous opinion of Rosecrans's subordinates impressed Halleck and Lincoln, they hid it well. Their dispatches during the next week made it clear that Rosecrans had pretty well exhausted his fund of goodwill with them. On June 11 Halleck wired, "I deem it my duty to repeat to you the great dissatisfaction that is felt here at your inactivity. There seems to be no doubt that a part of Bragg's force has gone to Johnston." Five days later, he was even more blunt: "Is it your intention to make an immediate movement forward? A definite answer, yes or no, is required." It had the sound of an ultimatum, so in his reply, Rosecrans was as equivocal as he dared be. "If immediate means tonight or tomorrow," he hedged, "no. If it means as soon as all things are ready, say five days, yes." That "five days" turned out to be seven days, seven hours, and forty minutes, but finally at 2:10 A.M., June 24, Rosecrans wired Halleck: "The army begins to move at 3 o'clock this morning."[27]

CHAPTER TWO

A Nine Days' Campaign

Preliminary movements had begun the day before. Rosecrans had dispatched Maj. Gen. Gordon Granger with the newly created Reserve Corps fifteen miles due west to the little crossroads of Triune. The Reserve Corps was scarcely more than two weeks old as an organization, and the portion of it available for field use in this campaign actually amounted to only a single understrength division so Rosecrans reinforced Granger with a division of Thomas's XIV Corps. Operating ahead of Granger was a cavalry division under Brig. Gen. Robert B. Mitchell. A road ran from Triune southeast to Shelbyville, and Mitchell's command was to ride down it like Cossacks, driving in the Confederate cavalry and whatever infantry pickets the Rebels might have out on their near left flank and pushing the lot of them clear back into the Shelbyville entrenchments. Granger would be right behind with support if Mitchell needed it.

Meanwhile, a single division of the XXI Corps, reinforced with a brigade of cavalry, was to march about the same distance in nearly the opposite direction. Maj. Gen. John M. Palmer would lead his division fifteen miles or so to the east-southeast to the hamlet of Bradyville, at the foot of the Highland Rim well beyond the right flank of Bragg's infantry position. Since he would be encountering nothing but cavalry, Palmer was to push on up the gap there and get his advanced elements out onto the Barrens. From there a back road could take him nearly straight south into Manchester, in the Confederate rear.[1]

Only after these movements were well under way did Rosecrans summon his corps commanders for their first briefing on this strange movement that had elements of the army already going in opposite directions as if they were meant to turn both Confederate flanks at once. Assembling at Rosecrans's Murfreesboro headquarters that evening were Rosecrans, Thomas, XX Corps commander Alexander McCook, and XXI Corps commander Thomas L. Crittenden. McCook was a member of the West Point class of 1852 and had served in the regular army until the outbreak of the Civil War. Though only thirty-two years of age, he had almost nine months' experience in corps command, including the battles of Perryville and Stones River. He was the highest ranking of the "Fighting McCooks," seventeen members of his family who served in the Union army.[2]

The forty-four-year-old Crittenden was the son of Kentucky's senior U.S. senator John J. Crittenden, who had striven mightily to prevent the outbreak of Civil War. The senator now had two sons in uniform, Thomas and his brother George. George was a Confederate. Thomas was a lawyer by profession and training but had served in the Mexican War, both on the staff of Zachary Taylor and as lieutenant colonel of the Third Kentucky Cavalry. In Mexico he had become good friends with the colonel of the First Mississippi Rifles, who, like his brother, was also on the other side of the lines these days. His name was Jefferson Davis. Crittenden, like McCook, had served with the Army of the Cumberland (and its predecessor the old Army of the Ohio) throughout the war, the last nine months of it in corps command. Both were brigadier generals, though McCook had three weeks' seniority over Crittenden.[3]

Thomas, McCook, and Crittenden had apparently had no previous explanation of just what movement was afoot because Rosecrans was taking considerable pains to try to ensure secrecy. He now explained that Granger's move was a feint intended to convince Bragg that the real attack was aimed at the Confederate left, on the west side of Shelbyville. That should fix Polk in position, while Rosecrans dealt with Hardee. To make Granger's feint more convincing, Rosecrans had dispatched Palmer to feint a feint. Bragg was supposed to believe that Palmer's force, half the size of Granger's, was intended merely to distract him. Thus, Rosecrans hoped, the Confederate commander would focus his attention all the more diligently on Granger and the Shelbyville front.

Rosecrans was aiming his real blow elsewhere. The Army of the Cumberland was to execute an enormous right wheel, pivoting on Granger's Reserve Corps, which itself would slide to the left. It was a complicated and daring maneuver, with more than one-fourth of the army making contact with the Confederates before pulling back and swinging to the left. McCook would come up behind Granger and then swing eastward and push through Liberty Gap, toward the center of Hardee's position. Granger would shift left to cover the Shelbyville Pike and keep up his bluff toward Shelbyville by threatening the Confederate cavalry pickets in Dug Gap.[4]

Meanwhile, Thomas, with three divisions, would march southeast on the Manchester Pike, headed for Hoover's Gap on Hardee's right flank. Leading his march would be a brigade of mounted infantry under Col. John T. Wilder. Wilder was an unorthodox officer. The previous fall, though devoid of any military training or experience before the war, the thirty-two-year-old Indiana businessman had ably and courageously defended Munfordville, Kentucky. When the Confederates brought up overwhelming force and demanded his surrender, Wilder, who had no Union professional officer to consult, came over under flag of truce to consult Confederate Simon B. Buckner, since Buckner was a professional and an honorable man. After capitulating on the basis of the insights gained in that conversation, Wilder was exchanged two months later and was soon back in service. He pushed aggressively to have his new brigade—three Illinois and two Indiana regiments—mounted and armed with the powerful new Spencer Repeating Rifles. Both ideas were much in line with Rosecrans's wishes for the army and soon had become reality. The Spencer had a seven-round magazine in the stock, took metallic cartridges, and could fire about seven or eight times as many rounds per minute as the conventional Springfields and Enfields with which most Civil War soldiers were armed. Wilder's "Lightning Brigade" possessed not only advantages in mobility and firepower but also very high morale. Wilder seems to have believed they could lick the world, and his men were inclined to agree.[5]

Rosecrans was not asking him to lick the world, only as many Confederate cavalrymen as might be covering Hoover's Gap, along with such infantry as they happened to bring up in support. It was a tall order, but the XIV Corps would be right behind to give support if needed. The goal was to be in complete control of Hoover's Gap by nightfall.[6]

Meanwhile, Crittenden was to leave one division in reserve at Murfreesboro and take another to join Palmer's already in position at Bradyville. This move would put him on the far left, well beyond the Confederate right flank. There he was to await orders. When the rest of the army had developed the situation properly, Rosecrans would give Crittenden the orders that would transform a fake feint into a genuine deep-penetrating turning movement. The meeting broke up, and each general received written orders. Starting time was just a few hours away, 3:00 A.M., June 24.[7]

Right on time and just as ordered, the various units moved out that night.

Leading the XIV Corps, Wilder's skirmishers struck the Confederate pickets in front of Hoover's Gap seven miles outside Murfreesboro that morning. Wilder had his men pause and wait for the infantry to close up and then sent in the Seventy-second Indiana of his brigade. The Seventy-second's colonel decided to deploy just two companies, one on either side of the road. That number proved to be sufficient; Confederates of the First Kentucky Cavalry skirmished briefly and then spurred their horses back toward the gap. Wilder had learned that the gap was another nine miles away, and the Confederates had built breastworks there. Storming such works would be expensive both in time and blood, and flanking them—through the hills— could be almost equally problematical. Thus Wilder was eager to keep up the momentum of his advance so as to deny the Rebels a chance to make a stand there. He ordered his brigade to remount and push on hard after the fleeing Confederates.[8]

Up to this point, things had not really begun to go wrong for the First Kentucky Confederate Cavalry. They had detected the enemy's approach, forced him to deploy, skirmished briefly with what they took to be a significant force of infantry, and now were doing what cavalry routinely did when confronted with solid formations of infantry. By all the normal rules, they should reach their breastworks in the gap well ahead of the tired foot-sloggers. Then they would have so many advantages working for them that they should have little trouble holding off the Union advance until Confederate infantry came up to support them. Of course, the normal rules made no allowance for John T. Wilder and the Lightning Brigade, and the Kentuckians soon found themselves in a horse race. Since Wilder's horses had been eating a good deal better, the Kentuckians lost and were soon scattering in all directions, seeking cover in the breaks and thickets and wondering what the war was coming to, with powerful infantry formations suddenly transforming themselves into powerful cavalry formations. The First Kentucky went entirely to pieces, leaving Wilder "a beautiful stand of embroidered silk colors" and Hoover's Gap. What had been a regiment of Confederate cavalry had all but ceased to exist, without having either delayed the Federal advance or sent notice to any higher headquarters. Other Confederate units would learn of the penetration more or less at random from scattered groups of fleeing cavalrymen on lathered mounts.[9]

Wilder now considered what to do with his success. Thanks to some of the Kentuckians who had failed to make good their escape and were now his prisoners, he knew a good deal more about the precise Confederate deployments at the southeast end of the gap. The Third Confederate Cavalry was camped near the village of Beech Grove, on Garrison's Fork just about a mile from his present position. About two miles farther, down the valley of Garrison's Fork, was a brigade of Confederate infantry. If those forces were allowed to take up a position anywhere between the hills that bounded the gap, they could make the place a Thermopylae. Wilder figured that in that case it would cost "at least a thousand" casualties to force a passage. So, even though his infantry supports were now six miles behind, having been unable to keep up with a running fight that had looked more like a fox hunt, Wilder determined to get to the far end of the gap and hold the place until they came up. He did, and as he was placing the regiments in position to receive the attack he knew must be in the offing, he could hear faintly, down the valley of Garrison's Fork, the sound of drummers in the Rebel camp beating the long roll that summoned the troops into line of battle.[10]

That camp belonged to the brigade of William B. Bate, the junior brigadier general in the Army of Tennessee. A month earlier, when a substantial portion of the army was transferred to Mississippi, a partial reorganization had taken place. Bragg had preferred to keep the Tennessee brigades of the transferred divisions here in their home state, where they could be expected to fight with higher morale. The loose brigades had been consolidated into a new division and placed under a newly promoted major general, Alexander P. Stewart. It would become an excellent division. Stewart was a devout Presbyterian and a West Point classmate of Rosecrans's. He had spent the intervening years in the Third U.S. Artillery and as a professor at West Point (where he taught Stonewall Jackson), Cumberland University, and the University of Nashville, the latter two as a civilian after his resignation from the army. Though he thought slavery wrong and secession ill-advised, he went with his state and was proving himself highly capable. He was destined for higher things and would end the war as a lieutenant general. This, however, was his first campaign in division command, and his inexperience showed.[11]

Bate was, if anything, more prepossessing than his superior. Ambitious and driven, he had gone from steamboat clerk to newspaper editor to politician. In the war he had gone from private to brigadier general, and within a few months he would vault from being the Army of Tennessee's junior brigadier general to being its junior major general. Still, he too was new to his job, having returned to the army from a long convalescence after being wounded at Shiloh too late to take part in the battle of Stones River. He would be leading a brigade into battle for the first time today, and everything seemed to be against him. For one thing, he and many of the other officers of his brigade were several miles from camp at a Masonic picnic when word first arrived that the Federals were coming through the passes. It took time for the couriers to hunt them up and for them to get back to camp. Then the stampeded cavalrymen brought only the sketchiest intelligence about the enemy's present whereabouts—generally such as they could see over the rumps of their own galloping horses. Consequently, he saw little choice but to detach a couple of regiments to cover routes that the enemy might possibly take depending on who they were and what they were after. Then with the remainder of his brigade, about half of it, he went looking for the Federals, doing the job the cavalry should have done.[12]

He found the Lightning Brigade waiting for him just on the Confederate side of Hoover's Gap, and being the kind of commander he was, pitched into them without further ado. Bate was a fighter. He hit Wilder head-on, was driven back by the concentrated fire of the Spencers, then tried the flank and failed there too. With nearly a quarter of his men down, Bate had to pull back and do some fairly ineffective shelling. Wilder had lost a total of 61 men, killed and wounded, Bate, 146. By the time the infantry of the XIV Corps arrived to make the Union position secure beyond doubt, the crisis had already passed.[13]

It was nearing sundown, though no one had seen the sun for most of the day. One of Stewart's officers described it as "a dark and rainy day," and by midafternoon the precipitation was coming down in sheets. Sloshing through the mud about 6:00 P.M. came the wet and bedraggled troops of Bushrod R. Johnson's and Henry D. Clayton's brigades in support of Bate. Stewart had finally got his division together and into position. The delay had not been entirely his fault. Like Bate, Stewart had suffered from lack of information because of the collapse of the First Kentucky Cavalry, and he had had to expend valuable time while his other two brigades sent detachments to try to locate the enemy, who were variously reported by civilians and fleeing cavalrymen to be practically everywhere. Though he had gotten word of the Federal attack about 1:00 P.M. and had immediately ordered his division under arms and ready to march at a moment's notice, it was not until 4:00 P.M. that he put them in motion toward Bate's position. By then it was too late to save Hoover's Gap.[14]

Six miles to the west, at Liberty Gap, the story was not much different. There McCook's column was led by a smaller facsimile of the Lightning Brigade. Col. T. J. Harrison's Thirty-ninth Indiana had been mounted and issued the fearsome Spencers. As his skirmishers approached the gap, they picked up three Confederate soldiers, detailed to harvest wheat on the Union side of the Highland Rim. From these prisoners they learned that the gap was presently held by only two Confederate regiments. Harrison's men pushed on until they made contact. Then Brig. Gen. Richard W. Johnson, commanding McCook's lead division, ordered him to stop and wait for the infantry to come up. They did shortly, and McCook, like Wilder further east, recognized the importance of taking the defile before the Confederates could occupy it in force. He ordered Johnson to clear the gap.[15]

Johnson's lead brigade belonged to one of the most colorful brigadier generals in the Army of the Cumberland. August Willich had been born in Braunsberg, Prussia, in 1810 and, as a member of the Junker nobility, was destined for the life of an officer. He entered cadet school at age twelve, the Prussian military academy at fifteen. By twenty-one he was a captain in the Prussian army. Prussian precision and military rigidity can do strange things to some minds, and at any rate a tainted intellectual wind was blowing in the Germany of that day. It stirred Willich, and he became a communist. He was court-martialed but allowed to resign from the army. In the revolutions of 1848 he fought to overthrow his king and, failing, fled to America. There he became first a carpenter and then the editor of a German-language newspaper in Cincinnati with a slant so leftist he earned the nickname "Reddest of the Red." When the Civil War came, Willich recruited fifteen hundred Cincinnati Germans within a matter of hours and helped organize the Ninth Ohio—now marching with the XIV Corps. Willich was headed for higher command. If the business of an army was to break things and hurt people, Willich certainly found nothing in his communism to hinder that, and his Prussian training made him especially good at it. His men found him a likable if strange old man, and when he taught them Prussian tactics and maneuvers done to Prussian bugle calls, they felt invincible.[16]

Ordering Harrison to stand clear, Willich deployed a regiment on either side of the road and plunged upward. Encountering the Confederate breastworks, he moved immediately to flank them on the adjacent slopes. A quick battle of maneuver followed, with the Confederates, two regiments of Brig. Gen. St. John R. Liddell's brigade of Patrick R. Cleburne's division, getting the worse of it. Johnson sent in a second Union brigade to support Willich, and the pace quickened. By evening, the Federals had pushed a half mile beyond the southern entrance to the gap, and though the balance of Liddell's brigade had finally come splashing up through the driving rain, there was nothing more to be done. Liddell broke contact and pulled his sodden troops back for the night. As Johnson summed up the action from the Union perspective, "The rebels were driven at every point . . . and Liberty Gap was in our possession."[17]

Thus ended the first stage of the Tullahoma campaign, scarcely fifteen hours after it began. Its most striking feature was the Army of the Cumberland's absolutely flawless execution of Rosecrans's plan. Union troops were in possession of two key passes in the Highland Rim. They had denied the Confederates the use of the best possible defensive positions and were now capable of deploying a good bit of their numerical superiority. All this spoke well of Rosecrans's plan, which carried complexity just as far as the army could execute and no farther. It also spoke well of his preparations. Much as his delay tried Lincoln's patience and aided the Confederate cause, he did make good use of the time to see that his men had the training, equipment, supplies, and rest they needed to function at a level of efficiency rarely achieved by Civil War armies. Whether that level of efficiency could have been achieved a good deal sooner is an open question, and Lincoln would probably gladly have settled for less if Rosecrans had moved sooner and thus produced a greater positive effect for the Union war effort. Still, none could deny that when it came to ensuring the successful operations of his own army—greater good of the war effort be hanged—Rosecrans knew what he was about. Naturally, the day's success also reflected extremely well on the skillful and resolute officers and men of the Army of the Cumberland.

Bragg had erred, plain and simple, by not keeping more force up in the gaps, and Rosecrans had made him pay for it. Yet the tactical problem the Confederate commander faced had not been a simple one. Keeping at least a brigade in each of the three northeastern gaps, Bell Buckle, Liberty, and Hoover's, might have served well against the offensive Rosecrans actually launched, but it would have impeded Bragg's ability to react had Rosecrans made a wide-sweeping flanking movement of the sort he was currently feigning to the far northeast around Bradyville. Also, Rosecrans had moved far faster and more powerfully than experience would have led almost any Civil War general to expect. Six months before, when Rosecrans had advanced from Nashville toward Bragg's position along Stones River, he had taken several days to cover an only slightly longer distance, with Confederate cavalry skirmishing vigorously in his front the whole time. If that performance had been duplicated in front of the Highland Rim, Bragg would have had time enough to meet Rosecrans wherever he chose. Finally, Bragg almost certainly did not consider the Highland Rim position indispensable—useful, perhaps, if the developments of the campaign allowed a stand to be made there, but not a prerequisite of victory. That was because he did not consider the position at Tullahoma hopeless. True, it could be turned, but it would soon become obvious that Bragg was not contemplating a static de-

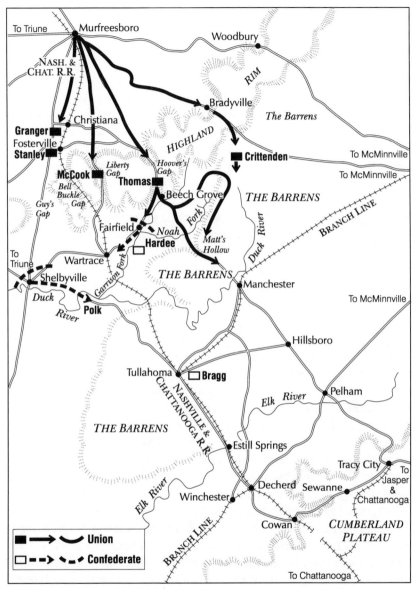

The Tullahoma Campaign

fense that waited for the enemy to do something to him. He was thinking about what he would do to the enemy.

Rosecrans and the weather promptly presented him with an opportunity. The rain that had begun on the twenty-fourth continued the next day, and the mud got deeper and the roads less passable. Perfection is a hard standard to maintain, and under these circumstances it became impossible. Also, the Army of the Cumberland began to experience its first flaws in execution. A special "Pioneer Brigade," a pet project of Rosecrans's in the months before the advance, proved no asset. Cobbled together out of handfuls of men detailed from every regiment in the Army of the Cumberland, it became ill-disciplined. At a time when the army's one crying need was skillful repair and maintenance of roads, the Pioneer Brigade was more hindrance than help, getting in the way of combat units as they struggled across roads the pioneers were too disorderly to improve. In the midst of all these less than perfect circumstances, Rosecrans asserted his perfectionism again. As he would not begin the offensive without having everything just right, so he would not continue it except on the same terms. When Crittenden's corps found it impossible to reach its assigned position for June 24 and the detached division of Thomas's corps likewise encountered mud too bottomless for the execution of its scheduled shift to the left, Rosecrans had Granger, McCook, and Thomas maintain their positions and wait throughout the twenty-fifth.[18]

A similar pause after an initially successful first stage of a turning movement had cost Joseph Hooker dearly eight weeks before at the battle of Chancellorsville in Virginia. During the previous year, Robert E. Lee and Stonewall Jackson had taught several Union generals the dangers of giving up the initiative. Still, seizing the initiative, even when the attacker pauses and allows the opportunity, was no easy matter. Robert E. Lee had several assets Bragg lacked: he was a military genius; he had Stonewall Jackson for a subordinate; and, significantly, he had J. E. B. Stuart for a cavalry leader.

Bragg's cavalry was one of his worst handicaps. Lack of fodder had put many of the horses in poor condition. Also, the Confederate practice of requiring cavalrymen to provide their own mounts provided an incentive for men who wanted to avoid hard service in the infantry to find whatever broken-down nag they could lay their hands on so as to remain in the cavalry. Discipline was often atrocious among the cavalrymen because the regimental officers were indifferent or worse, and much of the problem no doubt could be traced back to the generals who led the Army of Tennessee's mounted troops.[19]

Maj. Gen. Joseph Wheeler, an 1859 West Point graduate, was dapper and dashing but lacked efficiency in the workaday duties of a cavalryman, screening his own army and gaining intelligence of the enemy's. Still, compared to the other high-ranking cavalrymen of the Army of Tennessee, Wheeler was a paragon of professionalism. John H. Morgan had gained a bold reputation by making several raids into his home state of Kentucky, but he had little stomach for more prosaic duties. On the eve of this campaign he had disobeyed orders and set out upon more of his knight-errantry, a ride that would take him and what was left of his command all the way into Ohio—and the Ohio state penitentiary. Nathan Bedford Forrest could be an excellent cavalryman for practically any purpose if he could be convinced to pursue his commander's wishes. Having him in an army was something like operating in concert with a band of formidable but unpredictable barbarian allies. Earl Van Dorn could be very good indeed, but an unfortunate incident had removed him from the army.

These men's collective effectiveness was reduced by their personal problems. Morgan did not get along with Wheeler. Forrest did not get along with anybody. Van Dorn had apparently gotten along a bit too well with a certain Mrs. Peters and had his brains blown out by Mr. Peters a month before the start of the present campaign. Finally, when the armies began to move, Forrest had risen from the sickbed where he had been for a fortnight after receiving a wound the doctors had initially thought would be mortal in a dispute with a subordinate. Taken as a whole, the Army of Tennessee's cavalry leaders, though men of many admirable parts, were not an inspiring lot.[20]

On this occasion they were far from what Bragg needed. They did not provide timely warning of the Federals' approach or adequately delay their progress through the gaps. Nor, during the June 25 lull, did they provide the timely and detailed intelligence Bragg would have needed to formulate a plan for recovering the initiative. Forrest, commanding on the left, did not acquire the intelligence that would have revealed the presence of only one Union infantry division on that front—an obvious bluff. Wheeler, commanding on the right, did not discover Crittenden's XXI Corps, which had passed through the Highland Rim at Bradyville and was in a position that would have allowed it to descend on the Confederate flank and rear had the roads been dry. Because Wheeler detected nothing on his front, Bragg assumed nothing was there and transferred Wheeler to the Shelbyville sector to counter the larger Union cavalry presence there. That, of course, was precisely what Rosecrans wanted him to do. Elsewhere, the situation as known at Confederate headquarters remained too ill-defined for Bragg to decide on a response.[21]

And so June 25 passed with Rosecrans waiting for every last unit of his army to get into position and Bragg trying to figure out what positions Rosecrans had gotten into. The only action came late that afternoon when Liddell, whose Confederate brigade had been skirmishing with McCook's Federals in front of Liberty Gap all day, got the idea that McCook's men were in the process of pulling back through the gap and ordered his skirmishers to press forward "cautiously and slowly" and find out for sure. Of course, McCook was not going anywhere yet. Rosecrans's orders called for him to stay put in Liberty Gap, threatening Hardee's center, until Thomas launched the next stage of the campaign up at Hoover's Gap. Thus Liddell's skirmishers encountered not a retiring Union force but the skirmishers of Willich's brigade, dead set on holding their ground. The result was a skirmish scrap that swelled into a small but fierce battle, with each side reinforcing its skirmish line to full brigade strength and both sides emptying their cartridge boxes. Charge and countercharge surged across the woods and cornfields. After a couple of hours, Liddell pulled back. Willich lost about 50 men; Liddell had paid with 120 killed and wounded for the knowledge that the Federals still held Liberty Gap in force.[22]

And still the rain came down in what was becoming one of the worst midsummer wet spells in living memory. Through the mud that night the final division of the XIV Corps plodded into Hoover's Gap, and Thomas prepared to execute the plan that had originally been scheduled for the day before. Through the night the men of the XIV Corps toiled to get into position, and hooves, boots, and the wheels of caissons and gun carriages churned the roads into a thick mush. It was 10:30 the next morning before they were ready to go, but it was a miracle they were ready at all in that weather.

Thomas sent his corps storming out of the gap toward the Confederate position at Beech Grove, three divisions in line, one in reserve. Stewart's lone Confederate division fell back to the southwest, toward Wartrace. That was just what Rosecrans had expected and desired. Thomas was to seal off this Confederate force with one division and send the other two on to Manchester. At this point, however, the XIV Corps commander modified Rosecrans's design in favor of caution. Only the division of Maj. Gen. Joseph Reynolds would move directly on Manchester. The divisions of Lovell H. Rousseau and John M. Brannan would press toward Wartrace after the retreating Confederates, with the division of James S. Negley following them up closely in support. Slowly but steadily, they pushed Stewart back down the road toward Wartrace.

Ahead of Reynolds loomed the rugged hills that marked the edge of the plateau of the Barrens, above the valley of Garrison's Fork. They were not high for hills in Tennessee, about 150 to 200 feet, but they could be a definite obstacle if defended. Worse, the Manchester Pike cut through those hills and climbed up to the plateau by way of a narrow defile known as Matt's Hollow. A narrow slit of a ravine that led a winding course gradually up to the level of the plateau, Matt's Hollow had steep, tree-covered walls and a floor just wide enough for a narrow road and an even narrower brook. Some places it was not even that wide, and of course it was the road and not the brook that yielded some of its width. At such places two wagons could not pass, and at no place along its length could a wagon be turned around. The lush late June foliage met overhead so that the bottom of the ravine seemed like a tunnel, curving this way and that through green-tinted shadows. Altogether it was a very pleasant place in dry weather when one was not anticipating an ambush.

Reynolds was expecting something very like one and sent Wilder's Lightning Brigade riding roundabout to flank any Confederates that might be in position around Matt's Hollow. Wilder led his men northward, up the valley of McBride's Creek, a tributary of Garrison's Fork, then up onto the tableland and around the head of another valley to come riding back along the rim of the plateau ready to flank the defenders. When they reached the pike they found a column of very muddy soldiers marching toward Manchester. These were not Confederates, however, but Reynolds's men. Much to their surprise, the leading infantrymen had found Matt's Hollow undefended and pushed gingerly on up to the top. Now the whole division continued its march unhindered.[23]

About the same time Reynolds's men were emerging from Matt's Hollow early that afternoon, Braxton Bragg, now in Shelbyville, was meeting with Polk to discuss the Army of Tennessee's response. By this time Bragg was aware that Granger's continued skirmishing on the far side of Guy's Gap was merely a demonstration designed to draw his attention away from the main Union advance farther north, and he had a plan for dealing with it. In keeping with ideas he had been considering for several months, Bragg ordered Polk to take his corps on a night march northward up the pike toward Murfreesboro. They would pass through broad and gentle Guy's Gap before dawn, then turn northeastward and sweep along the Yankee side of the Highland Rim to take the Federals in Liberty Gap from the rear while Hardee pressed them in front.[24]

Polk immediately objected. One of his staff officers who was present said that he complained of "the character of the country, the heavy cedar growth, and the peculiar topography" and claimed that "the position he was about being thrown in [was] nothing short of a man-trap." Bragg held firm, insisting that the attack go on as ordered, and that seems to be how the conference ended. Not long after, however, further developments on Hardee's front led Bragg to cancel the operation. Ironically, despite Polk's fears, the operation had held the potential for major success had events in Hardee's sector allowed its execution. The distances to be covered were well within the capabilities of Polk's troops, even on muddy roads, as evidenced by their marching performance under even less favorable conditions the next day. Night marches were practical for Civil War armies, and troops who had made them often fought well the next day despite their fatigue. Proceeding as Bragg had ordered, Polk would have encountered only weak Union resistance.[25]

Several hours after Bragg had called off the attack, Rosecrans, pursuing his own plans in ignorance of Bragg's, gave orders for McCook to begin pulling his XX Corps out of Liberty Gap. Division by division it was to march back the way it had come. It would then proceed northeastward by roads along the base of the Highland Rim to exploit Thomas's breakout from Hoover's Gap.[26]

In carrying out Bragg's flank attack, Polk would have encountered only McCook's trailing division strung out in march order on the way out of the gap. Polk's corps contained eight brigades. The probabilities would have been much in favor of an overwhelming Confederate victory that not only would have allowed Polk to establish contact with Hardee by way of Liberty Gap but also put him closer to Rosecrans's base at Murfreesboro than Rosecrans was himself. That scenario would have presented all sorts of inviting possibilities for Bragg's Confederates. Of course, it would have been a daring operation, though no more so than Stonewall Jackson's famous flanking march at Chancellorsville the month before. But Bragg was not Lee, Polk was not Jackson, and such victories simply did not happen for the Army of Tennessee. Whether Polk, given his past record, would have carried out Bragg's orders energetically and skillfully is highly doubtful, even had Bragg continued to insist on their execution. As it was, Hardee's apparent failure to understand what his commander intended convinced Bragg that it was no longer practical to attempt to implement his plan.[27]

The bad feelings among the Army of Tennessee's top generals had produced a lack of communication. For months before the opening of the campaign, Bragg and his corps commanders would not meet if a letter would do or send a personal letter if one from a staff officer would do. They no doubt believed they were still carrying out all essential communication, but they certainly did not have a relationship that would have allowed them to understand one another's thoughts and intentions. Because the Army of Tennessee would be on the defensive, Bragg could not make specific plans for the coming campaign. Much would depend on what Rosecrans did. Bragg suspected, however, that Rosecrans would neither wreck his army against the Shelbyville entrenchments nor send it sweeping wide to the west. He expected Rosecrans to come through the Highland Rim gaps—just as the Union commander now had done. In that case, Bragg's plan had always been that Hardee would delay Rosecrans in front, either along the Highland Rim or around Tullahoma, while Polk struck the Federals in flank. Yet now when Bragg tried to implement this plan with the specific details that the circumstances dictated, Polk and Hardee quickly demonstrated that neither of them had had any clear understanding of it.[28]

Hardee, who seemed unable to think of anything but a static defense that simply held a given line until the enemy got tired of attacking it, complained that Tullahoma was not a suitable position for such a stand. In fact, both Bragg and theater commander Joseph E. Johnston had previously decided that Tullahoma was acceptable because Rosecrans would not dare reach too far around its northern flank. If he did, he would uncover his own communications. That would allow the Army of Tennessee to get into his rear as fast as he got into its, and as Johnston pointed out, the Confederates could well afford to swap bases with Rosecrans. In that case, the Union commander would have found himself sitting in the middle of the Barrens with his supply lines cut, while Bragg would still have had access to one of his chief sources of supply in south-central Tennessee and, better yet, would have been camped in the midst of the bountiful and strongly pro-Confederate Nashville Basin. None of this seemed to penetrate Hardee's awareness. If he had had confidence in his commander's wisdom, he would have reasoned that if Bragg's dispositions looked mistaken to him, he must not understand them. Instead, he simply took the situation as further proof of his long-held notion that Bragg was an idiot.[29]

The result was that at a time when Bragg intended Hardee to delay the Federal advance as much as possible, Hardee was instead pursuing the course he deemed best for saving an army whose commander was an idiot. He was retreating. As early as the evening of June 24, even as Bate's brigade was trying to retake Hoover's Gap, Hardee had directed Stewart, "if hard pressed tomorrow, you will fall back gradually toward Wartrace." Of course, Thomas had left Stewart alone on the twenty-fifth, but on the twenty-sixth, when the XIV Corps started its drive out from the gap, Stewart had naturally followed his orders and retreated toward Wartrace.[30]

This maneuver had a twofold effect. First, it made stopping—or at least delaying—Thomas more difficult. A retreat toward Manchester would have allowed the defenders to use Garrison's Fork, McBride's Creek, and Noah's Fork—as well as the intervening chains of hills—as defensive positions. Most important, it would have allowed the defense of Matt's Hollow, which should have stymied Reynolds's column for half a day despite the best efforts of the Lightning Brigade. A retreat toward Wartrace, however, fell back straight down the valley of Garrison's Fork, with no comparable defensive positions. Had Hardee ordered Stewart to fall back, when necessary, in the direction of Manchester, he could have used other troops to delay Thomas's advance on Wartrace—the center of his concentration—and the result would likely have been a delay of a day or more in the execution of Rosecrans's plan. And that would have been more than adequate to carry out Bragg's plan instead.

The second effect of Hardee's order to Stewart to fall back on Wartrace was to accelerate the speed of that retreat even beyond what the terrain and the disparity of numbers dictated. Stewart's subordinates reported that as often as not it was Stewart's order, rather than enemy pressure, that compelled their withdrawal to a new position. That the fighting was not especially fierce is borne out by the short casualty lists on both sides.[31]

Hardee's precipitate retreat and his complete abandonment of any attempt to defend Manchester are all the more curious in the light of his belief that the enemy could readily turn Tullahoma by going through Manchester. Bragg might not have thought so, but Hardee did. Thus his giving away of Manchester amounted to giving up any hope of fighting the enemy anywhere north of the Elk River or even the Cumberland Plateau. His attitude seems to have been that since the army could not possibly win with Bragg in command, he would bring about its retreat whenever possible until the government heeded his opinion and sacked his commander.

Word of Stewart's rapid retreat down the valley of Garrison's Fork to Wartrace convinced Bragg he would not have enough time to carry out his planned flanking attack, at least not until the Army of Tennessee was settled in its entrenchments at Tullahoma. So he gave orders for a retreat. At dawn on the morning of June 27, instead of moving out for a bold flank attack, the Army of Tennessee moved out in retreat toward Tullahoma. By 4:00 P.M., despite the continued rain and abominable roads as well as a nasty traffic snarl when some of Hardee's troops got tangled up in Polk's column, the soggy and bedraggled army was inside the Tullahoma lines.[32]

While the Confederates marched southeastward on the Shelbyville-Tullahoma Road, Reynolds's division continued in the same direction on the parallel Manchester Pike, ten miles or so to the north. Wilder's brigade, which had camped on the Barrens a few miles short of Manchester the night before, rode into town at eight o'clock that morning. By midday, the entire division was in Manchester. Meanwhile, Rousseau and Brannan had pressed halfway to Wartrace and still lost contact with the quickly retreating Stewart. McCook, having shifted around behind the Highland Rim from Liberty Gap, had pushed through Hoover's Gap and was moving up in support of Thomas, who had already shifted Negley from the Wartrace to the Manchester Road and was preparing to do the same with his other two divisions.[33].

Over on the Shelbyville-Murfreesboro Pike, in front of Guy's Gap, Granger's Reserve Corps division along with the cavalry corps under Maj. Gen. David S. Stanley, kept up their demonstration until orders came from Rosecrans to see if they could push through the gap and into Shelbyville after the retreating Confederates. About midmorning they made contact with the Southern cavalry holding the gap. Had Bragg's plan of the previous afternoon been put into effect, Polk's corps would already have been well past that point, and the gap would almost undoubtedly have been secured by one of his brigades. As it was, very little stood in their way.

The Army of Tennessee's cavalry, most of which was present, continued its poor performance, and Stanley's cavalry went into Shelbyville on the gallop, led by the "Saber Brigade," under Col. Robert H. G. Minty, the son of a British officer and himself a veteran of four years in the Royal Army. When the Confederates attempted a stand at the breastworks, Minty led the charge in person, leaping his horse over the works after the fleeing Rebels. Wheeler was present as well and tried some inspirational leadership of his own. When word came in that Forrest was still west of Shelbyville and was depending on the Duck River bridge there to make good his escape, Wheeler led a squadron of Confederate horse to try to hold the bridge. It was no use. Wheeler and his forlorn hope were shoved aside by the onrushing Federals. Cut off from the bridge, which the Federals captured intact, only Wheeler and a handful of others escaped capture by leaping their horses off the ten-foot-high bank into the rain-swollen waters of the Duck. The resourceful Forrest managed to find another crossing.[34]

The morning of Sunday, June 28, found most of the Army of Tennessee concentrated around Tullahoma and most of the Army of the Cumberland similarly gathered around Manchester. Crittenden's miserable XXI Corps soldiers were still laboring through the ooze of the rain-glutted Barrens some miles north of Manchester. Moving over the wet countryside with considerably more ease and relish were the men of the Lightning Brigade, who were traveling light and had mischief in view. Rosecrans, true to form, had felt compelled to stop, regroup, and resupply at Manchester. He was also unwilling to continue operations until Crittenden finally came up. Wanting nevertheless to keep up the momentum of an already highly successful campaign, Rosecrans dispatched Wilder on a raid to try to cut the railroad somewhere behind Bragg, preferably somewhere on the Cumberland Plateau.[35]

Wilder set out at reveille that morning and rode on down the turnpike to Hillsboro. There he turned due south toward Decherd, a little town on the Nashville & Chattanooga line about four miles from the Cumberlands. Halfway in between the Federal horsemen and that goal, however, lay the Elk River. Normally an insignificant stream easily fordable at numerous places, the Elk was now badly swollen by rains and presented an impassable barrier. When Wilder's men tried to swim their horses across, they were swept downstream by the powerful current. Improvising quickly, Wilder sent a detachment further downstream to destroy the road and railroad bridges at Estill Springs, then he took the main force six miles in the other direction to the turnpike bridge at Pelham. The Estill Springs detachment found the place too heavily guarded and had to retire. Wilder's own force had better success but tough going as they forded or swam each of the many flooded streams that emptied into the Elk, laboriously crossing their battery of mountain howitzers.

Somewhere along the line Wilder got information that a small Confederate detachment was on duty at Pelham with orders to destroy the bridge on the approach of Union forces. His troops made a stealthy approach, then rushed the bridge, capturing not only the structure but also two Confederates and seventy-eight mules. After sending prisoners and booty back to Union lines under guard, Wilder and his men pressed on. The next obstacle should have stopped them; the almost equally forbidding south fork of the Elk offered no bridge at all. With midwestern ingenuity they came up with a solution. It took them about three hours, but they disassembled a nearby mill, built it into a raft, and used that to float their howitzers across, swimming the river and towing the raft with their picket ropes.

And so they pressed on, reaching Decherd at 8:00 that evening. The eighty men in the Confederate garrison gave a very good account of themselves, first in a stockade they had prepared and then, after Wilder's men drove them out of that, in a nearby wooded ravine. The labor involved in bringing the howitzers this far now paid off handsomely as the little guns blasted the Confederates out of the covert. Once the Rebels had fled, Wilder's men got down to the hard but entertaining work of destruction. They tore up three hundred yards of track and punctured the water tanks, blew up a trestle on a branch line to Winchester, and burned the railroad depot full of Confederate rations. For good measure, they also smashed the telegraph. By that time, his scouts had detected a large Confederate relief force moving down from the north, the direction of Tullahoma, and Wilder thought it best to move along.

After riding back toward Pelham for some distance, they turned off into the woods and camped without fires about 2:00 A.M. The next morning they were back in the saddle bright and early, and Wilder was determined to break the Nashville & Chattanooga somewhere on the Cumberland Plateau. They rode up into the hills, occasionally admiring spectacular vistas of large bodies of Confederate infantry and cavalry gathering at Decherd and trying to find the Lightning Brigade. At the top, Wilder's men reached the town of Sewanee, the place Leonidas Polk had selected three years before as the future site of the University of the South. There, he imagined, young men would be educated without having their thoughts twisted by Northern ideas. Wilder's Hoosiers and Illinoisans were not interested in twisting anyone's thoughts, but they did have plans for the rails. Another branch line ran through Sewanee on its way from the main line to Tracy City, another plateau town four miles to the northeast. Having put their own midwestern twist into Sewanee's Southern railroad iron, if not its Southern thinking, Wilder's men rode on. He planned to cut the main line at two places, Anderson and Tantalon, and divided his force accordingly. He had not gone far, however, before learning that two Rebel troop trains were at Anderson and three at Tantalon. Disappointed at failing to cut the Nashville & Chattanooga anywhere but at Decherd, Wilder nevertheless decided not to presume any further on Southern hospitality, reunited his command, and set about getting back to Manchester. This was no simple proposition because yet another substantial Confederate force had now appeared at Sewanee, putting Wilder in the middle of a triangle whose three corners were the enemy. Undaunted, the Hoosier colonel put his command on the road for Chattanooga. Eight miles down the road, under cover of a torrential downpour, Wilder led his main body off into the woods while a small rear guard

continued skirmishing with the pursuing Rebels on down the road toward
Chattanooga. Once the Confederate column was well past Wilder's position,
the men of the rear guard dispersed into the woods and made their escape.
The main body cut back toward Pelham, and, as Wilder proudly noted in
his report, traveled through the mountains without guides "and came out at
the place we intended to strike." They camped at the foot of the Cumberlands that night and proceeded back across the Pelham bridge next morning, giving the slip even to the dreaded Forrest, who had been put on their
trail with two brigades of Confederate cavalry. By noon, June 30, the Lightning Brigade was back in Manchester, tired but with higher morale than
ever. They had not lost a single man on the expedition.[36]

Little had occurred around the main armies while they were gone. By the
evening of the twenty-ninth, the last of Crittenden's wet and weary soldiers
had plodded into camp. Rosecrans had spent the thirtieth getting the army
into position for the grand attack he planned to make on Tullahoma. That
took time because since the wheels of the artillery and the supply wagons cut
into the wet soil "as if it were a swamp," Rosecrans later reported. Reconnaissance patrols to the front revealed that Bragg was still patiently waiting
in his Tullahoma lines, which were depressingly strong. Still, alert to the
threat against his own supply line that Johnston and Bragg had foreseen,
Rosecrans prepared for a frontal assault. By the morning of July 1, all was
finally in readiness and the Army of the Cumberland moved forward. What
came next was somewhat anticlimactic but no doubt a considerable relief to
many a Union soldier, probably including Rosecrans: they found the powerful fortifications empty. Bragg had slipped away during the night.[37]

By the morning of June 29, Bragg had been prepared to receive the
Union assault. Wilder's raid had been a nuisance but little more. The three
hundred yards of torn-up track and the other damage at Decherd had been
the only hindrance to the operation of the main line of the Nashville & Chattanooga, and that had been quickly repaired. Bragg also knew that it was impossible to stop an enterprising horseman like Wilder from carrying out
such raids but that if Confederate cavalry were on hand to chase him and repair parties prompt in restoring such damage as he might be able to inflict
before being chased off, he need not be a fatal affliction for the Army of Tennessee. The Confederate commander said as much in a conference with Polk
on the morning of the twenty-ninth, adding that he intended to fight Rosecrans right here in the Tullahoma lines.

Polk offered no objection but promptly went out to find Hardee and tell
him how wrong this decision was. The two made an appointment to discuss

the matter with Bragg that afternoon. When the time came, Polk waded right in. Fighting at Tullahoma was all wrong; Bragg's "first duty" was to reestablish his communications. Bragg pointed out that they had been reestablished for some hours. "And how," Polk sneered, "do you propose to maintain them?" Bragg explained that he would do so "by posting cavalry along the line." In reply, Polk grandly stated the obvious but irrelevant fact that they did not have enough cavalry to prevent that sort of thing from happening again, and he added the illogical conclusion that the next time Rosecrans went after Bragg's communications, he would do it in such force that Bragg would not be able to dislodge him. Polk then launched into a veritable fable of horrors that would become reality unless his advice were heeded speedily. Cut off from Chattanooga, from which he was in any case drawing woefully few supplies, Bragg would, in Polk's highly imaginative scenario, find himself in a plight as bad as that of John C. Pemberton, the Confederate commander then trapped in Vicksburg. Bragg would have to retreat to the south-southwest into the hill country of northern Alabama, his wagons and artillery abandoned, his army starved, captured, or dispersed, maybe some of each. Rosecrans in the meantime would have taken Chattanooga and marched through Georgia and the Carolinas.

"That is all very well," Bragg replied, "but what do you distinctly propose to have done?" Polk replied that there was not a moment to be lost in starting their retreat. "Then," said Bragg, apparently somewhat shocked, "you propose that we shall retreat."

"I do," Polk insisted, "and that is my counsel."

Bragg next turned to Hardee and asked his advice. Hardee, of course, favored retreat in any circumstance as long as Bragg commanded the army, but he had a reputation to uphold and was not eager to appear to have advised retreat. Besides, the loss of territory would accomplish more toward Bragg's removal from command if the army commander seemed to have fallen back on his own without pressure from his generals. He observed that Polk's opinions should be accorded great importance but hedged that he personally "was not," as a staff officer recalled, "prepared to advise a retreat." Instead he offered the obviously absurd suggestion that Bragg deplete his already inferior infantry strength by stationing large detachments at key points along the railroad. That proposition assumed the truth of Polk's assertion that not letting a live bluecoat come within a country mile of the railroad was a Confederate necessity. By offering an unworkable and downright dangerous alternative to retreat, Hardee's suggestion made Polk's seem more reasonable—and was probably intended to.

The conference broke up with no satisfactory consensus. A staff officer who was present and took notes came away with the idea that Hardee's plan had been agreed upon, though that seems unlikely. Over the next twenty-four hours Bragg apparently reflected on Polk's dire predictions and the obvious lack of confidence of his top lieutenants. Perhaps he decided that Polk was right after all or that there was too great a chance that he was to be tested when the stakes were so high. Perhaps he reasoned that success was unlikely when the corps commanders seemed so confident of failure. Or perhaps he simply lost his nerve. At any rate, at 3:00 P.M. on June 30, precisely twenty-four hours after his conference with Polk and Hardee, Bragg issued orders for the army to withdraw beginning at nightfall. If his determination had lasted another twenty-four hours, his army, in its entrenchments, would have received the frontal assault of the Army of the Cumberland. If the Army of Tennessee could not have prevailed in those circumstances, it might as well have given up the war and gone home. As it was, though, by the time Rosecrans's lines moved forward at midmorning, July 1, the Army of Tennessee was already strung out in a long column marching southeastward, away from another potential victory.[38]

The obvious question now was where would Bragg turn at bay. His first choice was to hold the line of the Elk River, the raging torrent that had come near to thwarting the determined Wilder. Bragg issued orders for his troops to deploy behind the Elk, about eight miles southeast of Tullahoma at its nearest point. They were then to destroy the bridges at Estill Springs that they had previously saved from Wilder and the one at Pelham that Wilder had saved from them. That plan was sound enough, but Bragg was clearly shaken. The resolute and well-conceived Union advance and the constant carping and noncooperation of his own generals seem to have broken him down physically and emotionally. He struggled now with a collection of physical ailments, including a bad case of boils, and he was apparently unable to mount a horse to ride along his battle lines and survey the situation. Worse, his will seemed exhausted. Thus at 7:00 P.M. July 1, with the army just taking up its positions along the Elk, Bragg had sent to both Polk and Hardee asking, "Shall we fight on the Elk, or take post at the foot of mountain at Cowan?" Bragg's questioning his officers reveals how much he had been beaten down emotionally by his corps commanders. He was acting almost as if they and not he were in command of the army. Of course, they had been acting that way for some time.

The mountain referred to was the Cumberland Plateau. Cowan was a little town on the railroad at the foot of the Cumberlands. A defense there would have been highly questionable. The army would have been entirely dependent on supplies shipped by rail from Chattanooga, the only line of retreat in case of disaster would lead over the Cumberlands, and the odds were that the Federals would manage to get some of their own people—probably Wilder—up onto the plateau somewhere out beyond the Confederate flanks and perhaps bag the whole Army of Tennessee.

Polk and Hardee lost no time in responding and advising Bragg to retreat to Cowan and fight there rather than along the Elk. They simply did not want the army to accept battle with Bragg in command. As they anxiously awaited Bragg's decision, Hardee seems even to have entertained thoughts of mutiny and removing Bragg from command. At 8:30 that evening, Hardee wrote Polk a note marked "Confidential." "I have been thinking seriously of the condition of this army," he began. Bragg's poor health made him unfit to exercise command, and what if the army should have to fight a battle? "What shall we do? What is best to be done to save this army and its honor? I think we ought to counsel together. Where is Buckner?"

He referred to Maj. Gen. Simon B. Buckner, who had been transferred out of the Army of Tennessee the preceding December to command first at Mobile and then in East Tennessee. A member of the anti-Bragg Kentucky clique, Buckner would be the next most senior general in the army, after Polk and Hardee, when he arrived from Knoxville, which he had left four days earlier with such reinforcements as his department could spare for Bragg. Hardee was suggesting that Buckner should be in on whatever irregular proceeding the generals might undertake. "When can we meet?" Hardee concluded. "I would like Buckner to be present." Military organizations ordinarily take a dim view of officers meeting secretly to decide what to do with their commanders. In this case, it never came to that. Within hours of arriving on the Elk River line, Bragg complied with his lieutenants' directions and ordered the army to retreat to Cowan. A relieved Hardee wrote another note to Polk, sheepishly explaining that no meeting would now be necessary and adding, understandably, "I do not desire that any one but Buckner and yourself should know my anxiety."[39]

Having already abandoned several positions stronger than the one at Cowan, the Army of Tennessee was never really in earnest about making a stand there. In fact, the retreat paused there barely twenty-four hours. By the evening of July 2, the army was again in motion up the road onto the Cumberlands. By 3:00 A.M., July 3, the tail end of the column had passed through Sewanee, and Polk, riding just ahead of the rear-guard cavalry, visited the chosen site of the university of his dreams one last time before cantering off after his retreating troops. On the fourth—the day Vicksburg surrendered and Lee began his retreat from Gettysburg—the Army of Tennessee crossed the Tennessee River on its way to Chattanooga. By the evening of the seventh, the whole army had reached the town and encamped beneath the looming form of Lookout Mountain.[40]

Rosecrans had tried to mount a vigorous pursuit. Negley's and Brannan's divisions of the XIV Corps and Philip H. Sheridan's of the XX Corps reached the Elk River the evening of July 1 and exchanged fire with Confederate troops holding the opposite bank. The bridges, however, were destroyed, and the river was still all but unfordable. Even the aggressive Sheridan was able to do nothing to prevent the Confederates from breaking contact and withdrawing untouched over the mountains.

The river was dropping rapidly, though, and on July 3, Sheridan found a ford. He had his men stretch a rope across the river to aid the weaker ones in breasting the roaring current. Most of the division felt no need for such aid. "Placing their cartridge boxes on their shoulders," Sheridan reported, "[they] went in with a cheer, en masse, supporting each other, and the entire command was crossed without any loss, although the stream was deep and rapid." Yet, having got over, the division found it had very little to do. Only Confederate cavalry remained in the neighborhood, and with the main body of the Army of Tennessee now well clear and the Elk falling toward fording stage again, the Southern horsemen showed no propensity to linger. Rosecrans gave orders for the army to halt and wait for supplies to be brought up. The Tullahoma campaign, as it came to be called, was over.[41]

"Thus ended a nine days' campaign," Rosecrans wrote in his report, "which drove the enemy from two fortified positions and gave us possession of Middle Tennessee, conducted in one of the most extraordinary rains ever known in Tennessee at that period of the year." Only the rain and the mud, Rosecrans maintained, along with the resulting delays, had prevented him from cutting Bragg's communications and bringing him "to a very disastrous battle." Perhaps that was true, but the Tullahoma campaign had been a complex series of maneuvers with many variables that could have affected its outcome.[42]

If Rosecrans took a triumphant tone in his report, written in Winchester three weeks after the army halted, he could well afford to. His plans had been nothing short of brilliant, complex yet practical and perfectly adapted to his army's capabilities. He could view their success as a vindication of his slow, patient, methodical preparation of the army and gathering of intelligence while the authorities in Washington had fumed.

In part, the campaign was such a vindication. If all the war that mattered was being waged between Nashville and the Blue Ridge, Rosecrans's early summer campaign could not have been better conceived and planned. His delays, however, reduced the value of the campaign to the overall Union war effort. Instead of helping Grant at Vicksburg, Rosecrans had been helped by him, profiting from the absence of Army of Tennessee troops diverted to oppose Grant. As events developed, Grant was victorious at Vicksburg but no thanks to Rosecrans, who, with the nation's second largest army, had, for some six months, failed to pull his weight. And while concentrating on operations within one's own theater to the neglect of the greater ends of national strategy could, as in this case, sometimes yield a local success, it could also have the opposite effect. Before the autumn leaves fell that year, Rosecrans would have to face other troops, now occupied elsewhere, but who would be available for service in Tennessee by the time he got around to moving again.

Like his planning and preparation, Rosecrans's execution of his campaign had been, for the most part, excellent. One of the most significant factors was that he did not lose his nerve. At several times during the campaign a less resolute commander might have called the whole thing off and either stopped where he was or pulled back to Murfreesboro. That Rosecrans did not do so owed a good deal to his excellent intelligence. Rosecrans had detailed and accurate knowledge of Bragg's forces and dispositions before the campaign and so could form good estimates of Bragg's movements. In this campaign, Rosecrans faced few of the uncertainties that allow imagination to create the inward enemies that vanquished many a Civil War general.

If there was a fault with Rosecrans's conduct of the Tullahoma campaign, it was that he showed his old tendency to stop and wait until everything was perfect before proceeding with his operations. He maintained that the delays at Hoover's Gap and Manchester were the result of rain, and, in a sense, they were. Yet in each case they were circumstances that presented Rosecrans with the choice of pressing on as rapidly as possible with the force at hand or waiting until all was perfect. Ever the neurotic perfectionist, Rosecrans balked at the idea of making the best of a muddled situation and thus gaining an advantage on a foe who might be in even worse shape. Among the test tubes, beakers, and Bunsen burners of the laboratory, such patient precision might be indispensable, but in war it might allow an enemy—who had temporarily been put at a disadvantage—to recover and seize the initiative. A general who lost the initiative might not get it back again until he had been soundly whipped. Being able to strike the delicate balance between rashness, on the one hand, and a dangerous timidity, on the other, is no doubt a very large part of the art of war. If Rosecrans's practice of that art is subject to some latter-day criticism, it nevertheless proved to be more than adequate for the task before him in June 1863.

With the exception of its Pioneer Brigade, the Army of the Cumberland had functioned flawlessly, never putting a foot wrong throughout the campaign. Although the operations along the Highland Rim and on the Barrens had offered little opportunity for heroics, the quality of the army's performance is evident in the fact that all of Rosecrans's designs were executed promptly and effectively, except when extraordinary weather conditions intervened. Especially distinguished in these operations had been Wilder's Lightning Brigade. More would be heard from it in coming months.

Bragg and the Army of Tennessee in the Tullahoma campaign present a depressing contrast. Bragg's strategy was good. The choice of the position behind the Highland Rim was about the best possible under the circumstances.[43] Bragg's plan to use Polk to strike Rosecrans in flank was a good one, and his orders to Polk to that effect had every promise of producing spectacular results if Polk and Hardee had cooperated. That, however, was the problem. The Army of Tennessee's high command was a tangled mass of bitterness, jealousy, and hatred. It was now nearing the point of ceasing to function, and the Tullahoma campaign had increased its debility. Braxton Bragg, though an excellent organizer, disciplinarian, and strategist and a no worse than average tactician, was a decidedly mediocre politician. He genuinely tried to win the goodwill of his subordinates and superiors, but the result was often clumsy. He struggled against a natural bluntness so that he appeared alternately offensive and patronizing. A victorious general could probably have survived such a lack of skills in interpersonal relations, but it was Bragg's lot to have forced upon him as his first campaign an impossible dream based on wishful thinking. After the retreat from Kentucky, things had never been the same. Instead, as the Tullahoma campaign demonstrated, they just kept getting worse.

If Bragg lacked a vital attribute of a good general in that he did not have the ability to motivate his officers to enthusiastic cooperation, there can be no denying that he lacked the sort of army to command that Rosecrans had. The rank and file of the Army of Tennessee had plenty of courage and had already endured a great deal of hard campaigning and short rations. Their morale, however, seems to have been going a bit soft by this time. They had suffered defeat several times without a single victory, and they may have been coming to have a jaundiced view of their commanders, particularly if any of the commanders' attitudes toward each other had filtered down through the ranks. Also, many of the Army of Tennessee's soldiers, like many soldiers in all of the Confederacy's armies, fought neither for slavery nor for states' rights but merely to keep the semimythical "Yankee barbarians" away from hearth and home. When continued fighting no longer served that purpose, they would have no more reason to fight. This was especially critical for the Tennesseeans after the Tullahoma campaign, in which most of the remaining Confederate-held portions of their state had been lost. Rosecrans's provost marshal general reported taking over 1,600 prisoners during the campaign, 616 of whom claimed to have come in voluntarily, "being conscripts or tired of the war." Very likely the majority of Tennesseeans and others who slipped away from the army did not take themselves to Federal lines. In such rugged country, familiar to many of the men, evasion and return home would have been a more attractive option. The Tennessee brigade of Bushrod R. Johnson, which had fought as part of Stewart's division during the retreat from Hoover's Gap to Wartrace, lost 36 men to enemy action during the campaign and 335 to desertion.[44]

By far the greatest problem with the Army of Tennessee was its officer corps, particularly those highest in rank. Though devoid of military skills and virtues except, of course, physical courage, Polk, in contrast to Bragg, was a magnificent politician. He also possessed the friendship of Jefferson Davis and was all but impossible to remove. His continued presence was a tumor on the Army of Tennessee's high command, a tumor that had by now metastasized throughout the entire officer corps so that even such skillful division commanders as Cleburne and Stewart parroted their mentor Hardee—himself much under Polk's influence—in condemnation of Bragg. To be sure, the Army of Tennessee's commander had his faults, but no general, not even a Lee or a Grant, would have been likely to succeed against the circumstances Bragg faced.

In its results, the Tullahoma campaign was most striking in its incompleteness. Much territory had been gained for the Union, but the Army of Tennessee was still intact and at large, and East Tennessee, to Lincoln's continued dismay, remained under the Rebel heel. Indeed, the Washington authorities were anything but satisfied with Rosecrans and demanded that he finish the job. Rosecrans vainly requested that "the War Department may not overlook so great an event because it is not written in letters of blood," as were Gettysburg and Vicksburg. Yet as one of his own staff officers declared, "Brilliant campaigns without battles, do not accomplish the destruction of an army. A campaign like that of Tullahoma always means a battle at some other point."[45]

The Confederates were no more willing to accept the finality of the campaign's results. The authorities in Richmond were soon pondering the question of how Bragg's army might be sufficiently reinforced to allow him to reverse the verdict of those nine days and perhaps do what Rosecrans had failed to do: destroy the enemy's army.

CHAPTER THREE

We Must Force Him to Fight

As alarmed as the Confederate high command might have been about the loss of Middle Tennessee and Bragg's retreat to Chattanooga, no corresponding feeling of elation cheered the authorities in Washington. From their perspective, the Tullahoma campaign had been not so much a victory as a promising first step, and much of its strategic promise was related to other events in far-flung theaters of the war. Union victories at Vicksburg and Gettysburg convinced Lincoln, Stanton, and Halleck that the Confederacy was finally tottering to its ruin. A few more hard blows might complete its destruction. This was no time for methodical war and set-piece campaigns; rather, the men in Washington were more eager than ever for a war of momentum, now that the momentum was all on their side.

That, however, was simply not the way William Starke Rosecrans made war. By mid-July he had once again settled into a secure base—Winchester this time, with some of the army's units at Manchester and McMinnville—and was stockpiling supplies in preparation for a projected advance sometime in the vague future. Halleck and Stanton had also returned to their old pursuits, trying to prod Rosecrans into motion again, and another wearisome exchange of letters and telegrams ensued. Lincoln was more sympathetic toward the Army of the Cumberland's commander, yet he too remained less than satisfied. The liberation of East Tennessee was his most pressing immediate goal in that sector, and it was a task that remained to be done. To East Tennesseeans who petitioned him for prompt action to free their region of Rebel control, Lincoln wrote, "I do as much for East Tennessee as I would, or could, if my own home and family were in Knoxville." With that commitment, Lincoln, though patient, could not be indifferent to Rosecrans's seeming slowness to advance.[1]

By the first week of August, Halleck had become impatient enough to resort to a direct order. "Your forces must move forward without delay," he wired Rosecrans. "You will daily report the movement of each corps till you cross the Tennessee River." Rosecrans replied hotly that he was doing his best to get ready to move and asked if Halleck intended the order to take away his "discretion as to the time and manner of moving." That was precisely Halleck's intention. "The orders for the advance of your army, and that it be reported daily," he wired back to the reluctant general, "are peremptory." In this Rosecrans could see nothing but "recklessness, conceit and malice," and he determined not to obey. With the support of his corps and division commanders, he composed a telegram to Halleck requesting to be relieved of command if he were not permitted to delay the advance until at least August 17. To move any sooner, he insisted, would be to court disaster.[2]

When Rosecrans presented the telegram to his generals, Thomas agreed vehemently. "That's right," he blurted. "Stand by that, and we will stand by you to the last." The outburst was uncharacteristic of the reserved Thomas, but the opinion was not. If Rosecrans was simply a more gifted and mercurial version of Buell, Thomas was a more steady and methodical version of Rosecrans. All three generals made war the way they would have approached an exercise in geometry. War was not an art for them but a science, and they would wage it scientifically and methodically, preparing for every contingency and removing all uncertainty. It was not the way Lincoln would have had them do it nor the way Grant would have done, but as the Tullahoma campaign demonstrated, it could at times win limited but very impressive successes.[3]

The lone dissenter among Rosecrans's generals was his chief of staff, James A. Garfield. Garfield was a politician, and he was politically astute enough to realize that it was much to his advantage to be known in Washington as one who favored an advance. He had already made sure that Washington did know about it by writing to his friend Treasury Secretary Salmon P. Chase to complain of the Army of the Cumberland's inaction. Yet his discontent may have been more than a mere cynical ploy. As a politician who had already served in the Ohio legislature and also had connections in the nation's capital, Garfield was in a better position than anyone else at Rosecrans's headquarters to understand and appreciate a perspective larger than that of the Army of the Cumberland.[4]

Rosecrans ignored the chief of staff's remonstrances and sent the telegram anyway. It was not welcome in Washington, but it accomplished its purpose. Directing operations from the end of a telegraph wire several hundred miles long was a questionable enough undertaking in the first place. Sacking a general who refused to be maneuvered by remote control would mean taking a great deal of responsibility. In any case, Lincoln still had patience with Rosecrans and wrote him a kindly letter assuring him of his continued goodwill but admonishing him that other than purely military considerations had to be taken into account in the operations of the nation's armies. In the end, Rosecrans got his way, and the Army of the Cumberland remained idle until he felt ready to move again.[5]

It would not have been much comfort to the men in Washington or at Army of the Cumberland headquarters at Winchester, but other politicians and generals were also going through difficult deliberations just then as to what military policies promised best success. For months influential Confederates both in and out of the army had been urging that Southern forces be concentrated for a powerful blow against the Federal center—Rosecrans. Proponents of the scheme, from General P. G. T. Beauregard at Charleston, South Carolina, to Texas senator Louis T. Wigfall, believed that reinforcements for Bragg's army should be drawn from Virginia, Mississippi, and Charleston. After crushing the Army of the Cumberland, the Confederacy could set its western affairs to rights, forcing Grant out of Mississippi and perhaps even advancing to the Ohio River.[6]

Such hopes had dimmed somewhat in midsummer 1863. Vicksburg and Port Hudson had fallen and some 30,000 or so Confederate soldiers become prisoners of war—paroled, it was true, but demoralized. With the Mississippi securely in his grasp from Cairo to the Gulf, Grant was giving his full attention to chasing Johnston's 23,000-man army across the state of Mississippi, more than halfway to the Alabama line. Meanwhile, any surplus of troops that Robert E. Lee might have had—beyond the minimum required to defend Virginia—had just been reduced by about 28,000 on the slaughter fields of Gettysburg.

Still, the loss of Middle Tennessee looked as much like a beginning to those in Richmond as it did to those in Washington. The calamities of this year might be far from over for the Confederacy unless some decisive action were taken. Thus galvanized, the advocates of Confederate concentration west of the Appalachians stepped up their efforts. Apparently coming around somewhat to that view himself, Davis had Confederate adjutant and inspector general Samuel Cooper wire Bragg at the beginning of August to ask if he thought he could accomplish anything if Johnston's army were added to his own.[7]

Bragg had already been thinking about a junction of the two forces, though in a different direction. A fortnight earlier he had written Johnston to suggest bringing all but a few brigades of his own army to Mississippi for a combined blow against Grant. Bragg reckoned that Rosecrans would not feel up to advancing until September (an estimate that was overoptimistic by only about two weeks), and that would give the Confederates six weeks to deal with Grant. Johnston was uninterested. Now that Vicksburg had fallen, he had little hope for the success of the movement, and besides, he had more important business on hand, being engaged in an involved and unseemly argument with Jefferson Davis as to who was at fault for the loss of Vicksburg.[8]

Bragg first responded favorably to Davis's suggestion of a concentration on his own front but soon changed his mind. Between his army at Chattanooga and the Federals around Winchester lay the Cumberland Plateau. Pouncing on an unsuspecting foe was an inviting idea, but crossing that mountain barrier in the teeth of enemy resistance and with a very shaky supply service was definitely not. On further consideration, Bragg wired Davis that he did not believe he could be successful under those circumstances. Back in Richmond, Cooper fumed at what he saw as a prime opportunity slipping away and suggested to Davis that they order Bragg to carry out the offensive. Like Lincoln, however, Davis demurred. "However desirable a movement may be," he explained to Cooper, "it is never safe to do more than suggest it to a commanding general, it would be unwise to order its execution by one who foretold failure." Johnston's troops stayed in Mississippi, and the Army of Tennessee stayed in Chattanooga.[9]

Perhaps, however, Bragg could be more amply reinforced, and from the opposite direction. Along the East Tennessee & Virginia Railroad northeast from the Army of Tennessee's camps around Chattanooga lay a force of about five thousand infantry guarding East Tennessee under Simon B. Buckner, recently returned from their abortive dash to reinforce Bragg during the Tullahoma campaign. These Davis placed under Bragg's command. He could summon them whenever need arose or opportunity beckoned. Bragg designated the force the III Corps, Army of Tennessee, but for the moment left it where it was. Five thousand men would not be enough for an offensive that was doubtful with four times that number of reinforcements, so for the moment there was no point in further aggravating the supply situation around Chattanooga.[10]

Yet, beyond Buckner's camps in East Tennessee, that same railroad led into Virginia, and the possibility of reinforcing Bragg from Lee's Army of Northern Virginia continued to intrigue many Confederates, among them Lee's chief lieutenant and "Old Warhorse," James Longstreet.

Born in South Carolina in 1821 and raised in Georgia, Longstreet had graduated fifty-fourth in the fifty-six-man West Point class of 1842. He had done well as a junior officer in the Mexican War and had served in the U.S. Army until secession. Rising rapidly in the Confederate army, Longstreet had shown himself able to administer large formations and maneuver them around the battlefield. Unfortunately, that ability did not extend to knowing what maneuvers those units ought to undertake, as the battles of Williamsburg and Seven Pines clearly demonstrated. Yet many other battles demonstrated Longstreet's greatest strength—his calm, unflappable demeanor and reassuring presence. He was a motivation to his troops and a steadying influence to fellow officers of more nervous temperament. Lee had learned to give Longstreet plenty of direct supervision, leaving independent maneuvers to Jackson until that officer's death in May 1863. Lee's genius with Longstreet's solidity and ability to handle a corps had combined to make the latter's I Corps of the Army of Northern Virginia into a hard-hitting fighting force.

Unfortunately, Longstreet had grown proud, and his self-confidence had swollen into conceit. He criticized Lee behind his back, turned sullen and balky when Lee's orders did not suit him, and chafed at having to serve under the Virginian. With growing ambition, Longstreet began to scheme at getting out from under Lee and gaining command of an army of his own. The most likely opportunity for such a move had long appeared to be in replacing one of the Confederacy's two most maligned generals, John C. Pemberton at Vicksburg or Braxton Bragg. Longstreet had already requested such a move several times during 1863. In early August he renewed his request to Secretary of War James A. Seddon, lobbying Wigfall to the same end for good measure. His replacement of Bragg, he pleaded, was the only way to save the Confederacy. He further assured the authorities that he had no selfish motive in requesting it.[11]

Davis showed no inclination to shelve Bragg in favor of Longstreet, but he did seem interested in transferring Longstreet along with his contingent of the Army of Northern Virginia to reinforce Bragg. Yet decision did not come easy for Davis, and he liked to hash out his possibilities very thoroughly with his circle of advisers before taking action. In this case that circle included Lee, whose reluctance to part with a sizable chunk of his army further drew out the process of deliberation. By the end of the third week of August, Davis had yet to issue orders.

That so much time had been accorded both Davis and his Northern counterpart for decisions about what generals to keep and what policies to pursue was in large part a result of the peculiarly sticky strategic situation then prevailing in southeastern Tennessee. If Bragg was reluctant to take the offensive and Rosecrans all but mutinous in his refusal to do so, each man had the mitigating factor of facing a prodigiously tough problem of logistics and operations. The Cumberland Plateau that formed a wall between them was thirty miles of rugged, barren country with poor roads and virtually no food or fodder. Practically any route through them presented nightmarish supply problems and one or more powerful defensive positions where an army could be bottled up. Even having gotten across them, the commander who did so was likely to find himself fighting with his back to a towering escarpment and questionable line of retreat while his supplies—such as he might be able to get—were being hauled over execrable mountain roads by straining mules.

Little wonder, then, that neither commander was eager to attempt the feat except under ideal conditions. Bragg, though forgoing a chance to seize the initiative, could reasonably demur and force on Rosecrans the onerous task of coming over the mountain to get him. The Union commander, on the other hand, could not delay forever and sooner or later must attempt the dangerous maneuver.

Although Bragg had the age-old advantage of the defender, his task was far from easy. The best place to defend the Cumberland Plateau was atop its towering ramparts, preferably along the crest of the southeast wall of the Sequatchie Valley. Yet placing the army on top of the plateau (actually the Walden's Ridge portion of it southeast of the Sequatchie) would present even worse supply problems than taking it clear across, since it would mean putting the army in the most difficult possible position to supply and then keeping it there. And while the Cumberlands were full of wonderful defensive positions, those would avail Bragg only if he could get there with his army before Rosecrans had passed them. Yet Rosecrans's potential routes across the Cumberlands were spread over 150 miles of front, and Bragg could not hope to cover all the passes in force. A possible solution might have been to use his cavalry to patrol the top of the plateau aggressively and hope that it would provide him warning of Rosecrans's approach ample for taking up a defensive position and denying the Federals egress from the southeast side of the Cumberlands. Yet with so much front to cover, Bragg felt he needed his horsemen extending his area of surveillance on either flank. A Union lodgment on his side of the Cumberlands might be regrettable, but a Federal army going untouched and unnoticed around one of his flanks and into his rear could be downright disastrous.[12]

To complicate matters further, Union general Ambrose Burnside was in Kentucky with a sizable force, the Federal Army of the Ohio (not to be confused with the predecessor organization of the Army of the Cumberland, which had borne the same name). Burnside was threatening to move south through Cumberland Gap. During the Vicksburg campaign the IX Corps, about half of Burnside's strength, had been sent down to Grant to make the capture of the Confederate stronghold more certain. Now it was back, and indications were that Burnside would soon be advancing directly into East Tennessee from the north, threatening Knoxville and the vital East Tennessee & Virginia Railroad. From the Confederate point of view, the most frightening scenario would be for Rosecrans to link up with Burnside before attacking Bragg. The Army of Tennessee commander had to prevent that if he possibly could, and that meant deploying his forces more heavily on the northeast side of Chattanooga, watching the Tennessee River fords upstream from the city. Whatever Bragg may have thought the most likely path of a Union advance, the possibility of a Rosecrans-Burnside concentration was simply too serious a threat to be ignored. Thus deployed, Bragg waited for Rosecrans to make the next move.[13]

That move came on August 16. That same day, Burnside marched the Army of the Ohio southeastward from Camp Nelson, Kentucky, near Lexington, toward Cumberland Gap and East Tennessee. As he had been earlier that summer, Rosecrans was thoroughly prepared and moved with skill and dispatch. Spreading out from their camps scattered across the Barrens from Winchester to McMinnville, Rosecrans's divisions presented a broad front to deceive Bragg as to the main axis of his advance and to minimize traffic jams on narrow mountain roads. Crittenden's XXI Corps advanced on the Union left, its three divisions moving separately by three different roads over the Cumberland Plateau and down into the Sequatchie Valley and sending advance elements over Walden's Ridge and down into the Tennessee Valley. There they were joined by two cavalry brigades, Minty's Saber Brigade, and Wilder's Lightning Brigade.[14]

Their mission was to make the biggest possible show, and they proved to have no lack of chutzpah. Brig. Gen. William B. Hazen had overall command of the four-brigade advance force in the Tennessee Valley, and he had the troops marching this way and that, lobbing a shell across the river here, a few more someplace else, lighting surplus campfires and generally looking as numerous as possible. Just out of sight of the river, details went about their assignments of banging on empty casks and sawing up boards into scraps, which were then tossed into tributaries of the Tennessee and allowed to float down into Rebel view, all for the purpose of convincing the Southerners that someone was building boats nearby on a large scale. Indeed, Hazen had some of his men build the real thing, just in case they should come in handy.

True to form, Wilder's men were the stars of the show and enjoyed themselves immensely. On August 21, they were the first Federals to reach the north bank of the Tennessee opposite Chattanooga, and they reached it so suddenly that they captured the Confederate pickets stationed there and shot their relief detail to pieces, caught in an open boat on its way across the river. Then Wilder had Capt. Eli Lilly unlimber his Eighteenth Indiana Battery, attached to the Lightning Brigade, and see what mischief he could do in a cross-river target shoot. Lilly, sometime druggist of Greencastle, Indiana, lately turned artillerist, served up bitter medicine for the Rebels, sinking one Confederate steamboat, damaging another, and blasting the daylights out of a pontoon bridge the Southerners were holding in reserve on the south bank. Wilder noted with satisfaction the utter consternation of the Confederates, who seemed to be running hither and thither like so many frantic insects in a disturbed anthill. Presently, some of them manned a battery just west of town and replied to Lilly's guns. The Hoosier gunners silenced them in short order. Another Rebel gun crew made the attempt, opening up with a heavy, rifled 32-pounder in a well-dug emplacement. They got off one shot. Then in a spectacular demonstration of artillery sharpshooting, Lilly put a shell right through the embrasure, and no more was heard from that quarter. All in all it was a very satisfactory afternoon for Wilder's boys. Thereafter, they enthusiastically joined in the game of faking large-scale crossings of the Tennessee at every halfway practicable site from Chattanooga forty miles up the river to the hamlet of Washington.[15]

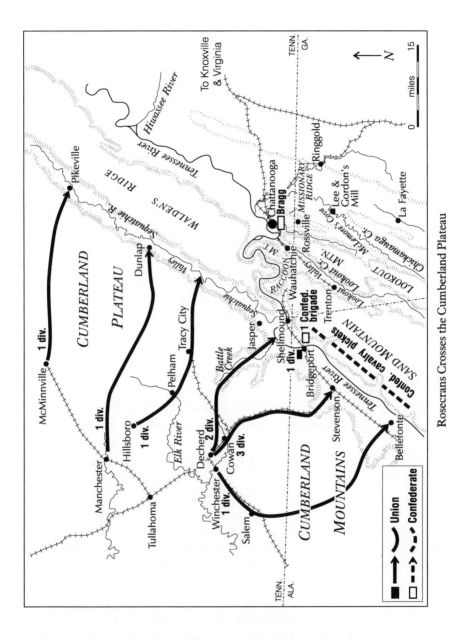

Rosecrans Crosses the Cumberland Plateau

August 21 was not nearly so enjoyable a day on the south bank of the Tennessee River. Bragg was absent, twenty miles away at an army hospital near Ringgold, Georgia, where he had gone partially for treatment of his list of physical ailments and partially to visit his ailing wife, who was also a patient. No one else in the Army of Tennessee seems to have had any more idea than he that action was imminent. The Confederate cavalry had been deployed well out to the flanks and had in any case been fascinated with what its officers saw as a movement by Rosecrans to link up with Burnside, who the day before had reached the Tennessee River far upstream near Knoxville. No Confederate seems to have imagined the Federals would do anything as cheeky as appearing directly across from the main Southern base at Chattanooga and shooting up the place.[16]

Bragg had not been so very wrong in discounting the possibility that Rosecrans would attempt to cross the river in the very teeth of the Confederate army at Chattanooga. It would have been well-nigh impossible—despite Wilder's bit of rowdy fun on the north bank—and in fact the Northern commander contemplated no such course. For the moment, Wilder, Minty, Hazen, and the other Federals in the upper Tennessee Valley presented no more threat to capture Chattanooga than they did Richmond. But they could be an infernal distraction.

Bragg hastened back to his headquarters to find reports of Union activity at dozens of places up and down the Tennessee for forty miles on either side of Chattanooga. Somewhere in all that mass of sometimes contradictory data must lie the true information that would reveal what Rosecrans was doing. The problem was sifting and weighing the many reports. The most intense activity seemed to be upstream, and that was the direction of the Confederates' greatest fears. Bragg and his top subordinates believed that Rosecrans would link up with Burnside, separating Bragg's forces at Chattanooga from Buckner's in East Tennessee. Burnside's twenty thousand men added to Rosecrans's sixty-two thousand would make so vast a host that there was no telling when if ever the Confederates might stop it. Bragg thus interpreted the Union presence in the Sequatchie Valley and upstream along the Tennessee as an effort to take Buckner in rear and then to carry out just the sort of program he most feared. To counter it, he ordered Buckner, who had already abandoned Knoxville in the face of Burnside's oncoming juggernaut, to fall back to the Hiwassee River, a stream that flowed down off the Blue Ridge and emptied into the Tennessee about thirty-five miles above

Chattanooga. He also shifted his infantry more heavily in that direction. He had already reinforced Buckner with a division from the Army of Tennessee, and now he deployed another division in detachments at all of the possible crossing points up the river to Buckner's position. There the anxious Confederates waited for action, listening to Hazen's men hammer and saw by day and counting their numerous campfires by night. At the same time Bragg drew in a lone infantry brigade that had been watching the Tennessee twenty-five miles or so downstream just across from Bridgeport, Alabama. The cavalry pickets along the crest of Sand Mountain, overlooking that downstream stretch of the Tennessee, would have to suffice. With his army concentrated between Chattanooga and the Hiwassee, Bragg was ready to counter the dreaded Union upstream movement, but by August 25 he had become painfully aware of another problem. He had lost Rosecrans.

At first, affairs had seemed to develop properly. After he had drawn Buckner in closer to Chattanooga, Bragg noted that the Northern formations in the Sequatchie Valley had turned and marched southwestward down the valley, apparently foiled in their scheme to crush Buckner against Burnside. The upstream Federals were still much in evidence along the Tennessee, but the powerful movement that their activities seemed to herald did not take place. Miscellaneous reports of other Union activity continued to trickle in, but it became increasingly apparent that Rosecrans's main force was yet to be located. The Confederate commander could only survey the forested ridges that crowded Chattanooga's horizon to the north, east, and west and reflect that somewhere out there beyond those heights his enemy was maneuvering with a view to his destruction.[17]

For Bragg, pulling in the downstream brigade opposite Bridgeport had been a most unfortunate move. Along the north bank within five miles of its old position, or hastening down to the river through several of the valleys that creased the rim of the Cumberland Plateau, were seven divisions of the Army of the Cumberland, the XIV and XX Corps. At the same time Crittenden's divisions had started by their three routes over the plateau farther north, Thomas's and McCook's men had taken three more southerly paths over the mountains. In a far-flung movement that had McCook's southernmost division sometimes as much as seventy-five miles from Crittenden's northernmost up in the Sequatchie, they made their way to positions along the north bank of the Tennessee from Shellmound, at the mouth of the Sequatchie, to Bridgeport, where the Nashville & Chattanooga as well as the

Memphis & Charleston had crossed the river before the bridge was burned. The broad-fronted advance speeded the movement by making use of different roads, and at the same time it added to the confusion of the intelligence reports reaching Bragg.[18]

With two corps concentrated around the intended crossings, Rosecrans on August 30 sent for Crittenden to bring his Sequatchie Valley forces down to the river to follow the rest of the army across, leaving only the four brigades in the Tennessee Valley to keep up the bluff. By the morning of September 1, all three of Crittenden's divisions were marching south, the movement Bragg had interpreted as a reaction to his withdrawal of Buckner from East Tennessee. Meanwhile, Rosecrans's men had begun their crossings. The army laid its single pontoon bridge at Caperton's Ferry after securing the south bank in a cross-river assault by a single brigade carried in the pontoon boats. The few Confederate cavalrymen were easily scattered. More troops were marching over the bridge and most of the army's wagons were rolling across it before the end of August 29. In the midst of their warlike advance, some of the Federals could not ignore the grandeur of their surroundings. "The Tennessee at this place is beautiful," wrote one diarist. "The bridge looks like a ribbon stretched across it. The island below, the heavily wooded banks, the bluffs and mountain, present a scene that would delight the soul of the artist." Other Union soldiers found more prosaic delights, and full a hundred of them went in swimming, "ducking and splashing each other, and having a glorious time generally."[19]

A couple of miles upstream Sheridan was frustrated in his task of contriving a makeshift bridge there. Given the resources and time available to him, this was no easy assignment. He had thought the job complete by the twenty-ninth, but part of his jerry-built engineering wonder had collapsed and the structure could not be made ready for use again until September 2.[20]

By that time troops still farther upstream had made good their crossing. Brig. Gen. John M. Brannan had made do with no bridge at all. At the mouth of Battle Creek his men began crossing on August 31, swimming and pushing their bundles of clothing and equipment on rails or logs in front of them. Their wagons they ferried across on makeshift rafts. By the time Sheridan's bridge was operational, Brannan's men were across. At the farthest upstream of the crossing points, Shellmound, Maj. Gen. Joseph Reynolds's division had an easier time. They had captured a fair number of flatboats upon reaching the river and so were able to ferry themselves, their wagons, and artillery across in style.[21]

The crossing was not entirely without its frustrations for Rosecrans. Though the army was using four different crossing sites, it nevertheless had only a very limited number of boats and bridges, and congestion was inevitable. Thus when Crittenden's divisions came up to the crossings they got entangled with the various supply and ordnance trains of the rest of the army, resulting in delay. Even those units that had reached the southern bank could not begin maneuvering away from the river until such mundane things as the wagons full of hardtack and bacon had crossed and caught up with their units. Still, by September 4 the operation was complete. Rosecrans and his army were on the south bank, along with every one of their guns, caissons, limbers, and supply wagons—in all, enough ammunition to fight two major battles and food to last the better part of a month.[22]

Rosecrans now set out to turn Bragg's position at Chattanooga as he had the Confederate position in front of Tullahoma earlier that summer. This time, however, the movement would be complicated by the mountainous terrain. Three long ridges lay between Rosecrans's army and Bragg's supply artery, the Western & Atlantic Railroad. The first was Sand Mountain, a high, broad plateau analogous to Walden's Ridge on the other side of the Tennessee. It featured rugged roads and few sources of food or water. Beyond it lay a narrow valley and then a much more formidable barrier, Lookout Mountain. Narrower than Sand Mountain, it was also higher and steeper and, worst of all, rimmed with a fifty-foot rock wall, the palisades, around its top. Crossing it was at best extremely difficult and, for the wagons and artillery without which the army could not function, it was impossible save at a very few "gaps." These were not really gaps at all but simply breaks in the palisades through which tortuous wagon roads struggled to the summit. The third ridge was Missionary Ridge, mild compared to Lookout, but still impractical for wagons except at the gaps, real gaps this time, and more numerous than on Lookout.

The terrain presented Rosecrans with an operational problem that had no good solutions. To keep the army in a concentrated mass would mean endless delays laboring through those narrow gaps, and by that time Bragg would almost undoubtedly respond and plug the gaps, taking up a defensive position that would be a dream for him and a nightmare for Rosecrans. If, on the other hand, the Union commander spread his army out to take advantage of several of the gaps, his corps would be a bit wider spread than good practice dictated, out of supporting distance of one another and vulnerable should Bragg detect the movement and respond aggressively. Still

this latter course offered the greatest rewards, and Rosecrans did not hesi-
tate to choose it.

He sent Crittenden's corps on the most direct route toward Chattanooga,
following the railroad through the gap that separated Sand Mountain from
Raccoon Mountain, a crescent of high bluffs towering over the south bank
of the Tennessee. Once past Sand and Raccoon Mountains, Crittenden
would move into the valley at the western foot of Lookout Mountain, where
he was to take up position at the crossroads of Wauhatchie. Thence he could
threaten Chattanooga via the north end of Lookout Mountain, where the
mountain sloped down abruptly from its spectacular peak to the banks of
the Tennessee. Hugging the curving riverbank and wrapping around the
northern foot of the mountain ran the railroad and wagon road. If they could
get into Chattanooga that way, so could Crittenden—unless Bragg stayed
put there to block him.

Thomas's XIV Corps would take several roads over Sand Mountain, then
unite in Lookout Valley and march south to cross the mountain by way of
Stevens Gap, twenty-four miles south of Crittenden's position. McCook
would swing even farther south, striking for Winston's Gap, forty-two miles
from the Tennessee and Crittenden, eighteen from Thomas. Once McCook
got his XX Corps over Lookout, Rosecrans wanted him to push even further to the southeast, aiming for Alpine, Georgia. It was a daring move, but
Rosecrans was reaching for the throat of the Confederacy's second largest
army, and certain risks had to be accepted.[23]

Rosecrans had the unbounded confidence of his soldiers. They had already advanced over a hundred miles by the strategy of "Old Rosey," as
they called him, and the present move appeared to be yet another of his brilliant maneuvers. As the corps swung south and east through their self-made
dust clouds on their divergent courses, the soldiers found the march very
much like those that had come before in the two and a half weeks of the
present campaign, with little or no contact with the enemy and even more
beautiful scenery. "The view is a magnificent one," wrote one soldier from
the gap between Raccoon and Sand Mountains. "One can see to the north
and west miles upon miles of country, stretching out until it is lost in the
blue misty atmosphere. Here and there you can see a plantation with its
houses and out buildings. . . . The river, as it winds along in its serpentine
course, looks like a silver thread reflecting the warm rays of the sun, a thing
of beauty in the distance." He surveyed the long moving columns of troops

with their shining rifle barrels and the white-topped army wagons that dotted the road behind them, and, in what seems to have been the army's consensus, he added, "What a living, moving picture for some artist to transfer to canvas, with its many colored features. It would take a master hand to do it small justice."[24]

In one way, the campaign offered a new experience for these blue-clad soldiers. Although Shelbyville's Unionists had received them enthusiastically that summer, most of the troops had been campaigning amid a hostile populace. Now, it was very different, particularly on the march through the Cumberlands of Tennessee and down to the river. This was the beginning of the cultural region of East Tennessee, and the people they encountered were the loyal men and women whom Lincoln had fretted more than two years to have delivered from Rebel oppression. The people were for the most part poor mountaineers who had suffered severely for their loyalty at the hands of the Rebel authorities. Men had been forced to hide for months in the woods and caves to evade Confederate conscription officers determined to put them in the ranks of those arrayed against their chosen government. Unsuccessful evasion attempts carried a price. Wilder's men in their rapid advance freed eight Union men from Confederate custody, five of them just minutes before they were to have been hanged. Yet in months gone by no bluecoated horsemen had been at hand to deliver such men, and numerous East Tennesseeans had paid with their lives for their loyalty. One widow related to some of Crittenden's men how her husband had been forced to dig his own grave and then stand in front of it to be gunned down.[25]

Despite their hardships and poverty, the people were openhanded in their generosity to the liberators. "They vied with each other in bestowing upon the boys their kindness," wrote one of Wilder's colonels, "sweet potatoes, all kinds of vegetables, ducks, chickens, pies, cakes, honey, and applejack brandy were among the gifts." When several of Rosecrans's staff officers stopped at a mountain cabin to ask for a drink of cool water, they were surprised at being welcomed in and seated at the kitchen table as honored guests. The lady of the cabin brought back from the springhouse not only water but butter and fresh milk too, delicacies the trail-worn Union officers had not seen for some time. The children of the family eagerly waved small United States flags, carefully hidden during two years of Rebel rule. In a letter to his sister regarding the march through loyal East Tennessee, one of the officers noted, "All the men want to act as guides for us, and three hundred have just enlisted in our ranks."[26]

As the army fanned out from the banks of the Tennessee River and headed for the passes of Lookout Mountain, the troops were marching through northwestern Georgia or extreme southern Tennessee, and the populace was again pro-Confederate or at least equivocal. Other than that, the march was much as it had been, dustier now that a dry spell had set in, but still along rough dirt roads through rugged, scenic mountains and thick forests of oak and beech broken by seemingly random clearings and their hardscrabble farms. They were at war, but for the moment there was little sign of the enemy.

By September 8 all three columns had reached their first objectives, Crittenden at Wauhatchie, Thomas's lead division atop Lookout preparing to descend through Stevens Gap, and McCook's similarly positioned eighteen miles to the south at Winston's. That afternoon Thomas's men on the crest of Lookout spied, "far off to the east, long lines of dust trending slowly to the south," and drew the conclusion that Bragg was abandoning Chattanooga. Rosecrans was riding with Thomas and by evening had received additional confirmation of the news. Rosecrans's plans, however were bigger than merely taking Chattanooga. He saw this as his opportunity to accomplish what had eluded him in the Tullahoma campaign two months before. He would destroy Bragg's army. A steady stream of Confederate deserters had been coming into his lines, and many of them told of utter demoralization within the ranks of the Army of Tennessee. Bragg was whipped, it seemed, and would not stop north of Atlanta provided he was suitably pressed. Rosecrans planned to press him so hard he might not make it to Atlanta at all.[27]

Without hesitation, during the night of the eighth and predawn hours of the ninth, Rosecrans issued new orders transforming his far-flung turning movement into an all-out pursuit. Crittenden was to move around the point of Lookout Mountain, through Chattanooga, and then southward on the trail of the fleeing Southerners. At the other end of the army, McCook was to move down off Lookout with his entire corps, angling southeastward for Alpine and Summerville in hopes of cutting off Bragg's retreat or at least tearing at his flanks along the march. In the center, Thomas was to debouch from Stevens Gap into a valley known as McLemore's Cove. The cove's far side was formed by Pigeon Mountain, a large spur of Lookout that branched northeast, away from its main ridge, a few miles south of the gap.

Thomas was to push on across McLemore's Cove and then up and over Pigeon Mountain through Dug Gap. That would lead him down into La Fayette, Georgia, squarely astride the road from Chattanooga to Rome. If Bragg were retreating by that route, Rosecrans would have him. If, however, Bragg were falling back toward Atlanta by way of Ringgold and Dalton, Thomas, like McCook, would be well positioned to strike eastward toward the retreating Confederates.[28]

Thomas had other ideas. When Rosecrans dropped by his headquarters on the night of the eighth, Thomas objected that the Army of the Cumberland ought to fall back immediately toward Chattanooga. That, he thought, had been the objective of the campaign, and now that Bragg had been forced out of it, the Federals should halt there until supply and organization had once again been brought to a state of near perfection before setting out on another advance. Rosecrans was adamant, however. He could hardly have failed to guess how Thomas's recommended course of action would be viewed in Washington. Besides, opportunity beckoned. There were all those Confederate deserters and their tales of Bragg's dire condition. The Federal commander smelled victory and was determined to pursue it.[29]

So at 8:00 the next morning Thomas's lead division, that of Maj. Gen. James S. Negley, swung down the eastern slope of Lookout Mountain and into McLemore's Cove. By 4:00 P.M. the division had reached the bottom. Rebel cavalry were in front of them now in some force, and Negley's men pushed on across the cove, skirmishing all the way. The Union cavalry was all out on the far-spread flanks of the Army of the Cumberland, with none scouting in front of the center here, to reveal what might be lurking there. Instead, it was apparently loyal citizens who first brought reports to Negley of a large body of Confederates up ahead at Dug Gap. That night the division camped not far from the stream that drained McLemore's Cove, Chickamauga Creek. There was more truth in the reports of Confederates ahead than Negley, Thomas, or Rosecrans dreamed at the moment. The entire Army of Tennessee lurked just the other side of Pigeon Mountain.[30]

After Rosecrans had vanished from the Confederate intelligence picture on August 25, both Bragg and his lieutenants had continued to believe that the Union plan of campaign involved some sort of link-up between Rosecrans and Burnside. The activity just across the river could be genuine, indicating a direct assault in the neighborhood of Chattanooga or just upstream as soon as the two Federal armies joined hands, or it could be a feint. But if it was a feint, what movement did it cover? Intelligence was extremely

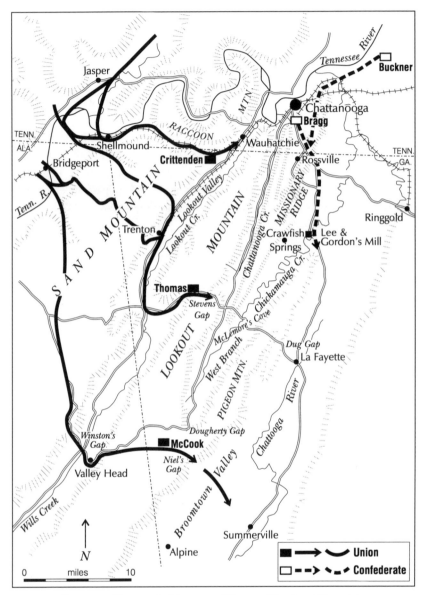

Rosecrans Crosses the Tennessee River and Lookout Mountain

sketchy, and the reports that did come in could be interpreted as indicating a crossing either well above or well below the town. The uncertainty created rising anxiety in the high command of the Army of Tennessee. Until his scouts and cavalry provided solid information, Bragg could only wait and keep on modifying his operational plans to fit the latest appearance of the situation.[31]

One other thing he could do was to request reinforcements. The obvious gravity of the situation gained hearings for his requests both in Richmond and at Johnston's headquarters in Mississippi. The latter dispatched two weak divisions, about nine thousand men, mostly troops Bragg had sent him that spring in hopes he could raise the Vicksburg siege. Bragg combined them with other troops to form a "reserve corps" under Maj. Gen. W. H. T. Walker.[32]

In Richmond, Bragg's pleas for reinforcements renewed Davis's interest in shifting troops west from the Army of Northern Virginia. The president summoned Lee to the capital for consultations. Lee was not eager to part with any of his troops, but Davis was insistent. Indeed, the president wanted Lee to go along and take temporary command of the reinforced Army of Tennessee. Lee was even more averse to this idea, and Davis did not press him. They made their final decision on September 5. Two of Lee's divisions, roughly ten thousand men, would go to the Army of Tennessee, but instead of Lee accompanying them to take command, they would be led by Longstreet, who was more eager than ever to have Bragg's job. Just days before, he had suggested that he ought to trade places with the Army of Tennessee commander, taking over that army and letting Bragg have his corps in the Army of Northern Virginia. Word that Bragg was to retain his position put Longstreet in an ill humor. To a friend he wrote, "I ought not to be under Bragg."[33]

Yet even as the president's scheme to reinforce Bragg was being conceived, Ambrose Burnside took from the Confederacy one of the chief means of effecting it. On September 2 his Army of the Ohio marched unopposed into Knoxville, to the cheers of its solidly Unionist population. That broke Confederate control of the East Tennessee & Virginia Railroad and meant that any reinforcements from Lee's army to Bragg's would have to travel a circuitous route down the various railroads of the eastern seaboard all the way to Atlanta, then back up the Western & Atlantic line to join Bragg at Chattanooga, or wherever he happened to be by the time they got there. It would be nearly two weeks before the first of Longstreet's troops joined the Army of Tennessee. For the moment, Bragg would have to make do with what he had.[34]

Even that prospect would not have been so grim during the first week of September if only Bragg could have been sure of where Rosecrans was and what he was doing. By August 31 enough information was available to confirm that very large Federal forces were crossing the Tennessee downstream from Chattanooga, in the vicinity of Shellmound, Battle Creek, and Bridgeport. That raised the specter of a Union lunge southward around Bragg's left, slicing the Army of Tennessee's communications in a region in which it could not hope to draw adequate supplies off the land. Such a move would have to be countered—powerfully—and Bragg knew he did not have the troops available to do that and hold Chattanooga at the same time. If the move was genuine and no feint, the gateway city would have to be abandoned.

Yet there was the rub. Bragg still could not know what Rosecrans meant to do with his bridgehead. The thought that he might find that he had given away Chattanooga in the face of a mere diversion gave him pause. He ordered the retreat, canceled the order, then, on the evening of September 7, renewed it as reports from pro-Southern civilians began to pile up in sufficient number to make clear that Rosecrans's forces were moving rapidly southward somewhere on the other side of Lookout Mountain. The army marched out of Chattanooga on the La Fayette Road early on September 8. Feelings in the ranks were mixed, some soldiers elated in the belief that the move was leading them to a battle, others discouraged at what looked for all the world like another retreat. By evening the corps of D. H. Hill (a replacement for Hardee, who had been transferred to Mississippi) had reached La Fayette, twenty-two miles south of Chattanooga. Polk's corps, along with Bragg's headquarters, was ten miles back at the place where the road crossed from the west to the east bank of Chickamauga Creek. There two leading local citizens operated a gristmill that gave the crossing its name, Lee and Gordon's Mill. Buckner's and Walker's troops were close behind.[35]

"A mountain is like the wall of a house full of rat-holes," Bragg later explained. "The rat lies hidden at his hole, ready to pop out when no one is watching." His problem on September 8 and 9 lay in the need to guess from which rat hole—mountain gap—Rosecrans's army would emerge. Guessing wrong could be disastrous, and the odds were much against guessing right. Rosecrans had outdone Bragg along the Highland Rim, the Cumberlands, and now the Tennessee River. Bragg apparently wondered if Lookout Mountain might finally be his undoing, and he expressed anxiety that Rosecrans might succeed in trapping the Army of Tennessee between La Fayette and Chattanooga.[36]

As when he had been in the latter place, intelligence reports were confusing and contradictory, but if he could not be sure what the enemy was doing, he would do his best to be sure the enemy was deceived as to his own actions. For that purpose he sent carefully primed "deserters" to Rosecrans with the story that the Army of Tennessee was in headlong retreat and about to come apart. Perhaps the Union commander could be coaxed into an indiscretion.[37]

Perhaps indeed. By late evening on the ninth, a picture was beginning to emerge from the murk of conflicting data reaching Bragg's headquarters, a picture so incredibly favorable to Bragg that he might well have wondered if his analysis was being colored by wishful thinking. This time the rat appeared to be popping out of a hole just where Bragg could best trap him. It seemed, at least, that a sizable Union force had marched down off Lookout Mountain through Stevens Gap and was now camping in McLemore's Cove, less than ten miles, by Dug Gap in Pigeon Mountain, from Bragg's main point of concentration at La Fayette and about the same distance from Bragg's right flank units near Lee and Gordon's Mill by way of a good road right up the valley of Chickamauga Creek. If the Federals were indeed where Bragg surmised them to be, Bragg now had an almost unprecedented opportunity to destroy a substantial piece of Rosecrans's army.[38]

Though Bragg could not be certain, his estimate of the situation in McLemore's Cove was precisely correct, even to the number of Union troops involved. Bragg guessed there were from four to eight thousand. The Federal unit, of course, was Negley's division of Thomas's XIV Corps. It had about five or six thousand men, and it was positioned in such a way that Bragg could hit it in front, flank, and rear, drive it into the narrow end of McLemore's Cove, and capture it entire. Thanks in part to Bragg's well-coached "deserters," Rosecrans was blithely unaware that the enemy he was so aggressively pursuing had stopped running and turned at bay. The result was an incredible opportunity for the Confederates.[39]

Bragg acted decisively. At 11:45 P.M. orders went out to Maj. Gen. Thomas C. Hindman, commanding a division encamped at Lee and Gordon's Mill, to march his troops thirteen miles southwestward into McLemore's Cove and strike the enemy in flank. He was to move out at midnight and strike the enemy early the next morning. Simultaneously, an order went to D. H. Hill, whose corps was encamped around La Fayette. Hill was to dispatch Cleburne's division, the best in the army, through Dug Gap to strike the Federals in front, making sure to coordinate his movement with Hindman's to ensure destruction of the Union force. The orders were clear, the objectives reasonable. The destruction of Negley's division was as certain as good generalship could make it. Bragg's subordinates needed only to carry out his orders and the Army of Tennessee's first clear-cut victory would be a reality.[40]

Yet at this point the strange dysfunction of the officer corps that had always plagued this army once again asserted itself. If the Army of Tennessee was yet to gain a victory, its constant if ever-changing handful of conceited, cantankerous, and incompetent generals was a good part of the reason. Various forces had propelled the misfits and malcontents into the ranks of the Army of Tennessee's general officers: politics, presidential cronyism (in Polk's case), or simple failure in the more prestigious theater of the war. It was an unpleasant fact of life for Bragg that he had to try to wage war with Robert E. Lee's cast-off generals.

Daniel Harvey Hill was one of them. An 1842 West Point graduate, Hill had served ably in Mexico before leaving the army to spend the decade of the 1850s as an educator. He went to war as colonel of the First North Carolina in 1861 and did well in early battles, rising rapidly to division command. Yet Lee became dissatisfied with Hill's performance in situations of broader discretion or responsibility for more than one division, and Hill proved a difficult character—carping and critical and prone to stir up strife. As did most officers whom Lee found wanting, Hill soon found himself assigned to other duties, the Department of North Carolina, then the Richmond garrison. They were definitely backwaters of the war and a comedown from the promise Hill had shown as a division commander. So, in accordance with Jefferson Davis's questionable penchant for viewing the western theater as the land of the second chance for generals whose careers had gone awry, Hill got orders for the Army of Tennessee, replacing the transferred Hardee.[41]

Thus it was Hill who, in the predawn hours of September 10, received the order to send Cleburne's division into McLemore's Cove. Somehow the assignment was too much for him, and he began to come up with excuses. Cleburne was sick in bed; several of his regiments were on picket duty; and the road through Dug Gap had been obstructed with felled timber by Confederate cavalry hoping to impede Negley's advance. Strangely, Hill claimed that Bragg's order had been nearly five hours in traveling about twelve miles, not reaching him until 4:30 A.M. Yet Hill's reply took well under three and a half hours to cover the same ground back to Bragg. Finally, though a march of six miles would have brought Cleburne's division into action, Hill insisted that this could not be accomplished before that evening, and he suggested that Bragg ought to forget the whole operation.[42]

Bragg was far from ready to give up, though, and, taking Hill's word for the problems at Dug Gap, decided to support Hindman instead with the two divisions of Buckner's corps. Buckner was encamped near Lee and Gordon's Mill and could follow along the same route Hindman had taken. At 8:00 A.M. Bragg sent word to Hindman and gave the orders that implemented his modified plan. Buckner's divisions were soon on the march.[43]

Meanwhile, Hindman had reached a position just four miles from Negley's flank and had settled down to wait and to take counsel of his fears. As colorful a man as one could hope to find in this or any other army, Thomas C. Hindman was a Tennessee native who had served with distinction in the Second Mississippi Regiment during the Mexican War before moving across the river to Helena, Arkansas, to carry his political career to further heights, including the U.S. Congress. He could be a man of selfless devotion, as when he and fellow Helena lawyer Pat Cleburne stayed in town to nurse the victims of a deadly epidemic. He could also be outrageously provoking—rude, insulting, and imperious—and he received a pretty much continuous stream of challenges to duels. He turned them down, but sometimes his enemies were too enraged to take no for an answer, as on the notable occasion when he and Cleburne were allies against several of them in a high-noon shoot-out on the streets of Helena. That one left them both badly wounded. Hindman also tended to take the direct solution to every problem, as when he scaled a convent wall to get himself a wife.

His record as a Confederate general was checkered. His most notable service had been in Arkansas, where his ruthless drive and efficiency had built him a respectably large army for that theater of the war and then his bullheaded impulsiveness had led him to wreck it in the unauthorized battle of Prairie Grove. All the while he cut a curious figure, short, slight, and dandified, with pink gloves and a rattan cane, long, curling locks cascading over his shoulders. Whatever else people might say about Thomas C. Hindman, and they generally said plenty, no one could say he lacked physical courage. No one had thought of saying he lacked moral courage either—until this day.

Whatever processes operated in Hindman's mind on September 10 are obscure. One thing is clear, and that is that by the time Buckner came up, about 5:00 P.M., Hindman, whose date of rank gave him command of the combined forces, was thinking more of saving his own division than of bagging Negley's. Despite having his available force more than tripled by Buckner's arrival, Hindman limited his activity to the most cautious of scouting while giving most of his attention to his own possible lines of retreat.[44]

Yet opportunity still beckoned. Negley was continuing to move eastward across McLemore's Cove, farther from the support of the rest of the XIV Corps. Shortly after noon, one of his brigades skirmished briskly with the Confederate cavalry covering Dug Gap. Bragg was aware both of the opportunity and of its fleeting nature. He now had information of Crittenden's force pressing down the La Fayette Road from Chattanooga as well as McCook's in the vicinity of Alpine. Clearly, Rosecrans's army was badly scattered, and Bragg was as close to any of its parts as they were to each other. He had an opportunity to beat the Federals in detail, but the rapidly converging Union columns would soon extinguish that chance and make his own situation difficult. That evening he strove to convey the urgency of the situation to Hindman. At 6:00 P.M. he wrote: "It is highly important that you should finish the movement now going on as rapidly as possible." At 7:30 P.M.: "The enemy is now divided. Our force at or near La Fayette is superior to the enemy. It is important now to move vigorously and crush him." He also sent oral communication that Polk's corps was covering Hindman's rear at Lee and Gordon's Mill against any possible threat from Crittenden and that Hindman must attack at dawn.[45]

But upon receiving these dispatches at 8:00 P.M., Hindman called a council of war, at which he and Buckner and their brigade commanders agreed to set aside Bragg's orders. Hindman's objections were a strange collection of strategic hobgoblins and other imaginary dangers, but he insisted on their reality, and Buckner, predisposed to believe that any plan Bragg devised must be inherently flawed, was quick to agree. Hindman sent a staff officer to inform Bragg of his decision as well as his estimate that another Federal division had now moved into the cove or was about to. He suggested that the army ought to forget about the troops in McLemore's Cove and turn on Crittenden instead. If an attack was to be made in the cove, Hindman wanted to delay his own attack until Hill had begun to drive the enemy.[46]

Bragg was appalled at these suggestions. Any attack on Crittenden would be a purely frontal assault and, even if successful, would probably succeed only in driving the Federal corps back onto its new base at Chattanooga. As for the force in McLemore's Cove, a central feature of Bragg's plan had always been that Hindman's flanking column should attack first, cutting off the Federals' retreat and preventing the affair from becoming simply another meaningless encounter that swelled casualty lists without bringing Confederate victory any closer. The report that additional Union troops had come down from Lookout Mountain changed none of Bragg's plans. He had ample forces on hand to deal with them; the more of them present, the worse their loss would be to Rosecrans. Bragg still had victory in his grasp if only just this once he could get somebody to carry out his orders.[47]

By the time Hindman's staff officer caught up with Bragg, it was midnight and Bragg was at La Fayette, where he had just arrived after a hard twelve-mile ride from Lee and Gordon's Mill to take a personal look at Hill's alleged difficulties and see what could be done about getting his corps involved in the attack after all. When he heard Hindman's message, Bragg responded—more emphatically than politely—that his "plans could not be changed and that [Hindman] would carry out his orders." In case he required further clarification, Bragg had a written order sent. It explained that McCook's advance was now seven miles south of La Fayette while Crittenden closed in on Lee and Gordon's Mill from the north and Polk deployed there to hold him off and protect Hindman's rear. It concluded, "General Bragg orders you to attack and force your way through the enemy to this point at the earliest hour that you can see him in the morning. Cleburne will attack in front the moment your guns are heard."[48]

What Bragg found when he investigated the situation on Hill's front underscored the importance of his being there. Cleburne, it developed, was neither sick nor in bed and could not understand why anyone had considered him incapacitated. Bragg gave orders to clear the obstructions out of Dug Gap and though Cleburne's men began the job after midnight, they were done before dawn, resting and waiting for the sound of Hindman's guns. To make doubly sure of success, Bragg ordered up the two divisions of Walker's corps to support Cleburne. Clearly, even without Walker's help, the obstacles to an advance had not been what Hill had represented them to be. If Bragg was angry with his new corps commander, he hid it well. Perhaps he was eager to maintain good relations with a subordinate general. As Hill noted, Bragg displayed his "usual cordiality." Well he might. If his generals followed orders, every Confederate would have ample reason to be in the best of humors before this day was over.[49]

The first light of day on September 11 found Bragg and Cleburne waiting at Dug Gap for the sounds of Hindman's attack. Cleburne had two brigades already through the gap and deployed for the advance. The sun rose behind them; the shadows retreated down the far mountainside and across the valley toward their position, but all was silent there. As the morning passed, Bragg waited with increasing impatience. He paced back and forth in frustration and during the course of the day dispatched several couriers and two staff officers to urge Hindman to get on with it. "Time is precious," Bragg wrote at 3:00 P.M. "The enemy in small force in line of battle in our front, and we only wait for your attack." Yet stillness rested over McLemore's Cove.[50]

Hindman was once again cringing at the thought of phantom blue-clad columns. He had well over fifteen thousand men. Negley, who had by this time been joined by Brig. Gen. Absalom Baird with elements of two of his brigades, had fewer than eight thousand. Waiting at Dug Gap or just the other side of it—ready to pour through in support of Cleburne—were twenty thousand more Confederates. Hindman was squarely on the left rear flank of the Federals in the cove, yet he did nothing.[51]

While he remained idle, Bragg could not launch Cleburne's attack. The much-maligned Army of Tennessee commander clearly had learned some things about battles during his tenure. A head-on assault was bloody and almost incapable of yielding truly decisive results. No matter how successful the attacker was, the defeated defender could almost always make good his escape. Only an attack that resulted in sealing off the enemy's escape route could produce the results for which the Confederacy could afford to invest more blood. Bragg showed a determination not to have Cleburne kick in the enemy's front door until he knew that Hindman had slammed the back door shut. In view of his obvious eagerness to get at the Federals—no one who saw him that day had any doubts about that—this could mean only that he realized the futility of simple frontal assaults.

By midafternoon Hindman had finally resolved his indecision by calling another council of war and persuading his fellow generals to agree with him that "any farther advance would be imprudent." So he wrote in a 2:45 P.M. dispatch to Bragg, adding that the enemy outnumbered him and that information he had received from Bragg led him to consider his rear insecure. This must have been particularly annoying to Bragg since the only information he had sent Hindman regarding his rear was that Polk was covering him. "I shall," Hindman concluded his dispatch, "therefore retire by Catlett's Gap to La Fayette. The orders are now given."[52]

As it turned out, Hindman met Bragg face to face before this message could reach him. Late in the afternoon, Hindman realized that the Federal column he so dreaded was withdrawing back into Stevens Gap. A desperately frightened James S. Negley (he had reason for his fears) had drawn his forces back when information from his scouts and loyal civilians had revealed Hindman's presence and his own observation had indicated that Cleburne was preparing to advance. Hindman pursued, and the resultant skirmish firing finally triggered Cleburne's advance. Bragg rode forward with Cleburne and confronted Hindman sternly when their forces came together. Bragg was furious at the lost opportunity. He had done all that a commanding general could reasonably do. His orders to Hindman had been clear and had left no room for discretion. The subordinate, in concert with Buckner and their brigade commanders, had simply defied them. A day of reckoning would come later. For now it was time to see what could be salvaged from the situation.[53]

By the morning of September 12, Thomas had all four divisions of the XIV Corps drawn up in line at the foot of Lookout Mountain covering Stevens Gap and ready to meet any Confederate assault. The corps' aborted advance toward La Fayette had saved Negley's and a good part of Baird's divisions from destruction, but it had also placed the Army of the Cumberland's three widely separated corps in a broad semicircle with Bragg in the center, well positioned to strike at any one of the corps before the others could come to its assistance. Rosecrans was disturbed at Thomas's failure to take La Fayette and thus keep on a line with the advancing XXI and XX Corps, but he was not in the least disturbed by Thomas's reports of a major Rebel concentration around La Fayette for the understandable—if shockingly mistaken—reason that he did not consider them true. He believed Thomas was dodging shadows and told him so, expressing his annoyance at the delay in pursuing what he still insisted on believing was Bragg's thoroughly demoralized army. Even when evidence began to pile up to show that Negley had encountered *something* out there in McLemore's Cove, Rosecrans continued to maintain that the withdrawal from the cove had been unnecessary.[54]

The next several days were to be a process of dawning unpleasant realization for the Army of the Cumberland's commander. On the eleventh, Crittenden's men had determined that Bragg had definitely retired down the La Fayette Road, not, as Rosecrans had considered more likely, the road that led toward Dalton and, far beyond, Atlanta. That meant Bragg was much farther west, and much nearer, than Rosecrans had thought, possibly nearer to each of his three corps than they were to each other. A reconnaissance down the La Fayette Road had revealed powerful Confederate forces on the east bank of Chickamauga Creek near Lee and Gordon's Mill. At the other end of the far-flung army, McCook had discovered Rebels in force on the La Fayette Road north of him. Worse, a prisoner his men picked up revealed that Longstreet's Army of Northern Virginia troops were on the way to join Bragg. This was Rosecrans's first hint of such a move, and it was a sobering thought.[55]

It took time for the various reports of Confederate presence and activity to reach Rosecrans from the distant units of the army. It took more time for Rosecrans to digest them and determine what they meant and still more time for his orders for a rapid concentration of the Army of the Cumberland to reach the three corps commanders. The question was whether the army could draw together and prepare to give battle before Bragg could gobble it up piece by piece.

Orders to McCook to close up on Thomas went out in midmorning of September 12, but away off in Alpine, he did not receive them and take up his march until the following morning. Also on the twelfth Rosecrans called Crittenden down to Lee and Gordon's Mill. He arrived there with the XXI Corps that afternoon but still seemed confused enough to lament that the Rebels were getting clean away from him, hope that Thomas or McCook could "hit them a side lick," and exult that if Thomas could just get into position at La Fayette, all the Confederates north of there would "be effectually bagged." In fact, "all the enemy north of La Fayette" amounted to the entire (by now heavily reinforced) Army of Tennessee, and it was Crittenden himself who was in imminent danger of being bagged.[56]

By the morning of September 12 Bragg had managed to lay aside his frustration at his generals' refusal to carry out his orders in McLemore's Cove.

He quickly realized that another opportunity lay just to the north of him. Crittenden's advance down the La Fayette Road put the Federal XXI Corps within easy striking distance of Bragg's concentrated army, and Thomas and McCook were still too far away to be of help to the isolated Federal force at Lee and Gordon's Mill. Bragg ordered Polk to move northward and close in on Crittenden, and directed Walker and Hindman to hasten forward in support. In all, Polk would have at his disposal thirteen brigades.[57]

That afternoon, Crittenden sent a brigade probing southward across the Chickamauga to the vicinity of Pea Vine Church, about three miles off. Confederate cavalry encountered the move and interpreted it as an entire division. When the report reached Bragg, he not unreasonably concluded that this would be easy prey for Polk. Acting at once, he sent a courier galloping off to his subordinate with a copy of the cavalry commander's report. "This presents you a fine opportunity of striking Crittenden in detail," Bragg added, "and I hope you will avail yourself of it at daylight tomorrow. This division crushed, and the others are yours. We can then turn again on the force in the cove." Additional reports that evening increased Bragg's confidence, and at 8:00 P.M. he sent a direct order to Polk: "Attack at day dawn tomorrow." Later he added another dispatch, urging Polk to make his attack "quick and decided." "Let no time be lost," Bragg exhorted.[58]

Instead of complying, Polk took up a course of action that was becoming depressingly familiar in the Army of Tennessee. He consulted with the other generals then present with his force and, having gained their agreement, wrote to tell Bragg what he planned to do instead of obeying orders. Instead of a single division, he claimed he was facing Crittenden's entire corps. He was correct in that all three of Crittenden's divisions were concentrated at Lee and Gordon's Mill, but that only made the opportunity that much greater. The bishop-general went on, however, to suggest that unknown hordes of Federals lurked behind Crittenden. Instead of making preparations to attack, Polk had taken up a strong defensive position and expected the enemy to attack him. Only if that event did not transpire and if Bragg would reinforce him with the whole of Buckner's corps—"so as to make failure impossible"—would Polk undertake to launch an attack of his own, and then not at "day dawn" but rather at some unspecified but more civilized hour thereafter.[59]

Polk probably believed that Bragg would not agree to reinforce him on so lavish a scale. Buckner's seven brigades would bring Polk's total up to twenty and leave Bragg with only six to watch the rest of Rosecrans's army to the south. If Bragg balked, Polk would have a ready excuse for inaction. If so, he underestimated his commander's nerve, for Bragg readily complied and put Buckner on the march northward. He wrote Polk informing him of this and adding that though Polk's defensive position was no doubt a strong one, Bragg hoped the bishop-general would not wait long for the Federal attack. "We must force him to fight at the earliest moment and before his combinations can be carried out."[60]

With Buckner's troops, Polk would have a better than two-to-one numerical superiority. Nevertheless, when Bragg rode up to view the situation for himself early on the morning of September 13, he found all quiet along the Chickamauga. Reconnaissance now revealed the Federal XXI Corps concentrated on the west bank at Lee and Gordon's Mill. Bragg counted the affair as another golden opportunity thrown away by the obstinate blundering of his subordinates and decided it would no longer pay to pursue the matter.

In McLemore's Cove two days before he had shown an unwillingness to make frontal attacks against an enemy whose line of retreat was intact. Yet other factors probably loomed larger in his decision to pull back from Lee and Gordon's Mill on September 13 and reconcentrate his army near La Fayette. For one, he was personally exhausted, having spent several nights in travel or in constant reading and analysis of the continuous screed of contradictory intelligence reports that reached his headquarters. For another, he could only have been deeply discouraged if not downright despairing about the apparently complete breakdown in the Army of Tennessee's command system. He may well have wondered how he could possibly hope to fight and win a battle under any circumstances with the subordinates then serving under him. Also, Bragg had just learned that reinforcements were on the way, the first of Longstreet's troops and two additional brigades from Mississippi. They were in Atlanta and would ride the rails up to Catoosa Station, several miles east of La Fayette. Bragg would naturally have wanted to wait for them to come up before bringing on a battle.[61]

Yet the final reason may have weighed heaviest with him. Bragg had been monitoring closely the reports of the movements of McCook's and Thomas's corps. It was as obvious to him as to any other trained military man that Rosecrans would not deliberately leave his army scattered once contact with the enemy had been made. The concentration of the Army of the Cumberland must then be in progress and would undoubtedly be carried out as rapidly as possible. Given the known positions of Rosecrans's units as well as the roads and terrain, a far less able general than Bragg could easily have calculated when that movement would be complete. Bragg's problem by September 13 was that any possible calculations indicated that the Union corps would be converging very soon. The sands appeared to have run out on Confederate chances for easy victory. To remain longer in the immediate presence of one of Rosecrans's corps was to court the disaster of having the others suddenly appear on one's flanks. It was time to pull out, and Bragg did.

A general obviously has to act on his best calculations, but just as obviously the best of calculations can fail to account for the unexpected exigencies of war. Such was the case with Rosecrans's attempts to draw his army together before Bragg could gulp down its scattered fragments. The Union commander could only have wished that his opponent's reckoning on that subject could be fulfilled. Instead, the affair took far longer than Rosecrans had hoped or Bragg had feared. The problem was with McCook's corps. Ordered to close up on Thomas, McCook had found that he knew far too little of the roads and terrain between his position and that of the XIV Corps. Indeed, he was embarrassingly ignorant of the enemy's positions and even the precise location of friendly units. Thomas was not much better off, and Rosecrans's headquarters made the mistake of assuming McCook knew more than he did. The result was that McCook made his march to join Thomas by a long and time-consuming detour. Rosecrans blamed McCook for the dangerous delay, and McCook reciprocated.

Still, by September 17, the XX Corps had moved into position on Thomas's right and the whole army had begun to sidestep to its left, moving northward along the west bank of Chickamauga Creek toward the mouth of McLemore's Cove and Crittenden's position at Lee and Gordon's Mill. For Rosecrans a tense week of maneuver on the brink of disaster seemed to be coming to a satisfactory close. His army was once more united. In front of him was the obstacle of a steep-banked stream, crossable only at bridges and fords. He was sliding sideways out of McLemore's Cove and toward a more proper connection to his new base of supplies at Chattanooga. Yet Rosecrans was about to reap some of the bitter fruits of his own methodical way of waging war. The six-week pause after the Tullahoma campaign that had so exasperated Lincoln, Stanton, and Halleck may or may not have been as inevitable as Rosecrans claimed it was. Nevertheless, it had allowed the Confederacy to reinforce Bragg until he was ready to meet even a united Army of the Cumberland. In early July, Bragg could have hoped for reinforcements neither from Mississippi nor from Virginia. Now, reinforced from both fronts to a combined strength of sixty-eight thousand men to Rosecrans's sixty-two thousand, Bragg prepared one final plan to catch the Army of the Cumberland and destroy it.

CHAPTER FOUR

Savagery and Confusion

Bragg knew he would have to act soon. Joseph E. Johnston out in Mississippi was clamoring for the return of the troops he had sent to the Army of Tennessee. The loan of troops from the Army of Northern Virginia was bound to be temporary. The large army Bragg now commanded would soon shrink back to its previous size; he had to act before that happened. In addition, though Bragg might well have to give up troops in future weeks, rumor had it that Rosecrans might be reinforced. Supposedly, twenty thousand of Grant's troops, the bulk of the Union Army of the Tennessee, were moving west from Mississippi, and there was nothing to prevent Burnside from coming south from Knoxville with his twenty-five-thousand-man Army of the Ohio.[1]

Yet aside from questions of relative numbers, the key factor demanding action from Bragg was Rosecrans's position. The Union commander was rapidly sidling his way out of danger. Once the Army of the Cumberland had reached the vicinity of Chattanooga, thus securing its supply line, there would be little Bragg could do against it even with the sixty-eight thousand men he now had. He thought he was still slightly outnumbered, but even the 10 percent numerical advantage he actually possessed would not allow him to besiege an undefeated Army of the Cumberland in Chattanooga. He would, in that case, have to approach the city carefully and could hope, at best, to win an indecisive victory that was likely to save neither his nor the Confederacy's future. In short, he had to act now.

That much was simple. Even the question of how to strike his blow was fairly straightforward; he would turn Rosecrans, moving north and getting between the Union army and Chattanooga. But as Carl von Clausewitz wrote, "Everything is very simple in War, but the simplest thing is difficult." Getting a grip on the precise whereabouts of Rosecrans's constantly moving army and figuring out just how and where to strike at it posed a problem of deceptive simplicity and perplexing difficulty. On the morning of September 15 Bragg informed his generals of his plan, but uncertainty about the Union position led him to delay the movement and revise his plans several times over the next few days. The two armies faced each other, Federals on the west bank of the Chickamauga, Confederates on the east. They were far enough apart to be out of contact save for scouts and cavalry patrols as each force constantly sidestepped northward.[2]

In its final form, as issued on the evening of September 17, Bragg's plan called for the Army of Tennessee to take possession of a three-mile-square block of northwest Georgia real estate. Crittenden, who had slid south to link up with Thomas and McCook coming north, by this time had his left flank and that of the Army of the Cumberland anchored at Lee and Gordon's Mill. From that vicinity, two roads led back to Chattanooga. One was the tolerably good La Fayette Road, running due north for a half dozen miles from Lee and Gordon's before bearing west to cross Missionary Ridge at Rossville Gap and descend into the town of Rossville and thence down the valley of Chattanooga Creek into the city. The other was the rough Dry Valley Road. It paralleled the La Fayette Road, farther west, for about two and a half miles north from Lee and Gordon's, running along the eastern foot of Missionary Ridge. Then it veered off farther to the west to cross the ridge at McFarland's Gap and merge into the La Fayette Road at Rossville.

Missionary Ridge was small compared to Lookout Mountain, but an army could cross it only at its gaps. Its southern terminus lay in the very jaws of McLemore's Cove, dividing the waters of Chickamauga Creek from those of Chattanooga Creek to the west. As the Army of the Cumberland moved out of the cove, it had to choose the valley of one creek or the other. That was really no choice at all. The best road, the La Fayette, lay west of Missionary Ridge, and to have chosen the east side would have been to give up entirely on covering the army's communications with Chattanooga. All that would have been left then was a race with Bragg for Rossville. Understandably, Rosecrans chose the valley of the Chickamauga. The Army of the Cumberland, once it was well concentrated, would move northward between the ridge on the west and the creek on the east, and it would do so—if it did at all—by the La Fayette and Dry Valley Roads. Bragg's plan was to seize the block of countryside just north of Lee and Gordon's where the two roads ran parallel to each other about three-quarters of a mile apart.

For Bragg the decision had to come there. It was the only practical point at which he could interpose his army on Rosecrans's communications. At Rossville or anyplace north of there, Bragg's own supply line would be as badly cut as Rosecrans's, and he could afford it much less. Between Rossville and the place where the two roads veered away from each other, it would be impossible to close off all the Federals' possible options for safe retreat. If Bragg was to succeed with his turning maneuver—if he was to accomplish anything decisive—he would have to do it between Lee and Gordon's Mill and the westward bend of Dry Valley Road.

At that northern boundary of decisive operations an east-west farm lane called the Dyer Road connected the two north-south roads, intersecting the La Fayette Road near the cabin and clearing of a farmer named Brotherton, three of whose sons were carrying rifles in Bragg's ranks. Federal units caught south of the Brotherton cabin and the Dyer Road would be operating with a line of retreat that ran off beyond their left flanks. They could perhaps be cut off and bagged. On the other hand, bluecoated units that got north of the Dyer Road would be relatively secure, having a potential line of retreat, the Dry Valley Road, running more or less straight to their rear, out of likely Confederate reach. Only by driving such units back south beyond the Dyer Road could Bragg hope to corner them. To win a truly decisive victory of the sort the Confederacy needed, Bragg would have to annihilate the better part of the Army of the Cumberland as an effective fighting force. Destroying an enemy army in head-on combat was ruinously expensive and all but impossible. Instead, Bragg would have to trap all or most of Rosecrans's army, and he would have to do it south of the Dyer Road.

These considerations dictated crossing Chickamauga Creek fairly close to the Union position at Lee and Gordon's Mill. Only during the early morning hours of September 18, when Bragg realized that Rosecrans would probably be able to cover all of the crossings for some distance beyond his left, did he make a final last-minute revision and extend his plan to include a crossing as far north as Reed's Bridge, four and a half miles northeast of Lee and Gordon's. The bridge there was to be seized by a division under Brig. Gen. Bushrod R. Johnson. It would march west from the railroad at Catoosa Station. During the day the arrival of additional brigades from Virginia was expected to boost the formation to two-division size, at which point Maj. Gen. John B. Hood of the Army of Northern Virginia, also expected to arrive that day, would take over command of this new provisional army corps while Johnson commanded one of its divisions and Hood's senior brigadier led the other. For most of the daylight hours, however, it would be just Johnson and four brigades, covered, in theory at least, by Forrest's cavalry.[3]

A little less than two miles further south, Walker's five-brigade Reserve Corps was to cross the Chickamauga at Alexander's Bridge. Still further upstream, just two miles due east of Lee and Gordon's (a bend in the Chickamauga caused it to meander in an easterly direction for some distance below the mill), Buckner's six brigades would cross at Thedford's Ford. Since it was likely that the latter two would encounter opposition, Johnson was to turn south as soon as he crossed Reed's Bridge and sweep up the west bank, uncovering the crossing for the rest of the army, which would follow Walker and Buckner. While the crossing was being effected, Polk would continue to threaten the Federals at Lee and Gordon's from the east bank, thus holding them in position.[4]

Inevitably, difficulties arose as the plan went into execution on the morning of September 18. The units of Johnson's division had never worked together before, and delays occurred as it marched westward from Catoosa Station. Forrest's cavalry was late coming up, and Johnson finally had to move on without them. Then, near Pea Vine Creek, he ran into Federal cavalry.[5]

This was Minty's brigade, one of the cavalry units assigned to screen the Army of the Cumberland's northern flank. Like the excellent cavalry officer he was, Minty had been diligently gathering information over the past twenty-four hours, and what he found had been disturbing—numerous indications of large bodies of Confederate troops moving north and much noise of railroad trains arriving at Catoosa Station. Equally disturbing to Minty was the fact that Crittenden, to whom he reported, took no interest in this information and professed to believe the Confederates were in fact retreating. Minty was having none of that, so at dawn on the eighteenth, he had patrols out on the roads to the east. They found heavy bodies of Confederate infantry advancing on all of them. The cavalry colonel sent couriers galloping off to every nearby Union formation and, at 11:00 A.M., undertook to slow Johnson's advance.

He did so with consummate skill, deftly mixing mounted charges with resistance by dismounted skirmish lines, each of which in turn fell back behind the next as Minty leapfrogged his regiments backward. Even Johnson had to admire the skill with which the Federal colonel used his artillery. Whenever possible, Minty hid his single battery and then greeted the Confederates with a surprise blast of canister as they came over a ridgeline or around a bend. Forrest eventually came up, but with only a small detachment of fewer than three hundred men. True to form, he pitched in at once, but his small force was not going to drive Minty anywhere, and Minty was

obviously not going unless driven. That remained the task of Johnson's infantry and artillery, who were again and again forced to halt and deploy from
march column to line of battle. The Confederate general finally had to shake
out a full divisional battle line to get over Pea Vine Ridge. Once across that
height, however, the Southerners could see Chickamauga Creek, about half
a mile ahead of them across gently sloping bottomlands. Minty made a final
stand in the yard of the Reed cabin, then limbered up his guns and took
them and his troopers across the creek at a gallop. The west bank of the
Chickamauga was indefensible at this point, so all the Federal horsemen
could do was direct a parting volley into the ranks of Johnson's yelling,
onrushing Tennesseeans, then show them their horses' hooves. No time
remained to destroy the bridge. By 3:00 P.M. the Confederates were filing
across.[6]

To the south, at Alexander's Bridge, the Confederates were even further
behind schedule. First, Walker's and Buckner's corps had gotten tangled up
with each other on the march, both needing to use a section of the same road
to reach their respective crossing points. Then, when Walker approached
the bridge, he found the far side of the creek—very defensible at this
point—occupied by a small but remarkably fast-shooting body of Federals.
They were a detachment of Wilder's Lightning Brigade. While the rest of
the outfit covered other possible crossing points, these men were left to
cover the bridge. They tore up the planking of the structure and used it to
throw up a barricade across the road some yards back. From behind that
cover they laid down such a heavy fire that Walker soon gave up and went
looking for some less well-defended crossing. By late afternoon he had
found one, about a mile and a half downstream, and succeeded in flanking
Wilder's men out of their position. As the sun dipped toward the top of Missionary Ridge, Confederate troops swarmed across Chickamauga Creek at
several points, well beyond the Union left flank around Lee and Gordon's
Mill.[7]

Near the mill, Crittenden had been much taken with Polk's demonstration on the east bank, and though for some reason he could hear no firing
from the direction in which Wilder's men, two and a half miles away, were
blazing away as fast as they could pump the levers and pull the triggers of
their Spencers, he could see large dust clouds on the other side of the creek
and downstream. Late that afternoon, he also received notice from Wilder
that the screening troops on the left could no longer hold the crossings. He
took it all very nonchalantly, merely shifting a single division around to extend his left. Clearly, Crittenden had not yet grasped the situation.[8]

That he did not reap the fruits of his complacence was partially a result of the late hour of the day and partially of the activities of the ubiquitous and formidable Wilder, who after being flanked out of his position at Alexander's Bridge succeeded in bringing most of his brigade together and placing them squarely across the path of a Confederate column that was advancing down the west bank toward Crittenden's flank. His Spencers and the gathering darkness brought the Southerners to a halt just a mile northeast of the Union flank. These Confederates were Johnson's men, now under Hood's overall command. The hero of several Virginia battlefields had finally caught up with Johnson just as the troops were beginning to cross Reed's Bridge and had led the now two-division column in its late afternoon and twilight march up the west bank. As darkness finally put a stop to the fighting, Wilder's men, on orders from Rosecrans, withdrew to a position on the flank of the Federal line, near the La Fayette Road.[9]

For Bragg it appeared that the frustrations of the past fortnight might be coming to an end. Even this day had seen its share of delays, including the stubborn stand of the Federal horse soldiers along the creek. Still he was across the Chickamauga and beyond Rosecrans's flank. His latest information placed the Union left in the neighborhood of Lee and Gordon's Mill. All he needed to do was push his troops southwestward the next morning and roll up the Army of the Cumberland. With that in mind he ordered Buckner's and Polk's corps across the creek first thing on September 19. By 9:00 that morning they were in position, Buckner forming up on the left of Hood where the latter's column had halted the night before, Polk and Walker in reserve, the whole line facing southwest, toward Lee and Gordon's Mill. Then, as crushing victory appeared to be again within reach, word came that Forrest's cavalry, scouting well to the north of the Confederate right flank, had run smack into a large formation of Union infantry. A major Federal force was somehow on the right rear of Bragg's army.[10]

The presence of those Union troops was the result of Rosecrans's key decision of the battle. The Federal commander's headquarters were now at the impressive Gordon-Lee mansion, about half a mile west of Lee and Gordon's Mill. He too had received timely notice from the efficient Wilder that the Union position along the creek was going to go, and during the afternoon he had sifted his scant information of Bragg's movements and contemplated what his own response should be. It turned out to be a series of orders initiating a great shuffling of divisions throughout the Army of the Cumberland. Within forty-eight hours, that shuffling would become so complicated that Rosecrans's headquarters would make a very embarrassing and costly mistake, but the early stages of this series of maneuvers were successful when the army absolutely had to have success.[11]

Rosecrans first ordered Crittenden to shift his entire corps north of Lee and Gordon's Mill, Thomas and McCook sliding northward to keep the line closed up. Rosecrans also ordered Granger, whom he had previously pulled down to Rossville Gap from Chattanooga, to send a brigade or two marching the five miles down the La Fayette Road to where it intersected with the Reed's Bridge Road. Still not satisfied, Rosecrans decided on a more drastic step. When at 4:00 P.M. Thomas arrived at the Gordon-Lee mansion with his leading division, Rosecrans directed him to leave his lead division, Negley's, to cover the creek south of Lee and Gordon's Mill and lead the other three on a night march up the Dry Valley Road and then by a local country lane that led into the La Fayette Road. The XIV Corps would thus shift from the middle of the Union line to the flank, leaving the XXI in the center. Thomas's, and the army's, left flank would then rest just east of the La Fayette Road at the clearing of a farmer named Kelly.[12]

For Thomas's men, this order meant stumbling forward over rough and dusty roads through darkness that was only slightly relieved by the light of fence-rail bonfires kindled by troops further up the column during one of the night's many halts. The fires added their own smoky touch to the surreal atmosphere of the march. After days of unpleasant heat, autumn was just beginning to touch the north Georgia mountains and the mercury that night plunged near the freezing mark. By the early morning of September 19, the men of Baird's division had reached their destination and dropped down in the Kelly field to boil coffee and munch their hardtack. Brannan's men were still marching but not far off. Reynolds's division had been delayed in its march and was still a couple of miles off.[13]

Even Baird's men had covered only five miles in the confusion and misery of that night march, but they and the other two divisions had changed the course of the battle. Without fully realizing it, they had been marching across the front and beyond the flank of the Army of Tennessee. Just as important, their position at the Kelly farm put them north of the Dyer Road and its connection to the Dry Valley Road. They now had two available lines of retreat, one running north and the other west, and they were beyond the point at which Bragg could have any practical hope of cutting them off and trapping them unless somehow he could drive them back southward—an unlikely event now because the Confederate army was south of their present position. Rosecrans had blocked Bragg's attempt to checkmate him.

The midmorning clash that brought Bragg to a shocked partial realization of this state of affairs was almost as accidental on the Union side as on the Confederate. While Baird's men were boiling coffee in the Kelly field and Brannan's were filing past them along the La Fayette Road to take up their place on the army's left flank, a messenger reached Thomas from Col. Dan McCook. A younger brother of XX Corps commander Alexander McCook, the colonel commanded a brigade of Granger's Reserve Corps. In answer to Rosecrans's order of the previous day, he had been sent down from Rossville to the vicinity of the Reed's Bridge Road. An early morning probe he dispatched toward the bridge had found it unguarded and destroyed it. McCook had also had a slight brush with some of the rearmost Confederates and came away with the impression that a single Rebel brigade had somehow gotten across the creek and was now trapped and ripe for destruction. The ambitious young colonel hoped he would be permitted to lead his own brigade on that mission, but now that Thomas was in place, Rosecrans wanted Col. McCook to rejoin the Reserve Corps at Rossville Gap, guarding that crucial point. So the colonel marched his troops off in disgust while Thomas made his own arrangements for dealing with the reported Confederate brigade.[14]

He sent Brannan forward to investigate, giving the lead position to one of Brannan's brigades under a twenty-six-year-old Kentucky lawyer named John Croxton. About 9:00 A.M. Croxton's men made contact with Forrest's scouting cavalry. Forrest would fight anyone, anytime, with any provocation or none at all. When Croxton's men loomed up through the woods to the west, the Confederate cavalry general promptly dismounted his brigades and threw them at the Yankees. Croxton was soon getting a good deal more than he had bargained for and sardonically sent back to Thomas to ask which of the four or five brigades in these woods was the one he was supposed to capture. The remainder of Brannan's division came up to support him, and the fight very quickly began to take on the shape of a pitched battle.[15]

It would be a strange battle in several ways, first of which was the terrain on which it was fought. The land between Chickamauga Creek and the La Fayette Road was gently rolling but almost completely wooded. A few clearings broke the continuity of the forest that rolled down to the cleared bottomlands along the creek. Three-quarters of a mile from Reed's Bridge a small clearing surrounded Jay's sawmill. Farmers named Winfrey and Brock had each cleared fair-sized fields between there and the La Fayette Road. Otherwise the canopy of treetops overhead was all but unbroken. Under the treetops, however, the foliage could vary considerably. Over most of this rolling terrain the woods were open, with little underbrush, and visibility was a little more than one hundred yards. In some areas, especially a quarter-mile-wide strip just east of the road, thickets of pine, cedar, and blackjack oak cut the range of vision to less than one-fourth that. West of the La Fayette Road, the foilage was much the same—thickets, open woods, and occasional clearings—but the terrain became gradually more hilly toward the base of Missionary Ridge.

In these woods no officer above brigadier could see all his command at once, and even the brigadiers often could see nobody's troops but their own and perhaps the enemy's. Chickamauga would be a classic "soldier's battle," but it would test officers at every level of command in ways they had not previously been tested.

Yet even the terrain and foliage could not account for all the confusion of September 19. An additional complication was that each army would be attempting to fight a shifting enemy while shifting its own position. It was, if not a running battle, at least a marching one. The forest would not have been so serious an element of confusion if each commander had been granted time to make sure of his opponent's position or even of the whereabouts of his own troops. Instead, each general would have to conduct a battle while shuffling his own units northward toward an enemy of whose position he could get only the vaguest idea. Strange and wonderful opportunities would loom out of the leaves, vines, and gunsmoke, be touched and vaguely sensed, and then fade away again into the figurative fog of confusion that bedeviled men on both sides. In retrospect, victory for either side would look simple when unit positions were viewed on a neat map, but in Chickamauga's torn and smoky woodlands, nothing was simple.

All Bragg could know by midmorning was that Forrest had run smack into a very powerful enemy force on the army's right rear, where no enemy was supposed to be. That it was a powerful force was borne out by the fact that Forrest quickly requested reinforcement. Bragg ordered W. H. T. Walker to send over a brigade of his Reserve Corps, and Walker gave orders to one of his brigadiers. He was nonplused, however, when shortly thereafter he discovered that Forrest had taken both brigades of that division. To judge by the sound of the firing, however, the unorthodox cavalry commander needed all the help he could get. Walker met Bragg on the field, and they discussed the obvious noise of battle to the north. Bragg wanted those Federals dealt with and ordered Walker to take the remainder of his corps—only another two-brigade division—and pitch into them at once.[16]

This was Brig. Gen. St. John R. Liddell's division, and it pitched in as ordered and with spectacular effect. Thomas had by now moved Baird's division into the fight alongside Brannan, and together they had been having things pretty much their own way against Forrest's dismounted cavalry and Walker's borrowed infantry brigades. Now, however, Liddell's line, advancing from the southeast, landed fairly athwart the flank of Baird's, which was facing due east. Along the edge of the Winfrey field and in the woods to the north, the Union line crumpled as Baird's division was routed, losing most of its artillery. Then the momentum shifted just as rapidly back the other way. Brannan swung right and counterattacked Liddell, hurling him back over the ground he had just gained and retaking Baird's guns, now standing forlorn as the center of a macabre woodland scene of bullet-pocked trees and a forest floor carpeted with dead men and horses.[17]

By early afternoon, six Union and seven Confederate brigades (three of the latter belonging to Forrest's cavalry) had fought each other to a frazzle in the woods between the Winfrey field and the Reed's Bridge Road, but the other four-fifths of each army were preparing to join the fray, which now expanded rapidly to the southward. Helping to complete the repulse of Liddell were troops of Richard W. Johnson's division of the XX Corps. They had started the day on the Union right, well down into McLemore's Cove, watching one of the passes of Pigeon Mountain. Even as McCook had started to move northward to take up his position on Crittenden's flank, Rosecrans, hearing the thunder of battle to the north, had ordered the XX Corps commander to detach a division to reinforce Thomas, and McCook had detached Johnson. A West Pointer and a competent officer, Johnson had served capably at Stones River. His command included the brigade of the irrepressible Willich, which was recommendation enough for any division.[18]

On receiving orders to report to Thomas, Johnson sent to the XIV Corps commander for instructions. He soon found out it was not that kind of a battle, as the only instructions Thomas could send were to "move in the direction of the cannonading." He did, and as he approached the scene of the fighting, Thomas met him and pointed him in the right direction, off into the woods toward Chickamauga Creek. That was about all a corps commander could do under these circumstances. Johnson made the best of it, advancing with two brigades in line and one in reserve and helping Brannan drive off Liddell's Confederates.[19]

More troops were moving up now and so was Rosecrans's headquarters. The commanding general left the comfortable Gordon-Lee house and moved up the Dry Valley Road to the spartan cabin of Eliza Glenn, whose husband had died in the Confederate army a few months before. The

Widow Glenn's house, as it was called, was located on a fairly imposing rise that looked out over a wide field rolling down to the east all the way to the La Fayette Road. It also marked the spot where the little country lane known as the Glenn-Kelly Road branched off from the Dry Valley Road and angled northeastward to join the La Fayette Road near Thomas's position. It was perhaps as good a site as any for the Federal headquarters, though Rosecrans would nevertheless soon be reduced to trying to follow the course of the battle by judging the distance and direction of the sound it generated.[20]

The next division up the Dry Valley Road was that of Maj. Gen. John M. Palmer. It had settled into its new position about a mile north of Lee and Gordon's Mill shortly before daylight that morning, completing the movement Rosecrans had ordered the day before. About midday, Rosecrans sent it up the road to strengthen Thomas, where its appearance was most welcome. With Palmer on hand and Reynolds at last approaching a short distance behind, Thomas felt strong enough to shift Brannan and Baird to the left, covering the Reed's Bridge Road. He then sent Johnson and Palmer plunging off into the woods toward Chickamauga Creek. Their advancing battle lines struck a large Confederate formation coming the other way and were soon hotly engaged.[21]

These Confederates belonged to Cheatham's division. When it had become apparent that the Army of Tennessee would have to fight toward the west rather than the south, Bragg had hastily cobbled together a new line of battle, shifting units through the woods to form a front that faced west-northwest, with Chickamauga Creek at the army's back and the La Fayette Road a mile or so in front of it. Buckner held the Confederate left, anchored on a bend of the creek. Next came Hood with his two divisions, and then Walker was supposed to form the army's right. By early afternoon, however, Walker's four brigades were pretty thoroughly chewed up and badly in need of rest and replenishment of ammunition. The only other major Confederate formation west of the creek was Cheatham's oversized division of Polk's corps, which Bragg had hoped to keep in reserve. With Walker used up and the Federal force around the La Fayette Road still apparently full of fight, Bragg was compelled to commit Cheatham.[22]

Composed of five brigades, the all-Tennessee division of Maj. Gen. Benjamin Franklin Cheatham was actually larger than Walker's entire Reserve Corps. Its men had great affection for and confidence in their division commander, the hot-tempered, hard-drinking Cheatham. A colorful figure with a shady past in the California mining camps and Tennessee politics, Cheatham was a bitter enemy of Bragg. At Stones River his performance had been disastrous, lending credence to reports that he had been drunk and had even fallen off his horse. At his sober best, Cheatham might have made a more or less satisfactory brigade commander, but he was out of his depth at the division level. Still, his men loved him. He led them into action shortly after midday.[23]

Almost immediately—Cheatham thought they had advanced only about 150 yards—they crashed headlong into two Federal divisions, only slightly superior to them in numbers but well led and well prepared for what they were about to encounter. As Palmer was about to advance his Federal division eastward from the La Fayette Road, a messenger from Rosecrans overtook him. The commanding general suggested that Palmer advance his brigades en echelon, that is, with the left brigade furthest forward, the center brigade a couple of hundred yards behind and to the right, and the right brigade still further back. Clearly, Rosecrans understood at least one of the reasons for the problems that had plagued Brannan and Baird. Confederates advancing from the southeast had flanked Union battle lines that faced straight east. From the echeloned formation, Palmer would be able to swing easily into a line that faced southeast or bring up his trailing brigades to fight directly to the east.[24]

The division commander took the advice, and so when Cheatham moved up from the southeast, Palmer was able to counter him, meet him head-on, and stop him. The southernmost of Cheatham's brigades, closest to the La Fayette Road, got so tangled in the dense thickets in that area that it stumbled into the Federal line almost flank first. The center and left brigades fought furiously but could achieve only a stalemate, blasting new tracts of woodland and exchanging volleys across a broad field belonging to a farmer named Brock. Cheatham brought up his two reserve brigades to spell them, but the situation continued to deteriorate, largely through the doing of the redoubtable Willich and his brigade. The German's soldiers once again used their patent tactic of firing while advancing and, with the aid of Johnson's other brigades, drove Cheatham's Confederates all the way back to the blood-soaked Winfrey field. Willich believed he could have gone farther if the troops on either side of him had advanced, and he was probably right.[25]

Cheatham's situation grew worse when Thomas put in Reynolds's division and two brigades of Brig. Gen. Horatio Van Cleve's XXI Corps division. Bragg countered with the division of Maj. Gen. A. P. Stewart. Nicknamed "Old Straight," the West Point–educated Stewart had left the regular U.S. Army years before to become a college professor. On this afternoon in the now hellish woodlands along Chickamauga Creek, he was living up to his nickname. When Bragg ordered him to advance, he demanded specific instructions as to where he should go, where he would find the enemy, and what he should do. Bragg, unfortunately, was no clairvoyant and could no more give Stewart specific instructions than Thomas had been able to give Richard Johnson a couple of hours before. Like Thomas, Bragg simply told Stewart he would have to march to the sound of the firing. Reluctantly, Stewart obeyed, but groping through the smoke-choked woods took time and made precisely coordinated attacks next to impossible. His two lead brigades engaged but could make no headway against the stubborn Federals.[26]

The deadlock continued, a nightmare struggle in which neither army seemed to be accomplishing anything. No ground was won, no enemy units destroyed; yet the men of each side fought on with desperate frenzy, blasting each other with artillery wherever they could drag guns through the forest and get a field of fire and everywhere lashing the woods with long, rolling volleys of musketry that shredded bark, twigs, leaves, and bodies. The fighting front had stabilized roughly along a country track known locally as the Brotherton Road, running southwest from the Winfrey field, through the woods to the Brock field, then through progressively thicker woods to open onto the La Fayette Road opposite the Brotherton cabin and field. The Federal line veered south before it reached the intersection, keeping a couple of hundred yards east of the vital La Fayette Road. For the moment, Rosecrans was succeeding in his goal of holding that thoroughfare as his army's primary connection with Rossville and its base at Chattanooga beyond. The Dry Valley Road he relegated to secondary status and all but forgot. It appeared he would not need it.

Yet even as the Federals held onto the stretch of the La Fayette Road north of the vital Dyer Road connection with the Dry Valley Road, trouble was brewing for the Union troops still south of that intersection. About 2:30 that afternoon both Rosecrans and Bragg had hit upon the obvious idea of striking the other's southern flank. With the armies engaged in a primal struggle for control of the La Fayette Road on the north end of the battlefield, it stood to reason that the enemy might well shift too much of his force in that direction, leaving himself vulnerable to envelopment on the south. At least, that is what the two commanders hoped. In fact, each army was still well strung out as the generals slid their units northward toward the bloody cockpit along the Brotherton Road. When Bragg and Rosecrans each probed—violently—for the other's southern flank, they not only launched their intended flanking columns right into each other but also trig-

gered a virtual melee as brigades and divisions moving up from positions
south of Lee and Gordon's Mill fed the inferno of battle around the fields
and buildings of a farmer named Viniard. The fighting that followed surpassed even the intensity of what had gone before and set the stage for the
explosive climax of the first day's battle.

The Federals advanced first. Even as Thomas sent Johnson and Palmer
into the woods farther north, the division of Brig. Gen. Jefferson C. Davis,
XX Corps, tramped up the Dry Valley Road and halted near the Widow
Glenn's. Davis asked Rosecrans for instructions and received orders to take
his men in on the right of Van Cleve. Davis, a colorful little West Point–
trained Hoosier who had once shot and killed a commanding officer who
had slapped his face and knocked him down, aimed to do just as Rosecrans
had ordered, but like everyone else in these woods, he had nothing by which
to guide his march but the sound of the firing. To be sure, there was no
shortage of that—the whole northeast quadrant throbbed with the roar of
battle—but judging precise positions by this uncertain clue proved to be
tricky. The result was that Davis, aiming to slide into line just on the right of
Van Cleve, instead careened forward a full half mile further to the right. Nobody on either side knew it yet, but along a division-sized front in the middle of the battlefield, the Union line simply did not exist.[27]

Davis's lead brigade walked smack into the Confederate skirmish line in
dense thickets where visibility was less than twenty yards, and the Federals
were as surprised as the Southerners at this sudden encounter. The Union
brigade was commanded by sturdy Norwegian Hans Heg, colonel of the
predominantly Scandinavian Fifteenth Wisconsin. The Confederates were
Tennesseeans of Bushrod Johnson's division. Fighting instincts took over
on both sides, and the two lines triggered searing volleys into each other's
faces. The range was murderous, the slaughter terrific. Within seconds half
of the Fiftieth Tennessee was down, and other regiments on both sides were
faring little better. At first Heg's momentum carried him forward and drove
the Tennesseeans back. Then Johnson, having just received orders from his
corps commander, Hood, to push for the Union flank, applied his numerical superiority and rolled the Federals back.[28]

Johnson's plan, in keeping with Hood's orders, was to swing his division
forward and to the right, savaging the flank of the Union troops fighting in
the vicinity of the Brotherton cabin. In this effort he was precisely halfway
successful. His right brigade and half the center brigade overlapped Heg's
flank and swung forward and to the right as planned, where they were soon
to wreak immense havoc. The other half of the brigade had its hands full

with the stubborn Norwegian. The Confederate division broke apart, and the feisty Heg, now presented with something a bit closer to even numbers, once again began to drive the remaining Confederates back through the tangled underbrush.[29]

Hood now threw in his own division, temporarily under the command of Brig. Gen. Evander Law, but in the thickets the rightmost of its three brigades veered off to the north, guiding on the sound of the fighting along the Brotherton Road. If Stewart or Cheatham had known of its presence, it would have been a very welcome reinforcement, but Hood would badly feel the loss of it before the afternoon was over. For the moment, he had things much his own way, driving the Federals even after Davis's other brigade moved up. The advantage of numbers shifted again, however, when from the south Maj. Gen. Thomas J. Wood's Union division added its two brigades to the fight. One of Van Cleve's brigades, detached when the other two marched north to join Thomas, was also swept into the swelling vortex of battle, which had by now spread to engulf not only the dense woods where Heg had been fighting but also the broad Viniard field just to the south.[30]

Overall Union command in this sector of the battlefield was being exercised by Crittenden, who was having his finest day as a corps commander. The army's divisions were intermixed now to the point that corps as such no longer existed, but Rosecrans gave Crittenden the assignment of overseeing affairs around Viniard field. With three of his own XXI Corps brigades, from two different divisions, and two brigades of the XX Corps, Crittenden energetically countered Hood's thrusts. He had hoped to do better and roll up the Confederate flank. When Wood's division hastened up the road from Lee and Gordon's Mill, Crittenden had sent word to Wood to angle off the road to the eastward and come in right on the flank of the Southerners fighting in the Viniard field. Rosecrans learned of the order, however, and countermanded it as too risky, much to Crittenden's disgust. He had to content himself with using the stray brigade of Van Cleve's division for the same purpose and succeeded in temporarily throwing Hood back. Hood called on Bragg for reinforcements, and the Confederate commander responded by ordering Buckner to send what help he could. Buckner, whose corps had, by the detachment of Stewart, effectively been reduced to a single three-brigade division, held the extreme southern end of the Confederate line west of the creek. He detached one of his brigades to go to the aid of the hard-pressed Hood.[31]

Bragg might have accomplished more by having Buckner commit his whole remaining division, Maj. Gen. William Preston's, rather than allowing him a discretion that he exercised in sending only a single brigade. D. H. Hill's corps was still on the east bank. Breckinridge's division was skirmishing with Negley's Federals around Glass's Mill, to the south, and Cleburne's, on Bragg's orders, was preparing to cross the creek at Thedford's Ford. Also moving up to the fords of the Chickamauga under similar orders was Hindman's division of Polk's corps. These forces would have been sufficient to secure Bragg's southern flank, and Preston's full division, rather than a single brigade, might have tipped the precarious balance in the Viniard field in favor of the Confederates. But Bragg had merely mortal powers of perception and no ability to see the movements and positions of troops—his own and the enemy's—beyond broad expanses of timber. No more did he possess the ability to divine the patterns of movement of the constantly shifting Federal army. Buckner was on the spot and would presumably know the degree of threat in his own front. In fact, he faced no serious threat at all but, being a pessimist, felt he could part with only a single brigade.[32]

Most important, however, was the fact that a Confederate success in the Viniard field sector would produce at best a minor victory. A couple of Union divisions might be roughed up, and Rosecrans might have to withdraw toward Chattanooga faster than he would have liked. Yet nothing that could happen on the Viniard farm could result in more than a single Federal division (Negley's of the XIV Corps, still deployed south of Lee and Gordon's Mill) being cut off and destroyed. That would be a small dividend for the investment of manpower the Confederacy had made in hopes of restoring its fortunes in Tennessee. It would be little enough, as well, to show for the gruesome slaughter even then in progress in the woods and fields west of Chickamauga Creek. If truly significant results were to be achieved in this battle, the Confederates would have to win on the northern part of the field, between Chattanooga and most of the Army of the Cumberland, and only that portion of the Army of the Cumberland that could be caught—or driven—south of the Dyer Road, and its connection with the Dry Valley Road, would be vulnerable. For Bragg, decisive victory could be won only on the right. His left flank effort under Hood was of value only if it could draw Rosecrans into weakening his own northern flank. Thus Bragg's orders both to Hindman and to Hill called for them to cross the creek and then move toward the Confederate right.[33]

Meanwhile, in the Viniard field and the adjacent woods, the forces were about equal with the addition of the brigade from Preston's division to Hood's force there. The result was some of the most frenzied and fluid fighting of the day. Battle lines surged back and forth. Cannon were captured, re-captured, and abandoned for want of any living horses to haul them off. The same ground was fought over half a dozen times. Gradually, though, the battle began to go against the Northerners. Crittenden's men were driven back nearly to the La Fayette Road. Out in the Viniard field they made a stand along a low ridge just east of the road. In the woods on the Union left, little remained of Heg's brigade, but a few hardy souls hung on grimly in the effort to keep the Rebels out of the La Fayette Road. A score or so of stub-born Norwegians had hunkered down in a log schoolhouse by the roadside and were fighting on in defiance of the famous Texas Brigade that had been the terror of many a Virginia battlefield.[34]

The gap between the Federals around the Viniard field and those farther north became Crittenden's undoing. He had realized its danger and hoped to plug it with Wood's two brigades. But Wood had been drawn into the swirling battle for the Viniard field and the gap had gone untended. The best Crittenden could do was belatedly send one of Wood's brigades up the La Fayette Road to clear it of the Rebels who were already beginning to swarm across it further north. That brigade, however, soon lost touch with Crittenden's force around the Viniard farm. Nothing more could be done about the exposed Union flanks, and once the Confederates began to lap around them, Crittenden's position started coming apart. Survivors of Davis's, Wood's, and Van Cleve's divisions streamed back across the La Fayette Road.

Crittenden and the other mounted officers spurred their horses into the fleeing throng, attempting to rally the men, but things had gone too far for that. Heg was shot from the saddle, mortally wounded. Crittenden himself was nearly captured. Fleeing among the buildings of the Viniard farmstead just west of the road, large numbers of Federals encountered a barnyard fence that blocked their retreat. The fence, along with the panic and jostling it created among men already running for their lives, delayed and bunched the bluecoats just long enough for pursuing Confederates to shoot them down in droves, leaving bodies piled atop each other amid the mud and squalor of the barnyard. No more shots came from the log schoolhouse, and around it Hood's now victorious Texans swarmed forward to the La Fayette Road. The remnants of four Union brigades now took shelter in a shallow ditch or dry streambed that ran about fifty to one hundred yards west of the road. It was only a couple of feet deep and several yards wide. Running through the lowest ground in the Viniard field west of the road, it offered scanty shelter at best to the large number of stunned and winded Federals who now crouched there attempting to avoid the withering fire of Hood's troops along the road and among the buildings of the Viniard farm.

Holding the ditch proved impossible, and another Confederate rush sent its living Federal occupants scampering the 100 to 150 yards westward across the gradually sloping field to the woods on the far side. When the Confederates tried to follow, however, they got a surprise. As silent spectators to most of the day's fighting in this sector, Wilder's Lightning Brigade had waited behind makeshift log and fence-rail breastworks along the western tree line of the Viniard field, their horses tied safely well to the rear. Wilder had occasionally sent forward a regiment, first to one side and then to the other, to check particularly threatening Confederate moves. As Crittenden's force crumbled, Wilder prepared to meet the Confederate onslaught. His men checked the actions of their Spencers and swallowed down whatever stirrings they felt of the infectious panic of Crittenden's men who stumbled through their lines and to the rear.

As Hood's men surged out of the ditch and up the gently sloping field in pursuit, the tree line in front of them suddenly blazed with a continuous rolling volley. Wilder's repeating rifles could lay down a volume of fire equal to or greater than that produced by the rest of the Union force around the Viniard field. The Confederate pursuit ended before it got fairly started, and now it was the Southerners' turn to crouch in the ditch and try to hang on to the La Fayette Road they had just won.

It was Wilder's job to get them out of there. When the unequal exchange of fire between muzzle-loaders in the ditch and repeaters behind the breastworks failed to get the job done quickly enough to suit him, Wilder ordered Lilly to advance a section of his battery. Supported by Wilder's riflemen, the Greencastle druggist got his guns positioned well forward and to the left of the Lightning Brigade so that they could fire into the ditch end-on, raking its whole length with devastating loads of canister. The cannon became, in effect, gigantic sawed-off shotguns spewing scores of three-quarter-inch lead slugs. The slaughter in the packed ditch was appalling. Wilder later admitted he had felt like ordering the guns to cease firing—anything to end the hideous spectacle before him. The surviving Confederates sprinted back across the La Fayette Road, leaving the ditch choked with the bodies of their fallen comrades. By this time the remnants of Crittenden's command had rallied, and now they advanced to reclaim the ground they had fought over most of the afternoon. Sheridan's division, the last of the XX Corps divisions to move north from Lee and Gordon's Mill, came up and helped secure the position and drive off the last stubborn Confederates.[35]

Even as Crittenden's men had struggled to hold the southern end of the Union line, a still more serious crisis had threatened the center. The same gap that had been the temporary undoing of Crittenden's force around the Viniard field proved disastrous to the Union forces north of the field as well. The half of Bushrod Johnson's division that had swung north landed on the flank of the Federals of Van Cleve's division who were battling Stewart's troops and the errant brigade of Law's division near the Brotherton Road. Such flank attacks were particularly devastating in the dense undergrowth that prevailed here because it was all but impossible to adjust and respond to them. Van Cleve's men could do nothing and streamed back in retreat. They found no place to rally short of the La Fayette Road and, crossing that thoroughfare, came to the Brotherton field. This reaped-down cornfield lay along the west side of the road, running about one hundred yards back from the road and roughly six hundred yards along it. Near the north end of the field the Brotherton Road joined the La Fayette Road from the east and the Dyer Road ran into it from the west. The Brotherton cabin stood on the west side of the road near the intersection. Down the middle of the field, parallel with the La Fayette Road and about fifty yards west of it, ran the crest of a substantial ridge. There the battered Union regiments prepared to make their stand.[36]

Yet for the Federals, the sad fact was that the Brotherton field was all but indefensible. Having lost their position in the woods several hundred yards east of the La Fayette Road, they were now faced with a situation in which the next good defensive position lay nearly half a mile west of the road. That position would still secure the Dry Valley Road and access to Chattanooga by way of McFarlands Gap, but Rosecrans understandably had shown no enthusiasm at the prospect of extricating his entire army over that poor road and had based his conduct of the battle thus far on holding the La Fayette Road as well. Worse, a withdrawal from the La Fayette Road would render the situation of Crittenden's command around the Viniard farm absolutely desperate. Maj. Gen. Joseph Reynolds, senior officer in that sector, would have known this and known that he had to attempt to maintain some hold on the La Fayette Road. His only choice, then, was to form his troops along the crest of ridge in the Brotherton field, where he had already brought together a substantial line of artillery.[37]

The Brotherton ridge looked at first glance like a much stronger position than it was. It loomed a good fifty feet above the La Fayette Road, and the vine- and bramble-choked forest floor across the road fell off even lower. Artillery could reach the ridge easily—for once, it seemed, not having to drag the guns through the woods to get into position. The drawback was that guns along the ridge would have no effective field of fire. Barely fifty yards beyond their muzzles lay some of the thickest, most tangled woods on the battlefield. For the infantry the Brotherton field was even more unfavorable. The normal position for an infantry line defending a ridge was well down the forward slope. Yet here that would have had the Federal infantrymen staring forward into a wall of leaves perhaps twenty-five yards away. They would be in the open; their attackers under cover. Clearly that was out of the question. So they took position along the very crest of the ridge. They still had no cover other than corn stubble, their field of fire was mediocre at best, and they were outlined as targets against the skyline for Confederate riflemen across the road.

To make matters worse, in the woods just beyond the southern end of the field was a ravine that provided excellent cover for snipers and attacking troops working their way in for a rush. Sometime around 4:00 P.M., as the conflict down around the Viniard farm was nearing its climax, Johnson's Confederates got into that ravine—the gap in the Union line still had not been plugged—and Reynolds's position along the ridge began to come apart. Its destruction was made sudden and spectacular by a renewal of Stewart's attack. The two brigades that had already been repulsed rallied and renewed their assaults, and Stewart's reserve brigade, under the hard-driving William B. Bate, came in to lead the attack with a hammer blow that struck the angle of the Union position, where the line of Reynolds's division along the Brotherton Road (facing southeast) met Van Cleve's makeshift line along the ridge in the Brotherton field (facing east). Both Federal divisions collapsed, though individual regiments sometimes fought fiercely before joining the general retreat.

It might have been a major disaster for Rosecrans if the Confederates had possessed enough fresh troops within supporting distance to exploit the breakthrough. Bragg had ordered Cleburne and Hindman across the Chickamauga, but they were not yet on hand. Johnson's tired soldiers now had to deal with the Federal brigade that had drifted northward out of the Viniard field fight in its effort to plug the gap in the line. Stewart's three brigades pursued alone, and they were tired and disorganized. Two of the brigades pushed westward, over the Brotherton field, through the woods beyond, and into a much larger field belonging to a farmer named Dyer. By this time, however, they were little better than mobs, their troops scattered over a very large territory all the way back to the La Fayette Road, nearly half a mile to the east. When powerful Union formations approached from both north and south, the Confederate brigadiers reluctantly recalled their troops to the east side of the La Fayette Road. The Federals advancing from the south were Negley's division, which Rosecrans had finally summoned up from Glass's Mill some time earlier. Moving down from the north behind the Federal battle line was Brannan's bloodied but still game division, dispatched by Thomas at Reynolds's request. The Union line was restored, with Negley's division taking position along the tree line at the western edge of the Brotherton field.[38]

Bate's brigade, following its slightly different axis of attack and veering a little to the north, followed up its success by driving straight north along the La Fayette Road. In theory, this line of advance could roll up half the Army of the Cumberland all the way to the Kelly field. In fact, the brigade's strength had been reduced by casualties and stragglers and its striking power weakened when it split into two separate groups. Bate himself and three of his regiments presently emerged into another long, narrow field along the La Fayette Road, this one virtually flat. It belonged to a farmer named Poe, whose house stood on the west side of the road, opposite the field on the east. The field was perhaps four hundred yards long, and Bate would have to advance the length of it. At the far end Reynolds and Brig. Gen. William B. Hazen of Palmer's division had put together another makeshift line of infantry remnants along with an impressive array of artillery. Bate was made of sterner stuff than his fellow brigadiers of Stewart's division, and he led his men onward into the field. After all, Confederates had crushed a similar Northern line in the Brotherton field.

This one proved to be different, however. Bate had only a few hundred winded men and no support in sight. Worse, the long, level field provided an ideal place for the use of canister, Civil War artillery's most dangerous load. Bate's ragged advancing line disappeared in the clouds of smoke belched out by the guns and dust kicked up by the huge patterns of canister as it skipped off the dry ground and into the Southern ranks. The encounter in the Poe field lasted five minutes at most, but by the time Bate and the other Confederate survivors got out of the field on the same side they got in, nearly a third of their comrades had been left behind.[39]

By the time the sun dipped toward the crest of Missionary Ridge that evening, Stewart's brigades were back to their starting points and the Federal line had been reestablished. The infamous gap was closed and the situation as near stable as it had been all day. Things might have rested that way for the night, except for a belated and somewhat misguided Confederate attempt to follow up on Stewart's success. Cleburne had gotten his division across the Chickamauga and into position behind Walker as ordered. Bragg could perhaps have thrown the fresh division into the fray directly behind Stewart, and latter-day critics would fault him for not having done so. Still the fact remained that the largest results were to be obtained on the right flank. Once Cleburne arrived, Polk decided to launch him in an immediate attack even though daylight was fading rapidly and no chance remained of decisive results that day. Bragg unwisely acquiesced in Polk's plan, and so the attack went forward.[40]

It had been a day of confused fighting, but this night attack surpassed everything that had gone before in sheer befuddlement. Cleburne hit the divisions of Johnson and Baird, the latter having closed up on Johnson's left flank. These Federals had just received orders from Thomas to withdraw to a superior defensive position closer to the Kelly field, and some of them were in the act of obeying when Cleburne's men struck, adding to the confusion. In the gathering darkness "friendly fire" incidents were frequent, as each side fired at the muzzle flashes of what it hoped was the enemy. Retreating units were blasted by their comrades who took them for advancing foes, while one regiment, nearly cut off and surrounded, made good its escape by marching past enemies who did not realize its allegiance. Afterward no one was quite sure what had happened except that it had been a very fierce fight. Baird thought the enemy attacked with more determination than at any time previously that day. Cleburne considered the firing to be the heaviest he had heard during the war. Each side was confident it had gotten the better of the exchange. When it was over, the Federals pulled back to the positions around the Kelly field as planned, and Cleburne's men camped in the positions they held when the fighting stopped. If Polk's goal had been simple man-for-man attrition, the affair might be considered adequately successful. As it was, 30 percent of the best division in the Army of Tennessee had become casualties while inflicting about equal losses on the enemy, and that was no bargain for the Confederacy. That and the fact that Cleburne's division was left in confused disarray were the fruits of Polk's evening adventure.[41]

The first day's fighting was finally over. It had not been a tactical masterpiece, but under the circumstances, it could not have been. Foliage and terrain made the generals' task extremely difficult. Each commander's problems were exacerbated because neither was precisely sure of the location of the other. That Rosecrans had a better idea of Bragg's location than Bragg did of his had been a fair portion of the latter's success. And clearly Rosecrans had come out ahead in this day's contest. He had managed to shuffle his units northward, one behind the other, in difficult country, across the front of an enemy about equal or slightly superior in numbers, even as the engagement swelled from the opening skirmish to a pitched battle. It had been a complicated series of maneuvers, and Rosecrans had nearly come to grief when that half-mile gap opened in his line. Still, it was equally complicated for the enemy, who had the disadvantage of having to take the offensive without knowing how Rosecrans would move next. The gap had been closed, the line restored, and disaster staved off. A sideways movement of a hotly engaged army could not be done in a neat and tidy manner, and Rosecrans had shuffled divisions and even brigades around as if corps headquarters did not exist. Thomas on the left and Crittenden on the right directed ad hoc commands slapped together out of units of all three corps. McCook had practically nothing at all to do, which was probably just as well. Most of Rosecrans's army was now situated so that it had viable retreat routes running to its rear and was no longer abnormally susceptible to being cut off and trapped. Another day of careful maneuvering should put the army in contact with Granger's Reserve Corps at Rossville Gap, its communications secure. Of course, Braxton Bragg would likely be heard from again before that result was achieved.

CHAPTER FIVE

They Fought Like Tigers

During the night of September 19, temperatures in the northwest Georgia hill country plunged to near freezing. Soldiers of both armies sought what warmth they could, reflected on the horrors of the day just past, and did what they could to help their wounded comrades. That, often, was little enough, and the cries of the wounded made the night terrible. While the soldiers endured as best they could, the generals planned the next day's action. Rosecrans and his corps commanders met at the Widow Glenn's and decided not to attempt precipitate retreat that night but to keep Thomas's left wing strong and continue pulling the right wing in as the army sidled toward Chattanooga. Granger and his three-brigade Reserve Corps would be left at Rossville Gap, three and a half miles beyond the army's left flank.[1]

Confederate preparations were more elaborate. Additional troops came in during the night, a brigade from Mississippi and two more from the Army of Northern Virginia. Also arriving was Lt. Gen. James Longstreet. Detraining at Catoosa Station, Longstreet and his staff made their way to Bragg's headquarters on horseback, miffed that the harried army commander had not seen to it that someone was waiting at the train station to welcome such important newcomers. In the darkened woods, Longstreet and his people had ridden up to a Federal outpost and, mistaking the soldiers' identity, exchanged words with them before realizing their error and bluffing their way out. They arrived at Bragg's headquarters late that night in a very foul mood.[2]

Incorporating the new troops into the Army of Tennessee was a relatively easy task; Longstreet was a different matter. Not only did he outrank every general in the army save Bragg himself, but he also possessed a formidable reputation. Bragg had to assume that the government had sent Longstreet west because it wanted him to exercise an important command, and perhaps Lee's most experienced lieutenant from the Virginia battles could actually be of some assistance. At any rate, Bragg decided to reorganize his army's command system overnight. He divided the army into two wings, each consisting of two corps and an extra division. Longstreet got one of them, and the other one had of necessity to go to the next-ranking officer in the army, Leonidas Polk. Longstreet's left wing included the corps of Buckner and Hood, plus Hindman's division, a part of what had until then been Polk's corps: seventeen brigades in all. Polk commanded the right wing, consisting of the corps of Hill and Walker along with Cheatham's division, the other half of Polk's old corps: fifteen brigades in all. It added another layer of command between Bragg and the troops who would actually do the fighting, and the Army of Tennessee already had enough places for things to go wrong. The confusion involved in changing command arrangements during the night in the midst of a major battle only made matters worse. It was not an ideal arrangement, but under the circumstances it may have been as good as any other available solution.[3]

What Bragg wanted the army to do the next day was considerably more straightforward. If the Army of the Cumberland were to be destroyed, it would have to be driven southward, toward McLemore's Cove and away from the routes to Chattanooga by either Rossville or McFarland's Gaps.[4] Therefore, Bragg planned to strike first with his right wing against Rosecrans's northern flank, overlap it or crush it, and then roll the Union army southward. For this purpose, the Army of Tennessee's divisions would attack one after another, in order, beginning on the right, so that the erupting conflict would sweep along the battle line from right to left like a great rolling peal of thunder. The idea was that as each successive Federal unit began to struggle against Confederate pressure on its northern flank—and perhaps to redeploy accordingly—it would be struck a hammer blow from the front and knocked out of line.[5]

Commanding the right wing of the Army of Tennessee, Polk would have the responsibility of starting the next day's battle, and so Bragg informed him at a midnight conference. Polk was to attack at "day-dawn" in the morning. Yet as usual in the Army of Tennessee—and for Leonidas Polk—things went wrong. On Polk's right, the extreme right of the army's main body, was Hill's corps. To its two divisions would fall the duty of being the first units to attack in the morning. At the close of the fighting on the nineteenth, Hill seems to have made only a halfhearted attempt to locate Bragg's headquarters near Thedford's Ford—he already had a considerable attitude

problem about his commander. Hill missed Bragg, but one of his staff officers ran into Polk, who informed him of the reorganization and told him to
have Hill report to Polk at the latter's headquarters near Alexander's Bridge.
Hill, who seems to have been miffed at being placed under the command of
a fellow lieutenant general, decided his new wing commander would keep,
and he grabbed a few hours' sleep before setting out in search of Polk. By the
time he did it was 3:00 A.M., and the couriers Polk had posted to meet Hill
and guide him in had long since returned to their camps and rolled up in
their blankets to get what sleep they still could. Since the night was dark and
murky with fog and smoke and Polk's actual headquarters camp was in a
cedar thicket half a mile from the bridge, Hill had little chance of finding it.
He did not waste much effort trying. Aside from posting the couriers near
the bridge to meet Hill—if he showed up within the next couple of hours—
and sending a single unreliable enlisted courier to look for him, Polk took no
steps to contact his key subordinate before turning in himself shortly after
midnight. Hill returned to his sector without any inkling that he was to
launch a daylight assault.[6]

Meanwhile, Breckinridge brought his division up from Glass's Mill,
where it had skirmished with Negley, and crossed Chickamauga Creek
around 10:00 P.M. Hill had left a staff officer at the ford to bring Breckinridge up to his place on the right, but when the latter ran into Polk and complained that his men were tired, the bishop countermanded Hill's orders
and directed Breckinridge to camp where he was. The action was characteristic of both men. Unfortunately for the Army of Tennessee, it also meant
that the rightmost division in the army, the one that was supposed to open
the next day's fighting, was a good mile and a half out of position that night
and though afoot by daybreak was still a good hour's march from its start-off
point at the time the attack was supposed to have begun.[7]

Bragg and his staff were up and in the saddle before dawn—and were increasingly distressed as minutes and then hours passed with no sound of firing to the north. Bragg dispatched staff officers to Polk and Hill and then
went to the front himself. Reaching Hill's corps, he found Hill with his division commander Cleburne and there learned of Polk's activities that morning. The wing commander had risen shortly before dawn, and only then had
he shown concern about the failure to make contact with Hill the night before. Still ignorant of Hill's whereabouts, Polk dispensed with him and sent
orders directly to the division commanders, Cleburne and Breckinridge, to
attack as soon as their divisions could be gotten into position. When the order reached Cleburne, Hill was with him. He countermanded Polk's orders

Dragging Artillery through Hills and Hollows in a Hard Rain. Alfred H. Guernsey and Henry M. Alden, *Harper's Pictorial History of the Civil War*, vol. 2 (New York: Harper and Brothers, 1868), 534

Chattanooga, from the north bank of the Tennessee, after the Federal occupation. Guernsey and Alden, *Harper's Pictorial History*, 540

Lookout Mountain from the Chattanooga Fortifications. Guernsey and Alden, *Harper's Pictorial History*, 561

The Fight at the Cravens House. Guernsey and Alden,
Harper's Pictorial History, 564

The Storming of Missionary Ridge. Guernsey and Alden,
Harper's Pictorial History, 566

until the troops of both divisions could draw rations and eat their breakfasts, at least an hour, he reckoned. In any case, both divisions were fearfully out of position. Cleburne's brigades had bivouacked in the final positions they had occupied in the previous evening's wildly confused night fighting. Breckinridge's division was still marching up from its camp near Alexander's Bridge, and the former vice-president had managed somehow to lose his wagon train. Polk had presently arrived on the scene, heard Hill's explanations, offered no protest, and then had wandered off in search of Walker, whose corps was supposed to be somewhere nearby.[8]

This was the situation when Bragg arrived. On further investigation he found the situation to be even worse. This was the first Hill and his division commanders had heard of a day-dawn assault, and Polk had apparently made no effort to get any part of his wing into position, either last night or this morning. The disarray of Hill's corps was only the beginning of Bragg's sorrowful discoveries. Cheatham's division lay entirely outside of Polk's sector, positioned behind Stewart's division of Longstreet's wing. At least two of Cheatham's brigades were so badly misaligned as to be almost at right angles to Hill's troops. Bragg finally gave up on getting the division into line for the attack and simply ordered it to pull back into a reserve position lest the assault be delayed endlessly. Walker's corps, which was supposed to be in reserve behind Hill, was well south of its intended position and almost completely behind Cheatham. In short, the right wing was a mess, and the bulk of its strength, which should have been concentrated up on the far right to crush the Federal northern flank, was instead bunched on the left of Polk's sector, ready to become entangled with Longstreet's command. As if all that was not enough, Polk had not bothered to reconnoiter the enemy position in his front, and he and his officers knew little of it save that since about sunrise it had been marked by the ominous sound of axes. The Northerners were constructing breastworks.

Bragg labored for several hours to get the wing into some kind of order for an assault. Even then preparations were far from perfect, but it was too late now for careful arrangement of troops. The chance to destroy Rosecrans was passing. At the same time, Bragg also directed a reconnaissance that revealed that Breckinridge, now coming up into his assigned position, was indeed substantially overlapping the Union flank. Opportunity still beckoned when at approximately 9:30 A.M., Breckinridge began his advance.[9]

Across the way, in the Union lines, Thomas and his men had spent the morning preparing for the Confederate assault. Thomas's main defensive line lay in the woods in a broad semicircle around the east side of the Kelly field, then back across the La Fayette Road and southward along the west side of the Poe field. Into this position Thomas had packed three of his own divisions plus those of Palmer and Johnson. Further south, Rosecrans was continuing to draw the rest of the army northward and demonstrating that he was prepared to make good on his promise of the night before and support Thomas with the entire army if necessary. Not long after sunrise, Thomas had become worried about the empty half mile between his left flank and Reed's Bridge Road. Loath to draw down his own reserves in the Kelly field, he had appealed to Rosecrans for troops to extend the flank, and not just any troops but Negley's division, the only remaining XIV Corps unit still separated from Thomas's command. Rosecrans promptly complied, pulled Negley out of his lines along the west side of the Brotherton field, where he had been since shooing away the remnants of Stewart's assault the night before, and sent him marching up the line to Thomas's position. Negley's place in the Brotherton field would be filled by Wood's division, one of two that Rosecrans now held in reserve. While Thomas waited impatiently for Negley's arrival, he gave orders shifting other units northward within his sector. Bragg was not the only one that morning who could calculate correctly where a Confederate attack could do the most damage.[10]

Thomas's men were far from idle during the chilly early morning hours. Some of the units were just moving into position in Thomas's perimeter at daybreak, and none of them had yet begun construction of breastworks. Shortly after dawn soldiers from all five of Thomas's divisions turned to the work of throwing together what protection they could from logs and fence rails. Soon the entire Kelly field perimeter rang with the sound of axes that had disturbed Bragg and other Confederate officers.[11]

The fact that the Federals would be fighting from behind log barricades in the coming battle would prove enormously important both to the length of the opposing casualty lists and to the ultimate outcome. Yet had Polk gotten his wing of the army into motion at day-dawn as ordered by Bragg, his troops would have encountered no Union breastworks at all. Indeed, they would have encountered considerably fewer blue-clad infantrymen than they did, as Thomas's and Rosecrans's efforts had continued to bring in reinforcements to the Kelly field sector throughout the morning. Those Northerners present at dawn were not completely positioned to receive an assault. Bragg later blamed Polk's failure to launch the day-dawn attack for the Confederacy's lack of a decisive victory at Chickamauga, and critics then and since sneered that his charge smacked of "sour grapes." Yet one of the Union division commanders within Thomas's perimeter conceded after the war that had the attack struck at dawn, "the battle would not have lasted an hour; we would have gone to Chattanooga on the run." That statement, however, misses the magnitude of the lost Confederate opportunity. If Thomas's lines had broken under a flank attack that morning, a fair proportion of the Army of the Cumberland would not have gone to Chattanooga at all. With Hill's victorious Southerners rampaging southward down the La Fayette Road after crushing the north flank of the Union line, Thomas's broken formations could only have fled southward through a collapsing position to join the rest of the army in attempting to flee through the bottleneck of McFarland's Gap before the Confederate advance cut it off too. Few of them could have made it and fewer of their guns and wagons.[12]

By 9:30, however, all such possibilities were already in the realm of the might-have-beens. Thomas's position was compact and densely manned with sturdy log barricades. Ample reserves were on hand and more were on the way. Save for the open country to the north, Thomas had no cause for worry, but it was there that Breckinridge struck.

The former vice-president's division advanced with its three brigades in line abreast, the right flank on the Reed's Bridge Road. The right and center brigades, commanded by Brig. Gens. Daniel W. Adams and Marcellus A. Stovall respectively, encountered only a weak line of skirmishers, which they quickly dispersed. These Federals were the men of Brig. Gen. John Beatty's brigade, the first of Negley's brigades to arrive at the Kelly field. Thomas, all but obsessed with the need to cover his dangling left flank, had not waited for the rest of the division to come up but had instead dispatched Beatty with orders to stretch his lone brigade all the way from the end of the newly built breastworks to the intersection of the Reed's Bridge and La Fayette Roads. It was a poor decision. Beatty's brigade was not strong enough to hold that much ground, and the result was an ineffectual skirmish line that Breckinridge's men easily brushed aside. The Confederates came on all but unscathed, while Beatty's brigade was badly bloodied and some of its component units did not rejoin the army for the rest of the day. Now in undisputed possession of the La Fayette Road well north of the Union flank, Breckinridge set about to restore the alignment of his two brigades and get them turned to advance southward, along the road, onto the flank of Thomas's position.[13]

Breckinridge's left-flank brigade was not having such an easy time of it. Brig. Gen. Ben Hardin Helm's Kentuckians had struck the northernmost curve of the Federal breastworks. Helm's men could not have known it, but they were bucking a stacked deck. They had to advance across an open grassy glade toward troops that were packed in tight behind log breastworks in the far tree line. Opposite the middle of the brigade the Union breastwork curved away to the northwest. The brigade's right wing, opposite the bent-back portion of the Union position, plunged forward looking for the enemy lines and not finding them, while the left half of the unit walked straight into the blazing muzzles of the Federal rifles and artillery. They split apart, the troops on the right wandering westward to link up eventually with the rest of the division and the left wing hurling itself furiously against the Union breastworks. For a few moments it appeared that their valor might accomplish the impossible. Color sergeant Robert C. Anderson of the Second Kentucky leaped to the top of the breastworks and planted his regiment's flag there, but the midwesterners on the other side stood their ground and fought back just as fiercely. Anderson toppled to the ground, dead. Helm himself, a brother-in-law of Abraham Lincoln, fell mortally wounded a few yards from the Federal works, and the Kentucky brigade's attack had spent itself without denting the Union line.[14]

Their slaughter was soon to be avenged, however, as Breckinridge's other two brigades finally plowed into the extreme left end of the semicircular Union position around the Kelly field and overlapped and crushed it. Federal troops fled their breastworks and dashed headlong into the Kelly field, hotly pursued by Stovall's Georgians, Floridians, and North Carolinians. West of the La Fayette Road, Adams's Alabamians and Louisianans pushed ahead with little opposition. Then the tide of battle swung quickly the other way. Adams' men, charging madly through thick underbrush, ran smack into a solid line of bluecoated troops who gave them a devastating volley at close range. These Federals belonged to Col. Timothy Stanley's brigade, another of Negley's units hastening to support Thomas. Beatty's remnants rallied behind Stanley's unbroken line, and together they hurled Adams's Confederates back out of the Union position. Adams himself remained behind, badly wounded.[15]

East of the La Fayette Road, out in the Kelly field, a desperate struggle raged on. Stovall's men had charged across the open field to within fifty yards of the guns of Battery A, First Ohio, but then had been driven back by blasts of double-shotted canister. Taking refuge in the edge of the woods on the north side of the field, the Confederates turned the tables on a Union brigade that now attempted to counterattack them, shooting it to pieces and sending its demoralized remnants fleeing out of the battle.[16]

Thomas still had ample forces available to stop this incursion by a single understrength Confederate brigade; besides the one Stovall's men had just demolished, at least three other Union brigades were available in reserve positions behind their divisional lines around the Kelly field perimeter and just to the south, but the momentum was now with Stovall. The Kelly field was squarely in rear of Thomas's entire position, and it now presented a scene of pandemonium, strewn with the dead and wounded of both sides, with demoralized troops fleeing, it seemed, in all directions and frantic staff officers galloping hither and yon trying to put together a concerted defense. Stovall's men laced the scene with rifle fire, and bursting shells told of the presence of a Confederate battery in support of Breckinridge's division. Some of them must have struck the Kelly farmhouse and barn, for the buildings presently became roaring infernos.[17]

To make matters worse for Thomas, at this point the Confederate assault entered its next phase. To the south of Breckinridge's division, Cleburne's had been late launching its attack because of its thoroughly disordered alignment, the result of the previous evening's fight and Polk's failure to have his attack orders transmitted. Finally, and still not in perfect order, Cleburne's three brigades surged forward against the outside of the Kelly field perimeter even as Stovall was wreaking havoc on the inside. In a broad semicircle arching around the field from north to east to south came the rattling crashes of musketry volleys and the chest-tightening concussions of the artillery. More dense white clouds of powder smoke drifted across the field to mingle with the dark wood smoke of the Kelly farm buildings. In the hour since Breckinridge's division had begun its advance, it had chewed up four Union brigades totaling substantially more than its own strength. Napoleon had once said that "big battalions" would generally prevail, but he had also said that in war, moral factors outweigh the physical. By 10:30 A.M., it appeared that unless someone managed to stanch the contagion of demoralization, the Union numerical advantage in Thomas's sector might not count for much after all and the Federal front would break, "big battalions" or no.

Into this scene presently marched the brigade of Col. Ferdinand Van Derveer. It was a good outfit to have in a tight spot. A diverse lot, with its northwoodsmen of the Second Minnesota, its Cincinnati Germans of the Ninth Ohio, and its leavening of Indiana and Ohio farm boys in the other two regiments, the brigade had been together since the early days of the war, when it had been Thomas's own. The men had confidence in themselves, their officers, and each other.

The situation into which they now marched was desperate, a hideous kaleidoscope of smoke, fire, sound, terror, and confusion. Ordered simply to move up from his reserve position behind Brannan's division and support Thomas in the Kelly field, Van Derveer entered the field with his regiments in two lines, both facing east, the general direction of the Kelly field lines. Of course, Stovall's threat lay to the north, but, nearly surrounded with sound and fury, Van Derveer's officers needed a few moments to determine which way their troops should face. Once they did, the men had the harrowing task of swinging their entire line across the open field to confront the Rebels along the northern tree line. Other brigades had come apart trying to accomplish such a feat. Van Derveer's did not. Finally fronting toward their tormentors in the woods, the Northerners began to give back some of the punishment everyone in the field had been taking for the last fifteen minutes, but with the Confederates under cover in the trees, it was an uneven struggle.

Van Derveer's men stuck to it nevertheless, and other Union regiments fell into line on their flanks, beginning to get the leverage on Stovall's tired men. Then the Ninth Ohio, without orders save from its German-speaking colonel, launched one of its trademark bayonet charges. For a moment the other combatants watched in awe. Then a sergeant of the Second Minnesota leaped out in front of his line bellowing, "Don't let the Ninth Ohio charge alone!" The rest of the Union line surged forward, and the moral ascendancy of Stovall's Confederates was broken. The tired men in gray and butternut scrambled madly for the rear ahead of an onrushing tidal wave of blue uniforms. Van Derveer's men chased them nearly to the Reed's Bridge Road before pulling back to the Kelly field.[18]

The Union position was restored for now, and Breckinridge's division was all but used up. It would be hours before its disorganized remnants could be gotten into attack formation again. Breckinridge believed that if ample reserves had been in position behind his division during the attack, "decisive results" could have been gained. Bragg had given Polk the troops—both Walker's corps and Cheatham's division sat out the first round of Confederate attacks on the northern end of the battlefield. Polk had simply failed to make use of his reserves, and thus Breckinridge's men had little chance to gain more than a local and temporary success.[19]

Meanwhile, Cleburne's division was dashing itself to pieces against the front of the Federal breastworks. It was the Irish-born Confederate general's worst outing since Shiloh. Part of his habitual success lay in his thorough preparation. This time he had no chance to prepare at all, and his brigades could hardly have been more completely out of position. Despite Cleburne's hurried attempts to deploy them properly for the assault, they wound up going forward piecemeal and unsupported, becoming entangled with each other and their neighboring division on the left and too late to be of any help to poor Helm on their right. As always, they fought ferociously, but this time their valor was wasted. Cleburne's best brigade commander fell and a great many other good soldiers too, and they achieved no result but to create a tense and noisy hour for Thomas's troops. The Union breastworks proved their value, making for grotesquely lopsided casualty figures. On the ground in front of the Federal position, Cleburne's division left just over thirteen hundred of its less than forty-seven hundred men. Hazen's Union brigade, one of several that turned back Cleburne's attack, lost a grand total of thirteen. Hazen himself noted that in earlier battles, in less intense fighting, his brigade had typically lost as many as four hundred men at a time. Clearly, the growing use of field fortifications was changing the face of Civil War combat.[20]

By this time, Walker's Reserve Corps was ready for action, but now the interaction between Hill, Walker, and Polk became muddled enough to be downright farcical if it had not resulted in so many deaths. Hill's skill as a commander seemed not to extend beyond simple combativeness, and he now proposed to take Walker's corps apart into its component pieces and throw these isolated brigades forward to support his disastrous first wave of attacks. Walker objected. Both men were known for their hot tempers and vented them in a rip-roaring argument while the men of Breckinridge's and Cleburne's divisions charged vainly or grimly tried to hang on behind the Federal perimeter. Polk, whose duty it was to command this sector and who should never have allowed such an argument to develop in the first place, did nothing. In the end, Hill had his way. One of Walker's brigades achieved the dubious result of reenacting the attack of Helm's brigade some two hours later, breaking apart on the curve of the Union breastworks and having its commander and nearly half its men shot. Another brigade retraced the steps of Adams's men. Like their predecessors, these Confederates enjoyed limited initial success by striking the flank of the Union position but then were driven off in disorder. The rest of Walker's corps suffered in futile attacks on the same breastworks that had broken Cleburne. Cheatham's division remained idle all the while. Taken as a whole, the performance of the Confederate right wing this morning had been one of the most appalling exhibitions of command incompetence of the entire Civil War.[21]

This failure was significant. Bragg's only hope of a truly important victory over Rosecrans lay in cutting off the Army of the Cumberland from Chattanooga. That could be done only at the northern end of the battlefield.

Unless Bragg could succeed in defeating and rolling up the Union left flank—driving the Federals south of the Dyer Road and thus denying them access to Chattanooga by both the La Fayette and the Dry Valley Roads—he could hope for no decisive results. If the Confederates failed in that task—no matter what else they might manage to do—the Union army would almost certainly succeed in withdrawing to Chattanooga, more or less intact, and securing its supply line. Confederate hopes of a meaningful victory rested that day on the shoulders of Leonidas Polk, and as he had on several previous occasions during the war and on at least one occasion within this very month, he failed. Of course, Bragg could be faulted for giving so important an assignment to Polk, but under the circumstances, he had little choice. Jefferson Davis had made plain to him over a year before that he expected him to work with Polk. That and Polk's rank meant inevitably that the bishop-general would frequently be in positions of great responsibility and frequently would fail. He may never have cost the Confederacy more dearly than on this day. All that remained now was to see how much combat damage the Southerners could inflict on Rosecrans's army and at what cost to themselves.

As the first unit of Longstreet's wing joined the assault late in the morning, it appeared that the Confederates would continue to inflict minimal damage at great cost to themselves. On Cleburne's left was Stewart's division. It too had experienced alignment problems that morning, and its right-flank brigade had gotten tangled with Cleburne's troops. So irritated did Bragg finally become at the resulting delays, the overall slowness of Longstreet's wing to prepare for battle, and the near paralysis of the Confederate right that he gave orders for every division up and down the front to advance at once. Before these orders could be delivered, Longstreet at last sent Stewart's division forward, initiating his half of the battle. Yet despite the different wing commander, this assault achieved no greater success. Stewart's men advanced across the Poe field from east to west, the same ground over which Bate's brigade of the same division had attempted to advance from south to north the evening before, only to be devastated by artillery fire. This advance proved no more successful, as the Federals, here ensconced behind breastworks just west of the La Fayette Road, quickly shot Stewart's brigades to pieces.

These Union troops also belonged to Thomas's command, the divisions of Reynolds and Brannan. For Thomas and his men, the day had thus far been an unqualified success. They had turned back every Confederate assault and punished the attackers severely. With the exception of the few tense minutes when Breckinridge's men got into the Kelly field and a similar period when one of Walker's brigades repeated the attempt, the Union position had never really been seriously threatened. It was a creditable performance by Thomas and his men, but it was no military miracle. Aside from Thomas's undoubted skill and steadiness, the toughness and fighting qualities of his men, and the ineptness of the morning's performance by Polk and Hill, the Union success on the north end of the battlefield was the result of Rosecrans's determination to hold that ground no matter what else he held or did not hold. His resolve to strengthen Thomas at all costs had led him to feed units to the XIV Corps commander until by the repulse of the last attack in the Kelly field, Thomas had under his orders some sixteen Union brigades. He had met and repulsed the attack of only fourteen Confederate brigades. Under those circumstances, Thomas's success was not too surprising. Nor had Rosecrans dispatched all these reinforcements unsolicited. Since two o'clock that morning, Thomas had sent thirteen separate appeals to his commander for more troops. Rosecrans had responded faithfully to these requests and before noon had even dispatched another four brigades to his northern flank. These, however, had not yet reported to Thomas by the time the fighting died down in the Kelly field sector. The only troops not then assigned to the XIV Corps commander were five brigades of McCook's corps plus Wilder's brigade, and these units were even then in the process of shifting northward to close up on Thomas. All of this moving of units had made the Federal left flank rock-solid, but shortly before noon it led to a serious mistake that left the Federal right flank fatally vulnerable.[22]

At the height of the crisis in the Kelly field, before Van Derveer's brigade had arrived to turn the tide against Breckinridge, Thomas had sent a staff officer to bring up Brannan's entire division to save his threatened left. This he did because he believed Brannan was in a reserve position several hundred yards behind the front. That had been the case the evening before, but during the army's nighttime maneuvering, it had changed. Thomas had contracted his lines a great deal to form the compact, densely manned perimeter around the Kelly field. His right division, Reynolds', had drawn in more than half a mile from the ground it had held the day before. The rest of the army was supposed to close up, slide north, and fill in the gap, but somehow they never quite made it. Brannan alertly plugged the hole, but somehow Thomas had never gotten word of the change.

And so it occurred that the staff officer from Thomas found Brannan not in reserve but in line that morning and gave him the order to march to the left and support Baird. Reynolds, who ranked Brannan, was nearby, and the two consulted on what to do about this extraordinary dispatch, which the staff officer assured them was most urgent. Things were quiet here at the moment, and Reynolds, whose lines angled back to approach Brannan's at the northern edge of the Poe field, thought that perhaps in a pinch he could cover the long open field with firepower alone, so he told Brannan to go ahead, and the staff officer galloped off toward Rosecrans's headquarters to tell the commanding general that he had just created a gap in the army's line.[23]

By this time Rosecrans had left the Widow Glenn's cabin and established his headquarters on the open northern end of an otherwise wooded knoll that overlooked the Dry Valley Road to the west and the Dyer Road to the north. To the east, a strip of woods blocked the view of the Brotherton field. The headquarters knoll was a busy place just now, as Rosecrans was in the process of moving several of his divisions toward Thomas and Chattanooga. The army commander, who had eaten little and slept less since the army had crossed the Tennessee River what seemed like an eternity ago, listened to the report of Brannan's withdrawal from the line and made a snap decision on how best to fill the gap. Wood, next in line to the south of Brannan, should slide north and make contact with Reynolds. Garfield, the chief of staff and regular order writer, was busy drawing up directives to the other divisions then in motion, so Rosecrans gave the task to another staff officer. The resulting dispatch was somewhat vague and said nothing at all about Brannan:

> Headquarters Department of the Cumberland
> September 20—
>
> 10.45 A.M.
> Brigadier-General Wood,
> Commanding Division, &c.:
> The general commanding directs that you close up on Reynolds as fast as possible, and support him.
> Respectfully, &c.,
>
> Frank S. Bond,
> Major, and Aide-de-Camp.[24]

What Rosecrans did not know was that Brannan had never left his position in line. After getting Reynolds's blessing for the move and informing Thomas's staff officer that he would go, Brannan had thought better of a maneuver so rash as opening up a division-sized gap in the battle line with an enemy attack apparently imminent. Surely affairs at the other end of Thomas's sector could not be so desperate as to warrant such a risk. Brannan decided he could not go through with it. He canceled his movement orders to his brigadiers and stayed in position. This wise decision, combined with the vagueness of Rosecrans's order to Wood, proved to be key elements in the coming debacle. The single ingredient still lacking was provided by the curious personality and unfortunate state of mind of Brig. Gen. Thomas J. Wood.[25]

Like his second cousin, the recently deceased Ben Hardin Helm, Wood was a native of Munfordville, Kentucky. An 1845 West Point graduate, Wood had won a brevet for gallantry in the Mexican War, stayed with the colors when the Civil War broke out, and performed with distinction at Shiloh, Perryville, and Stones River. A proud and sensitive man, Wood had had his feelings severely bruised a couple of times during this campaign when Rosecrans had administered embarrassingly public rebukes for what the army commander viewed as lack of promptness in obeying orders. The second such incident had occurred that very morning, when Rosecrans had wanted Wood to hurry up and take Negley's place in line and so hasten the latter's support of Thomas. Like any conscientious officer, Wood had wanted to be sure he understood his commander's orders before carrying them out, but Rosecrans had been in no mood for giving clarifications and Wood got a tongue-lashing in front of his staff. It was a bad habit of Rosecrans's.[26]

At 11:00 A.M. Wood received Rosecrans's order. Under the circumstances it was a curious one indeed. "Close up on Reynolds" indicated a lateral move, in line, toward Reynolds's position. Yet with Brannan still in line between Reynolds and Wood, this was impossible. In that case, to "support" Reynolds could only mean pulling out of line and marching behind Brannan to come up in rear of Reynolds. Yet if that were what Rosecrans had intended, he had certainly chosen an extremely odd way of expressing it. And if Wood were to withdraw from the line, this did not seem an opportune time to do it. The Confederates were obviously up to something over on the other side of the La Fayette Road, and their skirmishers were already engaging Wood's. Everything about this order seemed to demand that Wood get clarification before carrying it out, and even the staff officer who delivered it urged Wood to wait while he rode back to headquarters and explained the situation. Wood, however, was adamant. He was in no mood for getting clarifications—and possible tongue-lashings—from Rosecrans. He would obey immediately and literally, even if the order made no sense and appeared disastrous. To the consternation of his officers, he yanked his three brigades out of line and set them marching to the rear.[27]

Ironically, Wood, acting on Rosecrans's mistaken orders, had opened a gap in the Federal line at its weakest and most seriously threatened point. Had Brannan actually pulled out of line further north in the Poe field, Reynolds might indeed have been able to cover the gap with firepower by sweeping the field with the cannon and rifles of his division, posted on the northern edge of the clearing. Even if he had not, the Confederate force arrayed against that front, Stewart's division, had no supports immediately on hand and had it broken through could probably have achieved no more than it did in its limited breakthrough the previous afternoon. But Wood's sector had been the infamous Brotherton field. His men had been deployed in the edge of the woods on the western side of the field rather than on the exposed ridge top in the middle of the field as the Federals had been the previous day. That was an improvement because it meant that the Confederates would not be able to see or fire on the Union line until they themselves came under its fire, and at that point the attacking Southerners would be skylined on the open ridge top while the Federals would be sheltering behind low fence-rail breastworks in the woods. Still, the position would put the charging Confederates within about fifty yards of the Union line before they came under fire. If the Southerners were resolute, that would allow time for just one volley from the defenders. It would have to be a good one.

The worst of it—and what no one in blue could have known yet—was that directly opposite Wood's now abandoned position, Longstreet was massing the main force of his wing. The new general from the Army of Northern Virginia had taken a good deal of time sorting out the units of his wing and getting them ready to attack. Promptness was not one of Longstreet's virtues, and there was no denying he had a considerable amount of sorting out to do. If Polk had not been even slower and tasked with opening the attack, Longstreet's slowness would probably have aroused Bragg's irritation. Now, however, the Confederate left wing was finally ready. On Longstreet's right, Stewart was already opening the wing's attack—disastrously, as it turned out—against Reynolds's and Brannan's solid lines. On the far left, Hindman's and Preston's divisions waited their turn to go in. In his center, Longstreet had massed his main striking force, three divisions containing a total of eight brigades ranged five lines deep. Up front was Bushrod Johnson's division, two brigades up, one in reserve. Next came Evander Law's in the same formation. Finally came part of Maj. Gen. Lafayette McLaws's division, two brigades, commanded in McLaws's absence by Brig. Gen. Joseph Kershaw. The whole center attacking column was under the command of Hood, one of the hardest-hitting combat leaders of the Army of Northern Virginia. At 11:10 A.M., on orders from Longstreet, Johnson's Tennesseeans started up the east side of the Brotherton ridge to launch the assault.[28]

At the foot of the western slope of that ridge, less than two hundred yards away, the Union breastworks were mostly deserted, though at the southern end of the sector, the men of Davis's division were double-quicking by the left flank, trying to fill the gap left by Wood's departure. They were too late. To hold this position they would have had to have blasted the Rebels the moment they came over the ridge, but before Davis's men could take their places the yelling Confederates were upon them. Surprised, outnumbered, and flanked on both sides, Davis's division went to pieces. The rampaging Southerners next caught the trailing brigade of Wood's withdrawing division and wrecked it before it could get clear of the gap it had left. North of the gap, Brannan's division found itself assailed in flank and rear but resisted stoutly for a time before giving way and joining the rapidly developing rout.[29]

Johnson's men, still leading the Confederate assault, plunged ahead through the woods behind the Brotherton farm, then burst out into the open fields of the Dyer farm and one of the most incredible panoramas of the entire war. The open space was perhaps five hundred yards deep and about twelve hundred wide rimmed with hills on its far side to form a natural amphitheater. And it was the rear area of the Army of the Cumberland, now an indescribable scene of panic and confusion, as the shattered remnants of three broken Federal brigades fled madly through a tangle of reserve units, artillery, baggage and supply trains, and headquarters personnel. To Johnson, "the scene now presented was unspeakably grand. The resolute and impetuous charge, the rush of our heavy columns sweeping out from the shadow and gloom of the forest into the open fields flooded with sunlight, the glitter of arms, the onward dash of artillery and mounted men, the retreat of the foe, the shouts of the hosts of our army, the dust, the smoke, the noise of fire-arms—of whistling balls and grape-shot and of bursting shell— made up a battle scene of unsurpassed grandeur."[30] That the scene's beauty was much in the eye of the beholder could be attested by those who witnessed it from one of the hills that rimmed the western edge of the field. On Rosecrans's headquarters knoll things had become quiet and drowsy as noonday approached—so much so that Assistant Secretary of War Charles A. Dana, an unwelcome appendage to Rosecrans's staff who served as the eyes and ears of the dissatisfied Stanton, had even laid down in the grass for a bit of repose. His nap was rudely cut short by an excruciating crescendo of discordant sound as the battle roared into the far side of the Dyer field. Waking with a start, Dana was just in time to see Rosecrans, a devout Catholic, gazing wide-eyed toward the woods that screened the Brotherton farm and crossing himself. "If the general is crossing himself," Dana reasoned, "we are in a desperate situation." In fact, neither Dana nor Rosecrans, now watching in horror as Davis's fugitives fled into the field pursued by Johnson's Confederates, yet had any idea just how desperate.[31]

Davis's division was gone; so were the trailing elements of Wood and Van Cleve, both of whom had been on their way to Thomas. The only remaining units that retained any cohesion on this part of the battlefield were Wilder's Lightning Brigade, then moving up from the south toward the Widow Glenn hill, Sheridan's division, even now approaching Rosecrans's headquarters from the south, and several batteries of reserve artillery ranged along the crest of a ridge that edged the west side of the Dyer field north of the Dyer Road. The next stage of the conflict would be the struggle to control the Dyer field and determine whether these few Union formations could halt Longstreet's massive assault column.[32]

The Federals at first responded aggressively. From the ridge north of the Dyer Road the Union batteries opened up on Johnson's Confederates and Law's coming up behind them. From a hill on the south side of the road, next to the one where Rosecrans and his headquarters personnel were hurriedly mounting up and riding for cover, a brigade of Federal infantry charged directly into the onrushing Confederate masses in the open ground below. These foot soldiers were the lead brigade of Sheridan's division. They had a good position on the hillside, but McCook, who had just come up out of the chaos in the Dyer field, insisted on ordering them to charge at once. Down off the hill they went, bayonets leveled, but they were quickly overwhelmed by the left side of Hood's massive assault column and the right side of Hindman's division, now advancing on the far southern end of the Confederate line. Sheridan's next brigade tried to make a stand on the hill but was overwhelmed and swept away. The third brigade of Sheridan's division never got to the hill, making its stand on the low ground to the south. It fared slightly better but finally had to join the retreat.[33]

Sheridan's division was wrecked, and it might have seemed to Rosecrans, then making his own retreat along with the shattered remnants of the Federal right, that things could not have been worse there. In fact, they could have been a good deal worse. Part of the reason Sheridan's southernmost brigade had done as well as it had and the remains of Sheridan's division had been able to retire with any order at all was that their southern flank was solidly covered by the one remaining unbroken Federal unit on this part of the field. Wilder's Lightning Brigade kicked Hindman's momentarily victorious Confederates off the Widow Glenn hill and sent a brigade of them fleeing all the way back across the La Fayette Road, several hundred yards to the east.

Wilder next planned to fall on the flank and rear of the rest of Longstreet's wing as it turned north to confront Union troops still resisting in that sector. Breaking through that many Confederates would have been a challenge for the Lightning Brigade, but the Hoosiers and Illinoisans in the ranks did not believe they could be stopped. If they were wrong about that, no one had ever managed to prove the contrary. At any rate, Wilder was ready to try when a high-ranking fugitive from the Dyer field rode up. Assistant Secretary of War Dana had somehow gotten separated from the rest of Rosecrans's headquarters personnel, which, if noticed, could have caused no sorrow to them. Dana, however, was very frightened. He flatly forbade Wilder to make his projected counterattack and demanded an escort back to Chattanooga. Reluctantly, Wilder had to comply, and the Lightning Brigade retired from the field of Chickamauga unbroken and full of fight.[34]

Meanwhile, back in the Dyer field, Johnson, commanding the lead Confederate division, and Hood, commanding the entire central assault column, had more to think about than the feeble efforts of the Union left to reestablish itself. Their immediate concern was the presence of those Federal cannon along the ridge at the far side of the Dyer field. Maj. John Mendenhall had been there most of the morning with the reserve artillery of the XXI Corps. As the Union left collapsed, a dozen more guns had come thundering across the Dyer field behind lathered horses, up the ridge, and into battery. Now the crest was lined with twenty-nine guns, barking their defiance at the advancing Confederates as fast as their sweating crews could ram new loads down the hot barrels and manhandle the half-ton pieces to bear. Yet the momentum belonged to the Confederates, and Hood knew what to do with it. "Go ahead," he yelled to Johnson, "and keep ahead of everything."[35]

Johnson's division moved out due west along the Dyer Road and across the Dyer field. His left brigade got in among the Federal supply wagons near the place where the Dyer Road joined the Dry Valley Road. The wagoneers were attempting to flee by the Dry Valley Road toward McFarland's Gap, but Johnson's men captured a score of the wagons in a confused melee in the midst of a traffic jam. For a few minutes these Tennessee Confederates were within reach of the last road connecting the routed Union right with its base at Chattanooga. Yet they were too few, too late, and too disorganized to achieve decisive results. By this time only the battered fragments of half a dozen Federal brigades were still south of this point and liable to being cut off, along with assorted stragglers and rear-echelon people, the flotsam and jetsam of a retreating army. Nor could Hood have spared the force necessary to seize and hold the Dry Valley Road, compelled as he was to face the Union troops even then rallying at the foot of the ridge on which Mendenhall had his twenty-nine guns.[36]

Johnson's two other brigades meanwhile were moving to flank the guns on the ridge, getting astride the high ground south of them and advancing onto their right flank as they were heavily engaged with Law's division, which had swung straight toward them across the open field. For the blue-coated soldiers the collapse came with stunning suddenness. The infantry line at the base of the ridge, already badly demoralized, went to pieces. The gunners on the right were trying to limber up and get their cannon away from Johnson's flanking column. Then the Confederates overran the position, and everyone was trying to get away. For most of the guns it was too late, and well over half of them became prizes of the bloodied but jubilant Southerners.[37]

Hood now sought to exploit his advantage by pushing still further north. Longstreet agreed. To attempt to wheel to the left and drive the enemy southward, as Bragg had originally specified, was no longer a good idea in the changed circumstances of the battle. For one thing, there were no longer all that many of the enemy on the left to be rolled. For another, wheeling left would now expose Longstreet's wing to attack from the flank and rear by the unbroken Union formations to the north. The next Confederate move would have to be in the direction of the still resolute bulk of the Army of the Cumberland, Thomas's troops around the Kelly field and other Federal units now rallying to them.[38]

Whether Longstreet and Hood realized it or not, their struggle had by now been transformed from a contest to destroy the Army of the Cumberland into to an effort to do it what damage they could before it escaped to Chattanooga. That the battle at whose climax they now stood would be a Confederate victory was obvious. The question now was simply what price the Federals would have to pay for defeat. That price could still be considerable; a half day's fighting remained in which to determine the outcome.

If Hood or Longstreet had wondered whether the remaining Federals would fight resolutely, they quickly found out. As Law's division approached the northern end of the Dyer field they were met with a withering volley of musketry from a blue line drawn up behind a rail fence at the north edge of the field. This was Col. Charles G. Harker's brigade of Wood's division. Wood's center brigade, it had cleared the gap before the debacle but had not yet reached Thomas. Seeing the disaster unfolding in the field behind him, Wood had ordered the brigade back to try to contain the damage. For a time, it did. Law's men recoiled in disorder. These had been Hood's own troops back in Virginia, and he rode in to rally them but toppled from his horse when a Northern bullet shattered his right thigh just below the hip. He was carried from the field still muttering, "Go ahead, and keep ahead of everything."[39]

The reverse was temporary, however. Passing through Law's shattered ranks came Brig. Gen. Joseph Kershaw's division. Just arrived from Virginia, too late to see action on the nineteenth, this provisional division consisted of two brigades, Kershaw's own South Carolinians and a brigade of Mississippians under Brig. Gen. Benjamin G. Humphreys. Their regular division commander, Maj. Gen. Lafayette McLaws, had not yet arrived, and so Kershaw more or less led the formation. Still they were among the best troops in the Army of Northern Virginia, they were fresh and spoiling for a fight, and on this day they had the added advantage of wearing new bluish-colored uniforms, just issued to them during the journey southward from Virginia. As they advanced toward Harker's position, the Union rifles fell silent, and the Federal color-bearers rose and began to wave the flags vigorously back and forth, displaying the Stars and Stripes. Kershaw's men answered with a volley, and Harker's rifles spat back, yet the Confederates had made most of their advance under cover of their uniforms. They pressed hard against Harker's line, and the outnumbered Federals fell back, retiring over the last hill at the far northwest corner of the Dyer field and on through a valley of sparse, open woodland, then out into the open again and up the slope of another ridge, the last on which they could hope to make a stand. On its crest stood the modest cabin of a farmer named Snodgrass.[40]

Kershaw's men followed exuberantly but ran head-on into a devastating blast of fire from the ridge top that sent them back into the valley. Harker's men had found on the ridge not only a strong position in which to regroup but also reinforcements and a strong boost to their morale. The reinforcements consisted of Brannan's division, driven out of its old position on the edge of the breakthrough and now deployed further up the slope from the Snodgrass cabin on a series of wooded hills that together are known as Horseshoe Ridge. Also present were fragments of several other divisions, a regiment here, a company or two there. With its overall confusion and the beating many of its troops had already taken, the command on Snodgrass Hill and Horseshoe Ridge would have been far weaker than its numbers indicated save for the presence of George H. Thomas. The sound of firing behind his position had brought him over from the Kelly field. Taking command of the troops on the hills, he made his headquarters on the reverse slope just behind Harker's lines at the Snodgrass cabin. His presence put new spark and confidence into the confused and exhausted soldiers and steeled them to meet the Confederate onslaught.[41]

They would need all the nerve they could muster, for the Confederate attacks went on and on. Kershaw's first assault had come shortly after 1:00 P.M., and subsequent Rebel attempts to storm the ridge continued all afternoon. One after another, all the units of Longstreet's wing of the army, except for Stewart's division, joined the assaults. Yet the Confederate offensive became a curiously confused and disjointed effort. Longstreet had been relying on Hood to coordinate the attack, but even after he knew that Hood was down, Longstreet neither took over the active direction of the assaults himself nor assigned anyone else to do so. The result was a series of piecemeal attacks that frittered away the Confederate advantage in numbers. Longstreet also remained unaware of a five-hundred-yard gap between the Union troops around the Kelly field and those on Snodgrass Hill despite nearly riding into it, along with his staff, and drawing the fire of Federal skirmishers from Reynolds's division on the Kelly field perimeter. Thomas was painfully aware of the gap but had no troops to fill it. Longstreet had troops available to exploit it but seemed never to suspect its presence. The woods obstructed long views, and the prospect of sudden close encounters with enemy skirmishers was something no one could have relished. Of course, he could have advanced his own skirmishers, but he never seemed to grasp the need to know what was in that space. Perhaps James Longstreet simply was not the man to press an aggressive offensive movement. As always, he displayed admirable steadiness and aplomb, but those traits seemed to come at the expense of a great deal of complacency. In any case, the gap remained a tantalizing threat of disaster for Thomas, while Longstreet and his staff settled down to take a midday repast of bacon and sweet potatoes—unheard-of delicacies in Virginia—and Confederate soldiers struggled up the slopes of Snodgrass Hill and Horseshoe Ridge in frenzied but unsupported attacks.[42]

What the Confederate assaults lacked in generalship they nearly made up in fury. All along the Federal line the fighting was desperate. On Snodgrass Hill, Harker made clever use of terrain by arranging his brigade in two lines. One would stand and reload on the back slope while the other delivered a volley into the faces of the charging Confederates. Then a rapid passage of lines would put another solid rank of loaded rifles on the crest. Without breastworks or woods for cover, Harker skillfully shielded his men behind the crest of the hill. Farther up on Horseshoe Ridge more complex terrain made for a complicated fight, but the result was the same. Thomas's men threw back one Confederate charge after another. Yet the very persistence of the Southerners threatened to carry the position. Taking stock during a brief lull between attacks, Thomas learned that his men's cartridge boxes now contained an average of two rounds each and the XIV Corps' ammunition wagons had been caught up in the rout and were now somewhere on the road to Chattanooga, well beyond recall. It appeared that if the defenders of the ridge were going to stop the next Confederate rush, they would have to do it with their bayonets or their bare hands.

For Thomas, the news got worse before it got better. Far up on Horseshoe Ridge, at the extreme right of Thomas's makeshift line, the Twenty-first Ohio had been making one of the epic defensive stands of the entire war. These few hundred Buckeyes were the flank, and they had been severely tried as one Confederate advance after another had clawed for the vulnerable end of the Union line, the point of leverage that would throw Thomas's force off the ridge and away from the vital Dry Valley Road. The Ohioans had an advantage in that seven of their companies were equipped with Colt Revolving Rifles, a long-gun version of the successful Colt handgun. The rifle version was not an entirely satisfactory weapon, but it could deliver five shots in less than ten seconds, and firepower was what counted for the hard-pressed men at the sharp end of the Union's last possible defensive position. They performed near miracles of ingenuity in scrounging ammunition to keep their increasingly fouled and overheated weapons firing.

It appeared, however, that their valor and resourcefulness were to be for naught. The numerically superior Confederates sensed victory just beyond their reach and fought with redoubled fierceness. Some of them reached the crest beyond the Ohioans' flank and moved down to roll up the regiment's line. The lieutenant colonel commanding went down, but the major managed to get a couple of companies swung back at right angles to counter the move. By now there were more Confederates than Federals on this end of the ridge, though, and numbers were beginning to tell. The rapidly thinning blue line hung on and fought with fatal desperation.

While Thomas's troops had been taking up their position on the hills and then fighting stubbornly to hold them, six miles away Gordon Granger had

been making the decision of his life as a soldier. Stationed north of the battlefield at Rossville Gap with orders to hold that point, he had fretted
through the sounds of a day of battle. When a second day brought even
more intense thunders from the south and mounting clouds of white powder smoke, Granger faced his moment of truth as an army officer: was he to
obey orders and stay out of the fight or should he reckon that Rosecrans
needed him but somehow had failed to get the word to him? Taking his career in his hands, he chose the latter. Leaving a single brigade to cover the
gap, he took the two of Brig. Gen. James Steedman's division and marched
toward the sound of the guns.

Few of Granger's men had seen battle before, but as they reached the
northern fringes of the zone of the day's fighting, none of them could mistake the signs all around them. "The whole country was on fire," one of
them later wrote, "fences, woods, haystacks, houses." The sulfurous odor
of burned powder told them that more than wood smoke composed the gray
haze that lay across the landscape, and mingling with it all was the stench of
death. Soon they had no need to search for its source. Reaching the scene of
Breckinridge's morning advance, they saw the McDonald cornfield spread
out before them, strewn with bodies. "The hardest part of a battle is going
into it," recalled a sergeant of the Fortieth Ohio. They were in range of Confederates on the far northern end of Polk's wing now, and they began to take
incoming fire. "Double-quick!" came the command, and down the long
column the men leaned forward and trotted across the grisly field, steeling
themselves as best they could for what they all knew lay ahead.[43]

From his headquarters on the northern slope of Snodgrass Hill, Thomas
could see a large column of troops double-quicking toward him across the
McDonald field. He and the other officers nearby studied them and the dust
cloud they raised. Clearly this was a large formation of infantry and clearly it
was approaching the rear of Thomas's position. If they were Confederate,
the battle was all over but the shouting. Tense moments passed. Thomas
raised his field glass and tried to make out the colors waving above the jogging column, but his horse was skittish and cavorted about so that the glass
was useless. "Take my glass some of you whose horse stands steady," he
barked to his staff officers. "Tell me what you can see." One of them did so
and said he thought he saw the Stars and Stripes, but the dust was thick. No
one on the hill could be sure. Finally, Thomas sent a staff officer galloping
down the slope and across the field. A few minutes later he came spurring
his horse back; the approaching troops belonged to Granger's Reserve
Corps. Thomas was a taciturn man. He said nothing—merely mumbled

something into his beard—but the relief among the officers on Snodgrass Hill was too intense to require expression in words.[44]

While Granger's panting soldiers threw themselves to the ground and caught their breath on the back slope of the hill, Thomas conferred quickly with Granger and Steedman. He was delighted to learn that the wagons bouncing across the McDonald field behind Steedman's infantrymen contained ninety-five thousand rounds of badly needed ammunition. That was enough, Thomas reckoned, to issue about ten rounds per man to the hard-pressed troops along Snodgrass Hill and Horseshoe Ridge—no surplus, but a great relief. Though Thomas would have liked to use Steedman's division to plug the worrisome gap between Snodgrass Hill and the Kelly field lines, the growing crisis on the Union right, where the Twenty-first Ohio was fighting for the army's life, compelled him to commit the reinforcements there.[45]

Quickly Steedman's men were gotten to their feet and sent off again at the double-quick, this time jogging by the right flank through the woods at the northern base of Horseshoe Ridge. The first brigade came into position, halted, and faced to the front again, up the steep wooded ridge. The other brigade continued double-timing past them until it came into line on their right. Ahead of them the men of the left brigade could see a thin line of blue-uniformed men fighting at close range and even hand-to-hand, as the Twenty-first Ohio struggled on against the odds. On the right, Steedman's men could see only Confederates atop the ridge. Then the order came and the division plunged up the slope. The Ohioans had reached the last desperate extremity when a loud cheer rose from the back side of the ridge, and a solid bluecoated line of battle surged over the crest, through and around the thin line of exhausted Ohioans, and straight into the astonished Confederates.

If the Southerners were supposed to yield their hard-won position as a matter of form at the appearance of Union reinforcements, no one had given them a copy of the script. "They fought like tigers," recalled one of Steedman's brigade commanders, "and with a zeal and energy worthy of a better cause." They meant to hold this ridge. A bloody fight ensued at close quarters and raged back and forth over the ridge. Participants' estimates put it at anywhere from twenty-five minutes to an hour, but it ended with the Confederates receding once more down the bullet-riddled, body-strewn slope they had come up. A half-hour lull settled over the blood-drenched crest. Nearly half of Steedman's men were down; those still on their feet mopped their powder-streaked faces and peered apprehensively into half-empty cartridge boxes. It was still only midafternoon; the Rebels would be back.

And back they came, again and again throughout the long afternoon, pausing only to regroup and then pressing up the steep slope once more. Several times they were near breaking through, but each time Thomas's men managed to throw them back. The battered Twenty-first Ohio fought on, Steedman's division on their right now, Van Derveer's tough brigade of Brannan's division on their left. Harker's men, along with the fragments of half a dozen other commands, hung on to the open crest of Snodgrass Hill, with Harker exercising strict fire control and rationing his volleys—no one in blue had any ammunition to waste this afternoon.[46]

For the Confederates the afternoon was one of victory seemingly within grasp yet somehow still unattainable. Longstreet had been in high spirits after his initial success. To one of his brigadiers he had exulted, "Drive them, General. These western men can't stand it any better than the Yankees we left in Virginia. Drive 'em." For the moment at least, Longstreet seemed to have forgotten what had happened the last time he had tried to drive the eastern Yankees, outside a Pennsylvania town called Gettysburg. By midafternoon he had found that the western men were no easier to drive.[47]

Reporting his accomplishments to Bragg at headquarters and seeking support from Polk's right wing, Longstreet also found that his commander had a different view of the day's events. To Longstreet, Bragg seemed almost to consider the battle lost, and the general from the Army of Northern Virginia found this inexplicable. If Bragg was indeed in a bad humor, the reason would have been a realization that the two-week-long effort to destroy Rosecrans's army had failed. A victory that broke Rosecrans's southern flank and drove him north could be only a hollow victory that herded the beaten Federals back toward their base. Bragg's plan had hinged on the success of the Confederate right, and there Polk had failed. If Bragg was as lethargic as Longstreet years later made him out to be, he must have underestimated the opportunity that remained for doing significant further damage to the portion of the Army of the Cumberland that still remained on the field, at best even to capture several thousand Federals along with Thomas. Yet Longstreet and others from that day to this who would parrot his criticism of Bragg grossly overestimated the opportunity that remained for obtaining a truly decisive victory. By early afternoon it was clear that the Army of the Cumberland would be seriously damaged but not destroyed. The Confederate victory at Chickamauga would not complete the campaign, as Bragg had intended, but only begin it.[48]

"There is not a man in the right wing who has any fight in him," Bragg disgustedly told Longstreet when the latter requested reinforcement from that half of the army. At least that was how Longstreet recorded it in his memoirs. Whether or not Bragg actually resorted to such hyperbole, he did refuse to pull troops off the right wing and feed them into Longstreet's attack. That would have been impractical in any case and would have defeated the purpose of denying Thomas the Dry Valley Road by simply handing him the La Fayette Road instead. Bragg did, however, try to get the right wing rallied for another attack on Thomas's perimeter around the Kelly field. He sent Polk written orders to renew the assault "with his whole force and to persist until he should dislodge him from his position." He followed this order up by sending staff officers and by going to that part of the field himself.[49]

Finally, late that afternoon, the concerted assault by Polk's entire wing of the army, which was supposed to have happened nearly twelve hours earlier, became a reality. As the Confederates stormed toward the breastworks around the Kelly field, their chances of success received an additional boost. The Federals inexplicably began to withdraw.

Rosecrans had made his escape in the rout of the Federal right and was now well on his way back to Chattanooga. Having been in the midst of the day's disaster, he shared Longstreet's overestimate of its magnitude. Intent on rallying whatever fragments of an army might be left him someplace closer to Chattanooga, he sent orders to Thomas to retire to Rossville. These orders reached Thomas around 4:00 P.M. Ironically, they directed the worst possible course of action. If it was difficult to hold a position in the face of a numerous enemy flushed with success, it was even more difficult to withdraw in good order under such conditions. Thomas had hoped to hold on until nightfall, at which time it would have been relatively easy to disengage and withdraw. Now, however, he felt constrained to undertake this difficult maneuver by daylight, with the enemy still hammering at his troops. To make matters worse, the entire Confederate right wing launched its mass attack just as Thomas's troops began to pull back.

The result was disaster. The troops would have been hard-pressed to stop the Confederates while standing behind their breastworks. They found it impossible to do so while falling back across the open Kelly field. All vestige of a unified defense collapsed. Some units fought on, making a fighting withdrawal. Others disintegrated in a mad stampede for safety. A substantial number were captured. Thomas's plan called for the troops around the Kelly field to withdraw first, passing in rear of the position on Snodgrass Hill and Horseshoe Ridge, then down the ridge to the Dry Valley Road and McFarland's Gap. Quickly, whether in good order or otherwise, the troops who had held the perimeter all day moved back toward Snodgrass Hill.[50]

As Polk's troops overran the Kelly field, they broke into a chorus of Rebel yells, a vast, discordant shriek of triumph rising through the gathering dusk from the throats of thousands of men who believed they had finally succeeded in crushing the Army of the Cumberland. In fact, by far the largest part of Thomas's forces had made it intact—if not in good order—across Horseshoe Ridge and up the Dry Valley Road. The troops on Snodgrass Hill were next and then at last their comrades on the Ridge, finally vacating the positions for which so much blood had been spilled that afternoon. By that time the darkness was nearly complete, especially in the woods that blanketed the ridge.

The final parts of the battle of Chickamauga, much like the first, were confused and fitful affairs, uncertain but vicious encounters in darkened woods. Men blundered into enemy lines and were shot or captured, while others made good their escape almost under the bayonets of their foes. The Confederates reaped a substantial harvest of prisoners as they advanced over the vacated positions. In the desperate confusion of the fighting withdrawal, some Federals had not gotten the order to pull back. Others had lost their way in the jumble of woods and ravines. The Twenty-first Ohio had fought one of the most heroic defensive battles of the war that day. Yet, because its parent brigade and division had joined the rout back toward Chattanooga around midday, it had no proper chain of command linking it to higher headquarters and never got word of the withdrawal. It was finally overrun. A few of the men managed to creep off through the gloomy woods and hollows, but most went into captivity.[51]

The battle of Chickamauga had begun and ended in confusion, and much of what came between was equally muddled. Terrain and circumstances had combined to make the figurative "fog of war" extraordinarily thick on this northwest Georgia battlefield, and officers from army commander down to brigadier often had only the vaguest ideas of what they or their enemies were about. Now as the fighting sputtered out in the darkening woods atop Horseshoe Ridge, it left more confusion behind it. September 20 had been a Confederate victory, but what it meant or where it would lead remained as obscure to generals on both sides as the opaque blackness through which the battle-weary Northern soldiers tramped toward Chattanooga that night, while their Southern counterparts finally rested on the gruesome field of slaughter. A great battle had been fought, but the campaign for control of East Tennessee and the gateway to Georgia was still to be decided.

CHAPTER SIX

Like a Duck Hit on the Head

Victory or defeat in a Civil War battle was often a question of outlook. The general who first owned himself beaten very often was, and sometimes by no greater margin than that. George McClellan, in the Seven Days, and Joe Hooker, at Chancellorsville, had already demonstrated as much. Grant had shown the other side of the issue at Shiloh, when after the first day's pounding he had proposed to "whip 'em tomorrow," and did. In the aftermath of two days' fighting at Chickamauga, a Union offensive like the one that brought Grant success on the second day of Shiloh was not likely, but the same "whip 'em tomorrow" spirit that brought victory for Grant might have changed the history of the war if displayed at the end of Chickamauga's second day. It certainly would have changed the history of William Starke Rosecrans's life.

When at 3:40 P.M., September 20, Rosecrans reached Chattanooga, he was a beaten man, so physically and emotionally spent that upon his arrival at the headquarters of Brig. Gen. George D. Wagner, left with his brigade to garrison the city, he had to be helped out of the saddle. Shortly thereafter an officer who sought him out for orders found him weeping and seeking spiritual solace from his staff priest. An hour after arriving in Chattanooga, he received a dispatch from his chief of staff, Garfield, describing the situation on the battlefield and Thomas's gallant stand. The momentum had shifted, Garfield explained, and Thomas "will not need to fall back farther than Rossville, perhaps not any." He suggested that the day's disaster could be retrieved and urged Rosecrans to halt and regroup the rest of the army at Rossville, repairing there himself and bringing up ammunition and rations. Rosecrans, however, was beyond trying to recover the situation. Ignoring Garfield's recommendation, he instead sent his unfortunate order for Thomas to abandon the field his men had heroically held and withdraw to Rossville. Rosecrans promised to join him there, but though he sent forward a brigade of fresh troops along with some ammunition and supplies, he remained in Chattanooga.[1]

And so Thomas made his difficult fighting withdrawal in the face of the repeated Confederate attacks by the fading light of evening, and his tired troops marched northward through the darkness to the sound of Rebel yells back at the battlefield. They took position in the gap in front of Rossville during the night.

Garfield was in Rossville as early as 8:40 P.M. and from there wired Rosecrans, reporting on the "terrific battle" Thomas had fought and assuring the commander that "our men not only held their ground, but at many points drove the enemy splendidly. Longstreet's Virginians have got their bellies full." True, he admitted, the troops were terribly tired, hungry, and nearly out of ammunition, but, he added, with a touch of the proper spirit, "I believe we can whip them tomorrow. I believe we can now crown the whole battle with victory." He concluded by recommending that Rosecrans "not budge an inch from this place, but come up early in the morning, and if the Rebs try it, accommodate them." At 1:30 A.M., Garfield renewed his request that Rosecrans send supplies and "get here as soon as possible to organize the army and victory before the storm sets in." The soldiers retained enormous faith in Rosecrans, and his presence would have done much to restore their morale. Still the commander remained in Chattanooga. Morning brought a sober dispatch from the exhausted Garfield about the possible drawbacks of the Rossville position and the battered state of the army, but Thomas reported that all was quiet on his front.[2]

Much-needed encouragement for the faltering Federal commander came early that morning from a distant source. "Be of good cheer," Abraham Lincoln wired from Washington a few minutes after midnight. A 4:00 P.M. telegram from Dana had brought to the capital the first news of the disastrous second day's battle: "My report today is of deplorable importance," he wrote. "Chickamauga is as fatal a name in our history as Bull Run." He then went on to give the particulars as far as he knew them. Rosecrans checked in an hour later, reporting that the army had "met with a serious disaster; extent not yet ascertained. Enemy overwhelmed us." Other details followed. Though an 8:00 P.M. dispatch from Dana was more upbeat, reflecting news of Thomas's stand, the overall picture coming into Washington over the wires was grim.

Lincoln made it a point to try to buck up his sagging general, whose plummeting morale was evident in his dispatches. "We have unabated confidence in you and in your soldiers and officers," Lincoln assured him. "In the main," continued the president, "you must be the judge as to what is to be done. If I was to suggest, I would say save your army by taking strong positions until Burnside joins you."

Lincoln might retain confidence in Rosecrans, for the moment at least, but he was sorely disgusted with Burnside. As the crisis had developed in north Georgia over the past ten days, amid growing Federal knowledge of the transfer of Confederate troops to that sector, Lincoln had on September 14 ordered Burnside to unite with Rosecrans. The well-intentioned but bumbling commander of the Army of the Ohio had had other fish to fry in East Tennessee and had not gone. Now, after sending his encouraging message to Rosecrans, Lincoln reiterated his orders to Burnside in the plainest possible form: "Go to Rosecrans with your force without a moment's delay." Then, after a sleepless night waiting for each successive wire with additional news of the situation, the weary Lincoln stepped quietly into the White House bedroom of his secretary, John Hay. It was early, and Hay was still in bed. Lincoln came over and sat dejectedly on the side of the bed. "Well," he sighed, "Rosecrans has been whipped, as I feared. I have feared it for several days. I believe I feel trouble in the air before it comes."[3]

That morning Rosecrans, despite the president's efforts to boost his spirits and whatever help he might have gotten from his priest, remained demoralized. To Lincoln he wired, "We have no certainty of holding our position" in Chattanooga. News that Burnside had been ordered to join him and that William Tecumseh Sherman had also been ordered to march on Chattanooga with twenty thousand men of his tough Army of the Tennessee seemed to be more effective in raising Rosecrans's spirits. Indeed, the situation did not warrant despair. The Confederates still failed to appear in force before Rossville Gap, and the only action there was light skirmishing. The army there, as well as the units that had fled to Chattanooga, began to sort itself out and regain its organization. The soldiers' morale remained surprisingly high too. Maj. Gen. Lovell H. Rousseau, just arriving back with the army that day after a visit to Washington, wrote Rosecrans at 11:00 A.M. from Rossville, "I find the troops in fine spirits and ready to re-enter the fight, though they have suffered severe loss. . . . I have seen but one soldier today who is cowed. As I write, cheers are going up all over the field."[4]

For a time Rosecrans seemed to be regaining his nerve under all these positive influences, but that afternoon his spirits sagged. The pace of the skirmishing at Rossville picked up, and reports from cavalry and from sig-

nal corps observers on high ground spoke of mysterious dust clouds, unknown columns of troops at nearly every point of the compass, and even reports by prisoners that another entire corps of Lee's army had arrived, along
with practically everybody else in the Confederacy. Army commanders always received conflicting, confusing, alarming, and sometimes absurd intelligence reports, mixed in with the true stuff, and had to sort them out into
a realistic picture of what their foes were about. Rosecrans was ordinarily
fairly good at that, but on this day, after more than a week of inadequate rest
and nutrition and intense stress, he was unstable and ready to shy at
shadows. As a nightmare predictably conjures up those images the sleeper
most fears, so Rosecrans's present waking nightmare led him to credit all
that was worst in the raw data he received and blend it into a horrible scenario. At 5:00 P.M. he sent Thomas orders that were reminiscent of the situation the day before. He was to hold his position until nightfall, if possible,
and then withdraw, this time all the way to Chattanooga.[5]

The harried Federal commander need not have been haunted by such
hobgoblins of the mind, for the Confederates lacked the power to make
them real. As the first light of September 21 spread over the scenes of the
previous two days' carnage, neither Bragg, Longstreet, nor Polk had any
idea that the Union army had departed. In a dispatch to Bragg shortly before seven o'clock, Longstreet excused himself from reporting to headquarters because he dared not leave his lines with the enemy close by. Polk's first
inkling that the enemy had gone came shortly after dawn, when one of his
division commanders reported that his skirmishers had been all the way
across the La Fayette Road and beyond the McDonald farm without encountering any live, unwounded Federals. Bragg happened along at that
moment and discussed the matter with Polk, but the two apparently remained skeptical of the report. Bragg ordered Polk to keep his skirmishers
probing for the enemy.[6]

Around 7:00 A.M., Bragg and Polk rode over to Longstreet's headquarters to consult. Not until 9:00 A.M. were they certain that the Army of the
Cumberland had indeed departed the neighborhood. Once they were sure,
Longstreet particularly was full of ideas as to what the army should do
next—perhaps a movement on Nashville, or a swing into East Tennessee, or
a lunge across the Tennessee River around Rosecrans's flank to cut off the
Federals in Chattanooga. Bragg declined all these suggestions.[7]

Polk and Longstreet never understood and never stopped castigating
Bragg to their dying days. The problem was that every one of the proposed
moves, or any other major movement, was simply impossible for the Army

of Tennessee at that time. The troops were almost out of rations because the railroad line from Atlanta, at best a weak source of supply, had suffered several breaks and had lately been preempted to carry Longstreet's troops. As the last of those troops now joined the army, the problem got worse. Even the previous summer in Middle Tennessee, the army had suffered an acute shortage of the wagon transport necessary to carry supplies to its various units. The contingent from the Army of Northern Virginia now constituted nearly a quarter of Bragg's manpower, and not a single wagon had come with it. Supplying a stationary army under those conditions would have been sufficiently difficult; keeping the hardtack and salt pork rolling forward to an advancing army on a major strategic movement would have been impossible. Besides all that, practically any move except a direct march on Chattanooga from the south would have completely given up the only pitiful supply line Bragg had. Finally, Bragg had no pontoon train for crossing the Tennessee River. Forward movement was a logistical impossibility. [8]

Perhaps worst of all was the state of the army itself. Some eighteen thousand Confederate soldiers were killed, wounded, or missing—more than one out of every four men who had crossed the Chickamauga two days before. Longstreet's wing of the army had made its easy breakthrough but then had battered itself bloody against Thomas's rock-solid formation. Eight thousand of the soldiers brought by or assigned to Longstreet were among the casualties. The chain of command was in tatters. Hood was gone, of course, his right leg amputated just below the hip. Hindman was wounded too. Eight brigade commanders and dozens of regimental commanders had fallen. Twelve regiments had lost half their total strength in the two-day battle. The men who had survived were exhausted. [9]

Bragg did not, therefore, have the option of marching on Nashville, or taking East Tennessee, or flanking Rosecrans, or even mounting a vigorous pursuit of the retreating Federals. His last chance for a decisive victory over the Army of the Cumberland, for the immediate future, had faded away with the last light of the evening of September 20. All he could do now was follow slowly and cautiously after the retiring Union forces and try to get his own army into condition for further operations. All of that would have been a great deal more discouraging to Bragg than it actually was except that by the afternoon of September 21, every report seemed to indicate that he had already done Rosecrans enough damage to induce him to abandon Chattanooga and retreat back over the Cumberland Plateau, undoing all the gains of the previous six weeks' campaign. [10]

One of the first to bring such a report was the irrepressible Forrest. In the saddle early that morning, Forrest had taken his command up the road to engage in some skirmishing in front of Rossville Gap, the reports of which had helped unnerve Rosecrans. The Confederate cavalryman, however, was more interested in a Federal signal station he captured atop Missionary Ridge south of the gap. One of the Federal signalmen had possessed a nice pair of field glasses, and from the platform the Yankees had erected in a treetop, Forrest peered through the glasses and saw all the way to Chattanooga and the Tennessee River. Dust clouds indicated large movements, and wagons were crossing to the north bank of the river on pontoon bridges. The blue-coats, Forrest reckoned, must be running away, and to the fierce Confederate horseman that called for action—hit them hard and fast. Forrest never seemed to grasp the difference between a mounted raiding party and an army, and he naturally had neither understanding nor sympathy for Bragg's inability to follow up the battle as Forrest would have done with his cavalry division after a victory over a comparable force. "What does he fight battles for?" stormed the hot-blooded cavalryman after leaving Bragg's headquarters.[11]

Yet Forrest was not the only messenger with tidings of a Union flight from Chattanooga. Every indication was that Bragg need not further bleed his decimated army—assuming he could have gotten them up to the front in the first place—but could sit back and allow the fruits of the campaign to ripen and fall into his lap while he turned his attention to putting the Army of Tennessee back into fighting trim.[12]

Meanwhile, inside the city that the Confederates confidently expected to possess shortly, the Army of the Cumberland was indeed busy, but not in the way Forrest and the others surmised. The wagons going back across the river were carrying away the wounded and going to fetch new supplies of ammunition from the Union depot at Bridgeport. The combat troops, now perhaps thirty thousand of them, were working in relays around the clock to keep every available ax and shovel constantly employed in building breast-works and gun emplacements. Thomas had brought his contingent back from Rossville during the night of the twenty-first, and by 7:00 A.M. they had taken up their positions on the Chattanooga perimeter. Morale was higher than ever. Many in the army had their doubts about Crittenden, McCook, and Negley, other high-ranking generals who had left the battle-field of Chickamauga, but none seemed to doubt Rosecrans. During the tense twenty-second of September he rode his three-mile-long lines amid roaring cheers from his men, both those working on the fortifications and the remainder, who stood in line of battle, waiting for a Confederate attack.[13]

The twenty-third was another day of anxious waiting. "We are expecting a fourth of July today in the way of fire works," wrote an Illinois soldier in his diary early that morning, but hour after hour passed without the expected Confederate onslaught. "Eight A.M. and no fight yet. . . . Eleven A.M. and no enemy appears." Confederate soldiers came into sight, beyond practical rifle range, around midday, obviously taking up positions opposite the Army of the Cumberland. Still no attack came. The constant waiting took its toll. "Four P.M. and no fight yet, nor appearance of it. . . . It is wearing on the boys to be laying all day, in momentary expectation of the opening gun," observed the Illinois soldier, then added, "We are still digging away as though our lives depended on it." Morale stayed very high. Late that afternoon the men of Reynolds's division raised a large U.S. flag over their lines, setting off a storm of cheering left and right. Cheers swept the line again around dusk when Rosecrans rode along the front for at least the second time that day. Stopping to chat with the men of the Fifty-ninth Illinois out on the front line of rifle pits, he cracked, "Boys, I want you to reserve your fire till you can tell a black eye from a blue one; then fire and your front will be like the Irishman's pocket which was full and there was nothing in it. Do you understand how that was? Why the pocket was full of holes." It did not take much of a joke to bring a laugh from these tense men, and they roared with mirth and cheered him again. One wrote in his diary, "There is no question as to the hold Rosecrans has on the affections and confidence of his men. They thoroughly believe in him."[14]

The trouble was that Rosecrans no longer thoroughly believed in himself. This was especially clear in his handling that day of the situation on Lookout Mountain. Since the army had taken up its position in Chattanooga, Rosecrans had kept the Reserve Corps brigade of Brig. Gen. James G. Spears, four regiments of loyal Tennesseeans, on top of the mountain. On the twenty-third, when Bragg's army finally arrived and took up positions confronting the Army of the Cumberland, Forrest and his cavalry had moved along the broad top of Lookout Mountain until they confronted Spears's outpost regiment, the Third Tennessee, under the command of Col. William Cross. Characteristically, Forrest demanded the regiment's immediate surrender. Cross refused, though badly outnumbered, and sent to Spears for instructions. Spears in turn inquired of Rosecrans, who, rather than send reinforcements, instead issued what seemed to be his stock order of the past four days and directed Spears to pull off the mountain after nightfall, to the disgust of Granger, Garfield, and, ominously for Rosecrans's image in Washington, Dana. It would soon prove to be a costly mistake in more ways than one.[15]

Although many of the officers of the Army of the Cumberland might have considered Dana a pernicious War Department spy and the assistant secretary's personal behavior on the field of Chickamauga had been less than heroic, no evil intent or rattled nerves on his part were necessary to cause his dispatches to Washington to convey a disturbing sense of Rosecrans's loss of nerve. The general vacillated as to whether to hold the city or retire across the Tennessee, and when he did talk about holding Chattanooga, it was only if massive reinforcements would reach him very soon and no additional enemy troops showed up. Indeed, Rosecrans did not need Dana to poison the minds of his superiors against him; his own dispatches were alarming enough. "We can hold out for several days," he chirped weakly on September 22, and in an only slightly more encouraging vein later that day he wired, "If reinforcements come up soon, everything will come out right."[16]

Washington was not impressed, but the question of Rosecrans's further employment would have to wait. Chattanooga was the pressing issue. Lincoln wanted it held. "If [Rosecrans] can only maintain this position without more," he told Halleck, "the rebellion can only eke out a short and feeble existence, as an animal sometimes may with a thorn in its vitals." Rosecrans's musing about the possible necessity of evacuating the city aroused the Federal high command to an intense pitch of anxiety. This expressed itself first in frustration with Burnside. When ordered by Lincoln to go to Rosecrans in the wake of the battle, Burnside had replied that he would do so at once—that is, as soon as he finished an operation he was planning against Jonesboro, Tennessee. "If you are to do any good to Rosecrans," wired the exasperated Lincoln, "it will not do to waste time with Jonesboro. It is already too late to do the most good that might have been done, but I hope it will do some good. Please do not lose a moment." Burnside replied with excuses, delays, and questions, conclusively demonstrating his unfitness for independent command and sorely trying the patience of his superiors. "I telegraphed him fifteen times to [reinforce Rosecrans]," Halleck observed, "and the President three or four times."[17]

Finally, Lincoln, Stanton, and Halleck gave up on Burnside and set out to find what they needed elsewhere. The immediate catalyst for decisive action was the overwrought pitch of Stanton's nerves after several worrisome dispatches on September 23. Late that night, well after 10:00 P.M., the secretary of war decided it was time to act. He dispatched John Hay to ride out to the Soldiers' Home and fetch back Lincoln, who was spending most of his nights there. Hay thought the moonlight was beautiful as he galloped through the countryside, but not everyone would have agreed that night.

Five hundred miles away, the men of Spears's brigade were waiting for that same moon to set before beginning their stealthy descent off Lookout Mountain. Once Hay had arrived at the Soldiers' Home, he roused Lincoln and conveyed Stanton's summons. The deeply disturbed president dressed hurriedly, mounted, and rode off with Hay toward the city, remarking that "it was the first time Stanton had ever sent for him" like this. Others had similar reactions; Secretary of the Treasury Salmon P. Chase recalled, "The summons really alarmed me. I felt sure that a disaster had befallen us."[18]

When Lincoln, Halleck, Seward, Chase, and several lesser officials were assembled, Stanton stated his business. Rosecrans needed help now. Burnside would not go, and Sherman was too far away. Then he came to the point. "I propose to send 30,000 men from the Army of the Potomac. There is no reason to expect that General Meade will attack Lee, although greatly superior in force, and his great numbers where they are, are useless. In five days 30,000 could be put with Rosecrans."

Lincoln had enough experience by now with military operations to doubt that. "I'll bet that if the order is given tonight the troops could not be got to Washington in five days."

"On such a subject I don't feel inclined to bet," Stanton priggishly replied, "but the matter has been carefully investigated and it is certain that 30,000 bales of cotton could be sent in that time, and by taking possession of the railroad and excluding all other business I do not see why 30,000 men can't be sent as well. But if 30,000 can't be sent, let 20,000 go."[19]

What Stanton was proposing was the greatest transportation feat in the history of warfare up to that time. Never had so many troops been moved so far in so little time. It seemed impossible, and so it would have been practically anywhere else in the world, but the U.S. rail network had grown tremendously during the 1850s, both in extent and in organization. The track, engines, and rolling stock existed; more important, the know-how existed on the part of a number of railroad executives for coordinating the myriad technical details involved in an operation of this size. Indeed, Stanton had one of them on hand as an expert witness to bolster his case.[20] Incredibly to those not versed in the latest advances of the rail industry, the thing actually could be done, and after several hours of discussion, a reluctant Lincoln agreed that it should. At 2:30 A.M. the orders went out and the great endeavor began.[21]

The Army of the Potomac's two smallest corps, the XI and XII, would form a detachment under the command of Maj. Gen. Joseph "Fighting Joe" Hooker, the loser of Chancellorsville. In all, they would number about twenty-three thousand men. Hooker and the two corps commanders, Oliver O. Howard and Henry W. Slocum, made careful preparations for moving their troops, guns, and draft animals in an orderly and expeditious fashion. The railroad officials did the same, giving no excuse for Stanton to take over their lines and proving that they could do the job better anyway. Skillfully they forwarded the troops and their three thousand horses and mules and seven batteries of artillery through Ohio and Indiana to Louisville, Kentucky, then southward to Nashville, whence they pushed on to Bridgeport. The entire journey was 1,159 miles and was completed in nine days.[22]

Meanwhile, back in southeastern Tennessee, Bragg had moved his army into position around Chattanooga on September 23, establishing his headquarters at the Nail House atop Missionary Ridge overlooking the town. He had already turned his attention to remedying the problems in this army, and the chief of those problems, the one that had done most to deny it decisive victory during the past two weeks, was its high command.[23]

On September 22, while the army was gingerly approaching Chattanooga, Bragg sent a note to Polk requesting an explanation for the delay of the day-dawn assault he had ordered for the morning of September 20. Three days passed without a reply from the bishop, and Bragg renewed his inquiry. Still Polk gave no answer, but he did arrange a meeting among himself, D. H. Hill, and Longstreet. Hill and Longstreet were relatively new to the Army of Tennessee, and Polk may have feared that they were not yet sufficiently infected with his hatred and jealousy of Bragg. He need not have worried. Lee had purged Hill from the Army of Northern Virginia some months before because of the latter's inconsistent performance and also because he displayed a bitter, carping attitude that got him into trouble with nearly everyone. Hill fit right in with the command culture of the Army of Tennessee. Longstreet had come west to get himself an army command. He ranked every officer in the army but one, and that one was Bragg. So much the worse, then, for the commanding general as far as Longstreet was concerned. He had found material for criticism in Lee, and he would have no shortage with Bragg.[24]

The three agreed. Bragg must go. Polk had already importuned his old friend Davis with slanders of Bragg to such an extent that even he was reluctant to repeat them. He tried to get Longstreet to do the dishonors this time, but the latter declined. They decided therefore that Polk would write to both Davis and Lee while Longstreet wrote to his own friend Secretary of War Seddon. Both generals would emphasize the need to sack Bragg, accusing him of all manner of incompetence and even going so far as to complain that he had several times had the enemy at his mercy but had allowed him to escape. This took some considerable nerve in view of the fact Polk's and Hill's disobedience of orders was the prime reason for the failure of Bragg's plans.[25]

Finally, on September 28, Polk wrote his reply to Bragg's repeated queries. It was all Hill's fault, he explained lamely. Not surprisingly, Bragg declared the explanation unsatisfactory and issued orders the next day relieving Polk of his command and sending him to Atlanta, perhaps far enough from the army to prevent him from exercising his pernicious influence any further. It was, as Bragg observed several days later, something he should have done a long time ago. That same day, September 29, he issued orders officially relieving Hindman of command for his disobedience in McLemore's Cove on September 10 and 11, though the general's actual removal from the head of his division had already been more effectually accomplished by an unknown Northerner's minié ball. At any rate, the cleansing of the Augean Stables of the Army of Tennessee's high command had finally begun, but the task would not be done in a day.[26]

Polk was furious and raged against Bragg in yet another letter to Davis, while to his daughter he seethed, "I feel a lofty contempt for [Bragg's] puny effort to inflict injury upon a man who dry-nursed him for the whole period of his connection with him, and has kept him from ruining the cause of his country by the sacrifice of its armies." Davis now demonstrated how the Army of Tennessee's high command had gotten into its present sad state by taking Polk's side. "It is now believed that the order [relieving Polk] should be countermanded," he wrote Bragg, but the army commander remained adamant, pointing out that "the case is flagrant and but a repetition of the past." Rarely outdone in stubbornness, Davis now declared that Bragg could not suspend Polk from command without bringing formal charges against him. Very well then, Bragg produced the charges: disobedience and neglect of duty.[27]

Meanwhile, more trouble was brewing. On October 4 Bragg's enemies within the army held a secret meeting. The fruits of Polk's and Hardee's year-long campaign to subvert Bragg were apparent in the attendance of numerous corps, division, and brigade commanders. The ringleaders, predictably, were Longstreet, Hill, and Buckner. The last of these had his own designs on command of the army and was eager for Bragg's downfall. He got up a petition to Davis, denouncing Bragg, stating that the army had no confidence in him, and calling for his removal. A good many of the army's generals eventually signed it.[28]

The Confederate president had for some time been ignoring the reality of the command crisis in the Army of Tennessee. Now, hoping to harmonize his western generals under Bragg's command yet determined to sustain Polk in any event, Davis decided to visit the Army of Tennessee and see if he could set things to rights there. He left Richmond on October 6 and traveled first to Atlanta, arriving on the eighth. He met with Polk, summarily dismissed the charges Bragg had brought, and proposed to force the bishop-general back on Bragg whether the Army of Tennessee's commander wanted him or not. Polk, however, objected. For one thing, he was looking forward to his trial as the best anti-Bragg pulpit he was likely to get. For another, he flatly refused to serve under Bragg. Always ready to accommodate his old friend, at least in part, Davis agreed to transfer Polk to Mississippi and bring Hardee back to command a corps in the Army of Tennessee once more. The trial, in any case, would not take place.[29]

On the ninth, Davis arrived at Bragg's headquarters. Bragg immediately offered to resign, but Davis insisted he remain. Instead, he summoned to a meeting Bragg and the next four highest ranking generals with the army, Longstreet, Buckner, Hill, and Cheatham. It began as a discussion of the military situation and ended with all four of the generals denouncing Bragg and demanding his removal. Hill apparently did so in a way that was particularly offensive to Davis, but nothing about the meeting was pleasant either to Davis or to the army commander he had chosen to sustain. Over the next two days, Davis met with other generals who supported Bragg, and he also held private conferences with the disaffected generals, who again complained of Bragg and nagged for his removal. The president remained firm on that point, mainly because every possible alternative to Bragg—Johnston, Beauregard, or one of the malcontents themselves—was even more distasteful to him. Before leaving on October 14, he made a speech praising Bragg and warning that "he who sows the seeds of discontent and distrust prepares the harvest of slaughter and defeat."[30]

It had been only with considerable difficulty that Davis had prevailed on Bragg not to insist on resigning, and then only by agreeing that the general need never again "countenance disobedience of or non-compliance with orders from any officer, however high in position, regardless of consequences." That established, Bragg continued with the job of mucking out the Army of Tennessee's leadership even before Davis left. On October 11 he dismissed Hill, who went into oblivion for the rest of the war. Davis himself dealt with Forrest, who had gone into a rage about an organizational decision of Bragg's that he did not like and had threatened to kill his army commander. The cavalry leader was soon on his way to Mississippi.[31]

After the president's departure, Bragg attempted to improve the situation by reorganizing the army so as to break up cliques of malcontents. Doing so involved a shuffling of the army's units, save of course for Longstreet's Army of Northern Virginia detachment. When the rearrangement was complete, Buckner, who had taken to writing abusive letters to Bragg, found himself in command of a division rather than a corps. John C. Breckinridge had the opposite experience and rose from division to corps command. Cheatham continued as division commander but no longer led the oversized all-Tennessee division that had given him such staunch support. Yet in the end, a large number of semimutinous officers remained, and a great deal of intense disaffection continued to afflict the army. The cancer of discontentment had been allowed to fester too long. Both the new corps commanders, Hardee and Breckinridge, were inveterate anti-Bragg men, but by this time Bragg's options were few, and none was attractive.[32]

Somehow in the midst of all these distractions, the Confederates had managed to carry on operations against their blue-uniformed enemies as well. By the closing days of September it had become clear that Rosecrans was not evacuating Chattanooga after all. Yet because the Federal commander had abandoned Lookout Mountain, that might not be altogether a bad thing from the Confederate point of view. Lookout Mountain and the adjacent positions in Lookout Valley, to the west, and on the near slopes of Raccoon Mountain beyond, where the Confederate skirmishers deployed, commanded the Federals' only viable supply routes into Chattanooga. Both the railroad and the good wagon road ran eastward from Bridgeport, through Running Water Gap between Raccoon Mountain to the north and Sand Mountain to the south, thence down the valley of Lookout Creek and around the tip of Lookout Mountain into Chattanooga. The river itself was exposed to the fire of Confederate sharpshooters on the south bank, and the same was true for a mediocre wagon road on the north bank.[33]

That left only one way for Rosecrans to get supplies into the city—or get his army out, if it came to that. This was a perfectly execrable wagon road that took a long, roundabout route northward up the slopes of precipitous Walden's Ridge, across that barren and rugged plateau, and then down into the Sequatchie Valley before turning southward again and running down the valley to the Tennessee and on to Bridgeport. With its dirt roads, eyebrow ledges, and rickety trestlework, it was a harrowing journey for a mule wagon in good weather. On Thursday, October 1, the rains came. A long spell of dry weather now gave way to an even longer spell of very, very wet weather, and the dirt road over Walden's Ridge became a sixty-mile-long morass. Mules mired up to their bellies, wagons bogged down to the wheel hubs, and detachments of sodden and miserable infantry grunted and panted to heave them uphill through the orange-brown slimy muck. It required no master of logistic calculations to foresee that this route could not possibly supply the amount of food and forage the army needed.

Nor did Bragg propose to allow Rosecrans the unhindered use of it, poor though it might be. The day after the rains came, the Confederate cavalry came too. On October 2, Joseph Wheeler's horsemen descended on an inbound train of supply-laden wagons in the Sequatchie Valley, burning four hundred wagons with their loads and shooting hundreds of mules. The only good thing about the sorry mess from the Union perspective was that some of the wagons had contained commissary whiskey, which Wheeler's troopers appropriated, leading to the demoralization of virtually the entire unit. Wheeler was not subsequently as much of a threat as heretofore, but Rosecrans could not know this and had to deploy one of the four arriving Army of the Potomac divisions to cover his railroad in Middle Tennessee, lest the Confederates get to that and really make trouble.[34]

Things were bad enough as it was. Mules died by the hundreds, not from Confederate bullets but from too much hauling over the atrocious roads and not enough forage. The soldiers noticed that the starving animals had chewed the bark entirely off a large number of trees as high as they could reach. Some mules fell to their deaths from the narrow mountain road, and in the more level areas the road was lined with the rotting carcasses of animals that had died in the traces. As mules foundered and wagons broke down, the flow of supplies into Chattanooga dwindled to a trickle.[35]

By September 27 some units had no rations to issue the troops, and within days the morale of the Army of the Cumberland began to drop. When the officers were able to procure food, it was generally a good deal less than the regulation issue. On October 2, Rosecrans formally placed the army on two-thirds rations, but Lieut. Chesley Mosman observed in his diary that his own regiment had already been reduced to half rations for several days—when they could get anything at all. In some units the allotment soon dropped to one-fourth the normal amount. A time of near starvation followed for the Army of the Cumberland, as the men were forced to subsist on very little besides hardtack—and very little of that. "The continual gnawings of a growing appetite was a perpetual reminder of our condition," recalled an Ohio private. A sergeant from the same state later opined, "Possibly no set of men were more completely starved, during the war of the rebellion . . . save only the prisoners at Andersonville, and other rebel prison

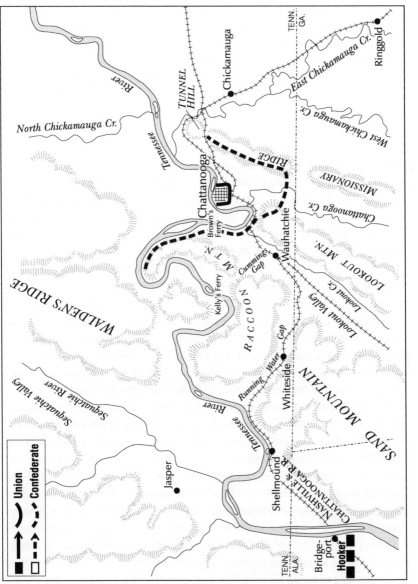

The Siege of Chattanooga

pens." So bad was the situation within Union lines that guards had to be posted over the army's horses and mules to prevent hungry soldiers from stealing the few ears of corn allotted to the starving beasts.[36]

Rosecrans had predicted that when his promised reinforcements came, he would retake Lookout Mountain, thus alleviating the supply problems. Now, however, he found that his problems with supply were preventing the arrival of his reinforcements. By the first week of October, Hooker's troops were at Bridgeport, but Rosecrans could not use them. The presence in Chattanooga of another fifteen thousand mouths to feed would have pushed the combined force over the edge into outright starvation long before a supply line could be opened. Still, in theory at least, Rosecrans was not checkmated, and he and his staff made elaborate plans for breaking this impasse. Somehow the right time for implementing the plans never came.[37]

Hunger gnawed at Union morale. "Never in the history of the Army of the Cumberland," an officer later wrote, "had the spirit of its officers and men been more depressed. The battle of Chickamauga had not only been fought and lost, but we also lost what was more than losing a battle. We have lost confidence in our commander." For the first time the men began to doubt that Rosecrans would get them through.[38]

Ironically, Confederate morale was also low and for some of the same reasons, primarily lack of food. The single-track railroad between Atlanta and Chattanooga had never been fully adequate to supply the army nor, for that matter, had a sufficiently efficient commissary system ever existed for collecting supplies and funneling them up the railroad. Now Bragg had a substantial additional number of troops, and the system could not feed them all. On top of that, to cut Rosecrans's access to supplies, his army had to deploy on an eight-mile line that ran along the foot of Missionary Ridge, then through the valley of Chattanooga Creek to Lookout Mountain and beyond. The difficulties in using the army's wagons to haul supplies over such distances and rugged terrain compounded the already acute shortage of rations. Bragg's men were better off than the Federals trapped in the town, but they were not eating particularly well for all that, and they were not happy. More fundamentally, the Confederacy had fared poorly that summer at Gettysburg, Vicksburg, and Tullahoma, and the events of the past few weeks had not convinced these soldiers that the tide of defeat would turn. Finally, the contempt of Bragg seeping out in the loose talk around so many corps, division, and brigade headquarters had to have worked its way down, at least in a diffused form, to the common soldiers.[39]

For a few weeks in October and November the mutual low morale led to what one participant called "a queer kind of war." The troops began to engage in wholesale fraternization across the supposedly hostile battle lines. The siege had not begun that way. During the days immediately following the September 23 Confederate arrival around Chattanooga, sharp skirmishing had flared up as each side adjusted its lines, and constant sniping had made the picket lines dangerous. By September 25, Confederate artillery atop Lookout Mountain started lobbing shells into the Union camps, scattering campfires, and, as an intended target reported, "making us hunt our holes."[40]

By early October, however, the situation in the front lines had changed. The troops made an informal enlisted men's agreement that they would do no firing unless there were a general advance. Pickets met, chatted, played cards, and swapped coffee, tobacco, newspapers, and other articles in no-man's-land. Some of the officers got into the spirit of things. When Brig Gen. Micah Jenkins thought the Federals opposite his division's position had their pickets deployed on his side (the west side) of Chattanooga Creek, instead of launching an attack to rectify his lines, he simply sent over a message asking if the two sides could not be content to stay on their own sides of the creek. The shelling went on for some time longer, but the Federals got used to it and no longer considered it a genuine threat. The Confederates eventually grew tired and gave it up.[41]

No-man's-land discussions could reveal much about the soldiers' state of mind. A private soldier of Jenkins's command, a member of the vaunted Texas Brigade of the Army of Northern Virginia, admitted to an Illinoisan, "We didn't whip you fellows much" at Chickamauga. The low morale that lay behind such fraternization was also reflected in the statements of some soldiers that they saw no reason to continue the war. One Confederate soldier cursed the war for a "piece of foolishness" and suggested to his ostensible Northern foes, "Let's all quit and go home." A Federal allowed that there was "some truth" in the man's statements. A Southern officer observed, "If the terms of peace had been left to the men who faced each other in battle day after day, they would have stopped the war at once on terms acceptable to both sides."[42]

He was wrong about that much, but this particular lot of soldiers, for the moment, might just have stopped it—or at least their involvement in it—on any terms or no terms. They were tired, hungry, cold, wet, and ready to go home. As the fog, chill, and rain of autumn settled down on the southeast Tennessee mountains, soldiers in all the varied faded shades of blue, gray, or butternut endured the same hardships together. "I was never tired of the service before, but I am pretty near it now," wrote one of them. "Will the rain never cease?" In the fellowship of shared suffering, men pledged to different causes temporarily forgot the principles and loyalties that had led them to war and remembered only that they were all human beings who desperately wished to be elsewhere and in different circumstances.[43]

Discontent prevailed in Washington as well, but it was different. More and more members of the Lincoln administration were coming to have doubts about Rosecrans's continued usefulness. In all probability, Rosecrans had been doomed since his flight from the battlefield of Chickamauga. Be the reasons what they might, a general who left a battlefield on which his troops were still fighting and fled thirteen miles to the rear simply did not have much future as a general. The two corps commanders who had been guilty of that offense had gotten short shrift. Before the end of September McCook's XX Corps and Crittenden's XXI Corps had been consolidated into a single new IV Corps, to be commanded by Granger, who had traveled the opposite direction on the afternoon of September 20. McCook and Crittenden were relieved of command and held no other comparably significant position for the remainder of the war. That was ominous for Rosecrans. Stanton shortly thereafter remarked that McCook and Crittenden "made pretty good time away from the fight to Chattanooga, but Rosecrans beat them both."[44]

During the days and weeks after the battle, the reports coming out of Chattanooga, both Dana's and Rosecrans's, had not helped the general's cause in Washington. Even aside from Dana's criticisms and his own missives of alternating panic and resignation, it was clear that Rosecrans had miscalculated, suffered defeat, and allowed himself to be bottled up in Chattanooga, ineffectually making plans while his army starved. Stanton and Halleck quickly turned against him, remembering the difficulties they had endured the previous summer in getting Rosecrans to fight in the first place. Treasury Secretary Salmon P. Chase and Navy Secretary Gideon Welles soon joined his detractors, and as early as September 27 Secretary of State William H. Seward suggested that Rosecrans be relieved of command.[45]

Besides his own poor performance, unreassuring dispatches, and the criticism by Dana, Rosecrans's fate may have been affected by two other factors. One of these was the revelation by Dana that what he heard around Rosecrans's headquarters led him to believe that Rosecrans, in writing his report of the battle and campaign of Chickamauga, would attempt to shift the blame for the defeat from himself to his superiors. While Rosecrans did not actually include such absurdities in his report, it would nevertheless have been dismaying to Lincoln to think that yet another failed general had joined the victims' and whiners' society, moaning that all his mistakes and misfortunes were someone else's fault and spending his time devising ways to dodge blame rather than defeat the enemy.[46]

The second factor was both more complicated and more dangerous. Back in May, Ambrose Burnside had ordered the arrest of Ohio Democratic politician Clement L. Vallandigham for "declaring disloyal sentiments and opinions with the object and purpose of weakening the power of the Government in its efforts to suppress an unlawful rebellion." A military commission found Vallandigham to be guilty, as indeed he was, and sentenced him to imprisonment for the duration of the war. Lincoln commuted this sentence to banishment to Rebel lines, but the wily Democrat slipped out of the Confederacy and into Canada, where from the north shore of Lake Erie he got himself the Democratic Party's nomination for governor in that fall's elections, to run against Republican John Brough. Though Lincoln wondered how "one genuine American would, or could be induced to, vote for such a man as Vallandigham," he also recognized the action of the Ohio Democrats as an attempt to repudiate his administration and the war itself. To Gideon Welles, Lincoln commented that he was watching that race with "more anxiety . . . than he had in 1860 when he was chosen" president.[47]

All of this bore on Rosecrans's case because the general was a very popular Ohioan and the election for governor was to be held on October 9, 1863, less than three weeks after the battle of Chickamauga. The president would run a serious political risk should he choose to sack Rosecrans virtually on the eve of such a crucial vote, particularly if there appeared to be any chance that Rosecrans might then decide to make common cause with the administration's enemies in the political campaign. All that would have put a different and not entirely flattering light on what was in fact an innocent if ill-advised proposal of Rosecrans's on October 3. To Lincoln the general wrote, "If we maintain the position in such strength that the enemy are obliged to abandon their position and the elections in the great States go favorably, would it not be well to offer a general amnesty to all officers and soldiers in the rebellion? It would give us moral strength, and weaken them very much." To the content of this note, Lincoln could not have objected. He had said repeatedly that holding on at Chattanooga would sap the rebellion, and he was not at all opposed to offering amnesty to surrendering Rebels. Rosecrans's note even contained an expression of proper sentiment with regard to the coming state elections, including, presumably, that in Ohio.[48]

Still, it was unsought advice in a realm outside of Rosecrans's responsibility at a time when the general might be thought to have plenty of other things, properly belonging to his duties, on which to bestow his thought. For that matter, what did a recently defeated general mean by proposing that his government offer peace to the enemy? Could something less than real victory be intended? Lincoln's reply suggested such a question: "If we can hold Chattanooga and East Tennessee, I think the rebellion must dwindle and die. I intend doing something like what you suggest whenever the case shall appear ripe enough to have it accepted in the true understanding, rather than as a confession of weakness and fear." One source close to the president opined that Rosecrans's suggestion "gave great offense and raised suspicions of political aspirations on his part." At best, the general's well-intentioned but inappropriate dispatch must have given Lincoln food for thought and indicated that Rosecrans still was not thinking calmly and clearly. Very possibly, it may have suggested to the president that the general was himself a victim of just such "weakness and fear."[49]

Nevertheless, Rosecrans publicly supported Brough and urged his officers and men to do the same. On October 9, Brough won a landslide victory over Vallandigham, garnering heavy majorities of both the civilian and the soldier vote, including 97 percent of the votes cast by Ohioans in the Army of the Cumberland. At this point, Rosecrans was no longer a political necessity, if Lincoln had ever considered him such, and the president might have dispensed with him at once. Instead, Lincoln continued to delay, grateful, perhaps, for Rosecrans's political loyalty and hoping the general could recover his self-possession and salvage his situation.

On October 16 a message arrived from Dana that made further postponement of a decision even more difficult. "Nothing can prevent the retreat of the army from this place within a fortnight," Dana wrote, "except the opening of the river." Rosecrans, he suggested, was not the man to do it. He "dawdles with trifles" and is "dazed and hazy," the assistant secretary reported. Lincoln could not deny the truth of that statement, having previously remarked to his secretary that Rosecrans was acting "confused and stunned like a duck hit on the head." At a cabinet meeting that day, the members voted in favor of replacing Rosecrans with Thomas, but Lincoln chose a compromise course. He had already decided to set up a sort of super-department called the Military Division of the Mississippi, incorporating the departments of the Cumberland, Ohio, and Tennessee. At the moment, those departments were commanded by Rosecrans, Burnside, and Grant, respectively. Setting up the Military Division of the Mississippi would go far toward eliminating the lack of cooperation that had kept Burnside from supporting Rosecrans. Lincoln decided to place Grant in command of the new arrangement and leave to him the question of whether to remove Rosecrans.[50]

Halleck and Stanton had already anticipated a possible role for the victor of Vicksburg, and Halleck, at Stanton's direction, had several days earlier directed Grant to report at once to Cairo, Illinois, to be ready for whatever service the country might have for him in the near future. On October 16, the same day Lincoln and his cabinet discussed Dana's alarming telegram, Grant reported by telegraph that he had arrived in Cairo. That evening in Washington orders were drawn up, and the next morning in Cairo Grant received a wire directing him to proceed immediately to the Galt House Hotel in Louisville, Kentucky, bringing with him his entire staff ready for immediate operations in the field. An officer of the War Department would meet him at the Galt House with instructions.[51]

Though no one in southeastern Tennessee knew it yet, the campaign for Chattanooga was taking a decisive turn, not in that city but in Washington, Cairo, and Louisville.

CHAPTER SEVEN

The Cracker Line

After the surrender of Vicksburg, Grant had had a frustrating summer. His plan for a follow-up offensive against Mobile, Alabama, had been set aside by Washington so that troops from his army could be stripped away to provide manpower for expeditions thought to be of more immediate political benefit. "The army," as Grant put it, "was sent where it would do the least good." Then, while visiting New Orleans in early September to confer with Maj. Gen. Nathaniel P. Banks about one of those ill-advised movements, Grant had suffered an accident. The large, powerful, and high-spirited horse he was riding shied at a passing train, slipped on a slick street, and fell on Grant's left leg. The leg, he later recalled in his memoirs, "was swollen from the knee to the thigh, and the swelling, almost to the point of bursting, extended along the body up to the arm-pit. The pain was almost beyond endurance."[1]

Grant was laid up with this injury for some time, and because he was Grant, people began to whisper about a possible return to "his former bad habits," a reference to an unfortunate episode years earlier when a bored and lonely young Captain Grant had given way to alcoholism while stationed at an obscure west coast fort. The gossip was false this time, as gossip generally is, but the whole affair, coming on top of everything else, could only have been extremely frustrating for Grant. Through it all, he could at least take comfort in the fact that he was now one of the nation's most successful generals, and lest he should wonder, Halleck wrote to assure him, "You need not fear being left idle. The moment you are well enough to take the field you will have abundant occupation."[2]

That was October 11, and Halleck already had a very good idea what the occupation would be. Grant reported at Cairo ready for duty just in time for the October 16 decision to give him the unified western command. The following day, Grant received the order to report to Louisville and set out immediately to go there by rail. The most direct route took him through Indianapolis, and there, as his train was about to leave the station, a messenger flagged it down to say that a special train from Washington had just pulled in bearing the secretary of war. Grant's train waited while Stanton dismissed his and came over to join the general and his entourage for the rest of the journey to Louisville. Grant and Stanton had never met face to face but had corresponded extensively by mail and over the wires. Presently the secretary of war swept into Grant's car, characteristically all business, all drive, all efficiency, and expecting everyone else to come up to his own exacting standards. "How do you do, General Grant?" he exclaimed, striding purposefully past the general. "I recognize you from your pictures," he added, vigorously shaking the hand of Grant's puzzled medical director, Dr. E. D. Kittoe. Several moments of embarrassment followed as Grant's chief of staff, John A. Rawlins, corrected the error and introduced the secretary to the real Grant.[3]

After that difficult beginning, the conversation developed slowly and awkwardly as the train rolled across the southern Indiana countryside. Stanton explained the new command Grant would be taking and showed him two sets of orders from which the general could choose. They were identical in setting up the Military Division of the Mississippi under Grant's command. They differed only in that one called for leaving the present department commanders in their places (Grant, of course, being replaced by Sherman), the other for replacing Rosecrans with Thomas. Grant had no special liking for either man, but Rosecrans particularly had proved difficult and insubordinate when he had served under Grant in northern Mississippi the previous fall. Grant needed no time to make the decision: he would take Thomas rather than Rosecrans.[4]

They reached Louisville after dark that night in a cold, drizzling rain, Grant still hobbling about on his crutches and the secretary of war nursing a bad cold. They spent the next day in Louisville discussing forthcoming operations, and that evening, while General and Mrs. Grant were out visiting with relatives who lived in town, Stanton received an alarming message from Dana to the effect that if something was not done immediately, Rosecrans was likely to abandon Chattanooga. This was not, in fact, true, but Dana might have thought so. Stanton thought so and was well-nigh beside himself—all the more so when he could not at once find Grant. High-strung at the best of times, the nervous secretary of war now became more or less unstrung and began asking everyone he met—including random hotel guests—where Grant was, demanding that they find him immediately and send him in. Happy and relaxed, the Grants came back around 11:00 P.M. from their pleasant social evening. Grant recalled that as they neared the Galt House, "every person we met was a messenger from the Secretary, apparently partaking of his impatience to see me."[5]

Grant went immediately to Stanton's room, where the austere secretary of war was pacing forcefully from one side of the room to the other in his dressing gown. He filled Grant in on the present crisis, such as it was, and urged that something be done at once. Grant complied by having the War Department's order assigning him to the western department telegraphed to Rosecrans immediately, along with a personal order assuming command and another to Thomas directing him to "hold Chattanooga at all hazards," and promising to be on the scene in person as soon as possible. At the other end of the telegraph wire, Thomas was angry. He was part of the faction of Army of the Cumberland officers still loyal to Rosecrans, and he was essentially like Rosecrans in his approach to war and thus fully approved of his commander's actions. Indeed, Thomas would have been even more cautious and slow. Thomas resented not only the removal of Rosecrans but also the implication in Grant's telegram that Chattanooga might be abandoned. Nevertheless, he was a soldier, so he swallowed his resentments and immediately replied to Grant's telegram, "I will hold the town till we starve."[6]

The next day Stanton headed back for Washington while Grant set out for Chattanooga, leaving his wife, Julia, with the kinfolk in Louisville. On the evening of October 21 he arrived in Stevenson, Alabama, where Hooker had his headquarters, and there he met Rosecrans traveling north. The former commander of the Army of the Cumberland had left within twelve hours of receiving word of his relief. "I can't bear to meet my troops," he had explained to Thomas, and so he had left before notice of his departure could reach the troops. Now he was on his way to Cincinnati "to await orders." He stopped by for a chat with Grant and shared his ideas about what to do next. Grant considered Rosecrans's plans excellent. "My only wonder," he later wrote, "was that he had not carried them out." For William Starke Rosecrans, the need to have everything perfectly in order before proceeding had finally brought ruin. "Poor 'Old Rosey,'" an Army of the Cumberland soldier wrote eight months later, "where are you now? 'Weighed in the balance and found wanting.' Yet no officer ever more completely had the confidence and love of his army. We thought ourselves invincible, and the intensity of our belief in him and ourselves is shown by the terrible list of

Chickamauga dead." Regretfully, however, the soldier had to add the con-clusion of wisdom and reflection gained since that time: "His conduct of that field in no wise lessened the slaughter."[7]

And so the next morning Rosecrans boarded the train for oblivion while Grant and his party mounted horses for the grueling ride up the Sequatchie Valley and over Walden's Ridge. An autumn storm had swept in that morn-ing with fierce wind-driven rains, but Grant had business in Chattanooga. He had his crutches strapped to his saddle, and then Rawlins lifted him onto the horse as easily "as if he had been a child." They rode through mud some-times up to the horses' bellies, struggled through swollen streams, and passed the continuous litter of broken wagons and dead mules. After spend-ing the night in a little hamlet in the Sequatchie Valley, they set out the next day up Walden's Ridge, negotiating a steep, winding trail with numerous washouts. Where the way was too precarious to go mounted, staff members carried Grant. Then as they came down the east side of the ridge, Grant's horse slipped and fell, causing intense pain to his bad leg but apparently not compounding the injury. Finally, on the evening of October 23, Grant ar-rived in Chattanooga, "wet, dirty, and well," as Dana put it in another dis-patch to Washington.[8]

In Chattanooga, Grant went straight to Thomas's headquarters. His re-ception there was cool. Thomas and his staff had heard that Grant was on the way, but no one had thought he would arrive this soon. Perhaps that was why Thomas seemed deficient in hospitality. In any case, there had never been much warmth between these men, and Thomas was still smarting from Rosecrans's removal and Grant's order to hold the city. Whatever the reason, when Col. James H. Wilson, the advance man on Grant's staff, who had already been in Chattanooga for a few days, walked into the room, he found Grant and Thomas sitting in awkward silence on opposite sides of the fire, Grant, his wet uniform steaming in the warmth of the blaze, had a pud-dle of water under his chair, the result of his dripping clothes. Wilson sug-gested that perhaps some dry clothes should be found for Grant, and Thomas seemed to come to himself and bestir his staff members to care for Grant's needs. Most of their offers Grant declined.[9]

He did, however, ask to meet with the various heads of the Army of the Cumberland's staff departments. One by one they were summoned to head-quarters to give their reports on the army's current situation. Though Grant sat "immovable as a rock and as silent as the sphinx" through their presenta-tions, he showed his quick grasp of their subject matter by following up the reports with "whole volleys of questions." Of special interest was Brig. Gen.

William Farrar "Baldy" Smith, a West Point classmate whom Grant had not seen since their years at the academy. Smith had been Rosecrans's chief engineer, and he happened to be the chief source of ideas about breaking the Confederate siege of Chattanooga. An odd character, Smith was alternately brilliant and dismal, always eccentric. He was at his best this month, with a plan for what Grant called "opening up the cracker line."[10]

Grant now asked Smith for a full account of his plan, and Smith explained the position of the two armies and the surrounding geography so clearly Grant felt as if he could see the landscape without leaving Thomas's headquarters. Just below Chattanooga the Tennessee River turned south for three miles until it reached the foot of Lookout Mountain. Then it curved away from the mountain and ran back to the north for several miles. This double curve was called Moccasin Bend because when viewed from the top of Lookout Mountain it looks like an Indian moccasin with its toe against the mountain. Below Moccasin Bend, the river runs northwest to round the northern end of Raccoon Mountain before turning southwest again toward Bridgeport and Stevenson. A wagon road crossed the base of Moccasin Bend, starting just across the river from Chattanooga and running westward to a place called Brown's Ferry, opposite Raccoon Mountain. Just across from the ferry was a gap in the mountain, Cummings Gap, and the road that led through Cummings Gap came down on the west side of Raccoon Mountain at Kelly's Ferry—just a pontoon bridge and an easy haul from the Union supply depot at Bridgeport.

Using this new route, loaded supply wagons would have a relatively short haul and good roads from Bridgeport to Kelly's Ferry, across the pontoon bridge, and through Cummings Gap to Brown's Ferry. A pontoon bridge there would allow them to cross Moccasin Bend and reach Chattanooga. All this could be done at once, provided the Confederates were party to the arrangement. Since Confederate troops occupied the south bank of the Tennessee from Lookout Mountain all the way around the bend north of Raccoon Mountain and could be expected to object to such an operation, something was going to have to be done about them.[11]

Smith believed he knew just what that was. Three forces would converge suddenly on Brown's Ferry, seizing the west bank of the Tennessee there along with the northern end of Lookout Valley and Raccoon Mountain. First, a brigade would pile into flatboats and pontoons and make a daring predawn passage down the Tennessee River, round Moccasin Bend under the guns of the Rebel army, and land on the west bank opposite Brown's Ferry. Second, another brigade, having marched across the Moccasin Bend wagon road, would be ferried across in the boats that had landed the first wave. Third, coming in to meet them from the south would be heavy manpower: Hooker's three divisions would march along the main highway—through Running Water Gap, south of Raccoon Mountain—and then northward down Lookout Valley to link up with the two brigades opposite Brown's Ferry.[12]

The plan was a masterpiece, and Grant liked it at once. He wanted to see the ground for himself, however, before sending in his troops, so early the next morning he was back in the saddle and riding the Moccasin Bend wagon road for a personal reconnaissance with Thomas and Smith in tow. Leaving their horses in the woods a short distance back from the river at Brown's Ferry, they went down to view the site on foot. On the opposite shore, within easy rifle range, was a Confederate picket post with about twenty soldiers. Grant felt sure they must have recognized his party as being composed of officers rather than enlisted men, yet they held their fire while Grant and his companions examined the area and firmed up their plans—a good indication of why healthy armies do not allow the sort of lax front-line policies that had come to prevail around Chattanooga.[13]

Satisfied that the plan would work, Grant gave orders to execute it as rapidly as preparations could be made. Grant left the detailed planning and administration to Thomas and Smith. That afternoon, amid careful security measures to preserve secrecy, work began on the needed pontoons, and Thomas detailed an officer to round up any flatboats he could find. He also selected the assault units, Hazen's brigade for the dangerous river-borne assault, John B. Turchin's to back them up in the second wave from Brown's Ferry. The operation was scheduled to begin at 3:00 A.M., October 27. Hazen carefully studied the ground himself and arranged to have signal fires lit at carefully predetermined points on the Union-held shore so that his boat crews would know the precise moment to turn toward the Confederate side for the final run-in. When Hooker seemed to get balky and found obstacles to proceeding with his end of the plan on schedule, Grant did what Rosecrans would never have dreamed of doing and told Smith to go ahead without him. The two brigades ought to suffice, and if they needed help Grant could throw men into Lookout Valley from Chattanooga by way of the Moccasin Bend wagon road faster than Bragg could across the nose of Lookout Mountain. A new driving force had arrived at the top of the Union command structure in Chattanooga.[14]

The Confederate high command presented a stark contrast. After Davis's departure and Bragg's continuing attempts to suppress insubordination and break up mutinous cliques in the officer corps, relations among the top brass of the Army of Tennessee had continued along their dismal course. The leading figure of the malcontents was now Longstreet, who sulked because his commander in chief would not comply with his demands to have his army commander relieved. His bad frame of mind did not seem to improve either his alertness or his tactical or strategic perception. Bragg had assigned Longstreet responsibility for the left end of the Confederate line, from Chattanooga Creek, around the shoulders of Lookout Mountain, and across Lookout Valley to the slopes of Raccoon Mountain and the banks of the Tennessee River just beyond. His were the troops against whom Hazen, Turchin, and Hooker would contend in opening the "cracker line."

Longstreet seemed unable to grasp the concept of what the Army of Tennessee was trying to accomplish at Chattanooga. If his deployment of troops is any indication, he believed the only possible threat to the Confederate envelopment of Chattanooga would have to come from inside the city. Yet the Confederates had known for some time that reinforcements were on the way to the Federals in the beleaguered city, and Longstreet himself was fully aware that Hooker's force was camping on the far bank of the Tennessee just beyond Raccoon Mountain. Nevertheless, he deployed all his troops in the Chattanooga Valley and on the northeast shoulder of Lookout Mountain, facing the city. Until Bragg ordered him to do so on October 9, Longstreet had not placed a single man in Lookout Valley or on Raccoon Mountain. Even then he sent only two regiments to form a thin skirmish line and snipe at boats trying to use the river or at wagons on the north bank road. The force was adequate for that purpose but made no provision for dealing with the advance of Hooker's troops should that officer decide to move up the main highway and around the southern end of Raccoon Mountain.[15]

Bragg should have caught these errors, but he was keeping his distance from Longstreet's sector. Perhaps it was because Longstreet had come west as the vaunted general from the Army of Northern Virginia, Lee's warhorse, who presumably knew what he was doing. Of course, Lee himself knew better and usually kept his own headquarters as close as possible to Longstreet's; some officers needed more supervision than others. Indeed, Longstreet's reputation had been won under the close and watchful supervision of the South's foremost general. Another reason Bragg may have stayed away from Longstreet's sector is that general's appalling attitude. He scarcely veiled his contempt and loathing for Bragg, and he clearly resented any exercise of authority on Bragg's part. The commanding general may therefore have hoped that by minimizing contact with his recalcitrant lieutenant and allowing him as far as possible to carry on his corps' affairs without oversight, he could avoid a more explosive clash at a time when he had enough problems with general officers.[16]

Whatever the reason, Bragg kept to his own side of Chattanooga Creek and left Longstreet to handle all facets of command at the west end of the line, including the intellectual problems for which the bluff corps commander from the Army of Northern Virginia was entirely unequipped. As cavalry brought news of Union efforts to repair an important bridge in Running Water Gap, scouts reported activity in Hooker's camps, pickets disclosed a stronger Federal presence on the far bank of the Tennessee opposite Lookout Valley, and signal officers high atop Lookout observed westward troop movements on the other side of Moccasin Bend, Longstreet proved as helpless to analyze the data and divine Union intentions as he had been to grasp the strategic significance of the terrain or the armies' positions. Back in Virginia those had always been Lee's jobs.[17]

To make matters worse, Longstreet was engaged in a squabble involving the officers of the division on his far left, Hood's old outfit, over who was to succeed the wounded general. The officers of the division favored Brig Gen. Evander M. Law, long-serving and capable commander of the division's Alabama brigade. Longstreet, however, wanted to fill the slot with his favorite and longtime protégé Brig. Gen. Micah Jenkins, commander of the South Carolina brigade of George Pickett's division. That brigade had been detached during the Gettysburg campaign and so had missed the division's hour of glory and slaughter on Cemetery Ridge. Now it was detached again to accompany Longstreet to Tennessee while the rest of the division recuperated from its Gettysburg ordeal; Longstreet inserted it into Hood's old division and made Jenkins the division commander. Despite the South Carolinian's outstanding combat record, the division's officers were loath to accept an outsider. Longstreet forced Jenkins on them over their protests. Bad blood developed between Jenkins and Law. Just what passed among these two and their corps commander that month remains unclear, but they were the officers responsible for Lookout Valley and Raccoon Mountain, and strange considerations seem to have been driving their decisions during the last week of October.[18]

On October 25 Bragg passed on to Longstreet some of the intelligence his sources had produced pointing to a Union movement on the Confederate left, and he ordered Longstreet to make a reconnaissance toward Bridgeport. Longstreet ignored the order. He conceived the notion that Hooker was going to go wandering off to the southwest, crossing Lookout Mountain far behind Confederate lines and performing who could guess what feats of mischief there without any visible means of supply. Still Longstreet claimed that was the real threat and began edging a couple of his brigades southward along the crest of the mountain, contrary to Bragg's directions.[19]

Meanwhile, down in Lookout Valley, Law, two of whose regiments were the only force Longstreet had stationed there, warned that trouble was brewing and that the Confederates had best have a full division there. Longstreet made a slight concession to this request and let Law have the other three regiments of his brigade; the rest of the division stayed put. The balance of Law's brigade arrived in the valley on October 24.

The next day Law left on a brief furlough to visit Hood, recuperating some miles to the south in north Georgia, probably for the purpose of discussing Longstreet's machinations to put Jenkins in command of the division. While he was gone, Jenkins, for reasons that have never been adequately explained, pulled the three additional regiments back around to the east slope of Lookout Mountain without notifying Law's second in command of the move.

Law got back to division headquarters on the night of October 26—actually past midnight on the morning of the twenty-seventh—and was appalled to find his three regiments camped nearby, meaning that the thin line of skirmishers in the valley was again unsupported. Furthermore, he learned that Jenkins had just departed on a furlough, leaving Law temporarily in command of the division. Law determined to put the extra regiments back in the valley at once, middle of the night or not. He routed the troops out of their tents and began forming them up for the march around the shoulders of Lookout and down the west slope. It was slow work in the opaque darkness, for the bright moon had set a short time before and a dripping mist had rolled up from the river. As Law's troops stumbled into line, the unmistakable crack of a rifle shot stung through the damp blanket of fog from the direction of the river, then another, and then the swelling, rhythmless drumbeat of a fierce and growing fight. Law was too late.[20]

The men of Hazen's brigade were up shortly after midnight and marched down to the Chattanooga riverfront to launch the elaborately planned operation for opening the "cracker line." They discovered that the boats would not hold as many passengers as advertised and that even with reduced loads they were so crowded that the men had to stand and balance precariously, packed so tight the oarsmen had difficulty rowing. A waggish soldier quipped that it "reminds me of a picture I saw of George Washington crossing the Alps," bringing chuckles from his comrades and a stern rebuke from an officer.

By 3:00 A.M. the boats were ready to shove off. The bright hunter's moon—having run through its cycle and come full again since the harvest moon of the September night when Lincoln had galloped worriedly into Washington from the Soldiers' Home—now had set, and the mist thickened the gloom and promised additional protection. Hugging the Union-held right bank, the awkward flotilla set off on its nine-mile journey past the Confederate positions at the foot of Lookout Mountain. Rounding Moccasin Bend, they let the current carry them north again, away from the dark form of Lookout Mountain that blotted out the southerly constellations. With the mountain and its garrison behind them, so too was the most dangerous part of their voyage.

Finally, about 5:00 A.M., General Hazen, waiting on the right bank with his overland detachment near the large signal fire at Brown's Ferry, saw his waterborne force drifting out of the murk upstream. With relief, then irritation, and finally alarm, he watched as the boats appeared to be drifting past the target area. "Pull in, Colonel Foy, pull in!" he called to Lt. Col. James Foy of the Twenty-third Kentucky, whom he had chosen to lead the force in the boats. "Pull across the river—head for the ridge—dig in." Foy and his men obeyed, oarsmen hauling furiously at their sweeps to bring the unwieldy craft across the strong current. The Confederates on the far bank, who until now had made no response to the movement, answered with rifle fire. Foy and his men scrambled up the bank, momentarily confused in the darkness from having come to shore a little too far downstream. Reorienting themselves, they pushed ahead and drove the Confederates away from their left-bank positions. True to Hazen's instructions, they then began to ply their axes to erect breastworks on the crest of two low hills just beyond the ferry landing.

The Rebels Foy's men had driven off were pickets of the Fourth and Fifteenth Alabama regiments of Law's brigade, commanded this morning by Col. William C. Oates of the Fifteenth. Oates mustered his few available reserve companies and hastened to counterattack. In the inky predawn darkness his force collided with Foy's at close range, each side sensing the other's presence by sound and by the flash of their rifles. For a few minutes the issue was in doubt. Foy's troops fell back toward the landing in more or less disorder. Back at the ferry, however, the boats had been kept moving back and forth across the river, bringing over the rest of Hazen's brigade and some of

Turchin's as well. They were soon too many for Oates's small force, and the
Confederates had to give way. Oates himself went down with a bullet in the
thigh. Law arrived shortly thereafter, along with the remaining three regiments of his brigade, but could do nothing against the rapidly growing Federal force on the left bank and knew enough not to get any more of his men
killed trying. In disgust he pulled his brigade back to the slopes of Lookout
Mountain and notified Longstreet of the disaster. Over in the Federal lines
others also knew what the night's action meant. As daylight spread through
a drizzling rain, Hazen exulted to his troops, still vigorously fortifying the
position they had just taken, "We've knocked the cover off the cracker box."[21]

Indeed they had. By 10:00 A.M. a pontoon bridge spanned the Tennessee
River at Brown's Ferry and the basic conditions were in place for restoring
the flow of supplies to the Union troops in Chattanooga as soon as the
wagons could be set rolling along the new "cracker line." Much now depended on how quickly Hooker could arrive to keep the line open and Bragg
could act to close it.[22]

Grant and Thomas had been urging Hooker for several days to get his
force in motion. The eastern general had hoped to have his men on the
march by the morning of October 26, but the needed preparations did not
get done by then, forcing a one-day delay. Early on the morning of the
twenty-seventh the two divisions of the XI Corps and a single division of the
XII Corps tramped across the pontoons at Bridgeport and swung northeastward through Hog Jaw Valley along the main highway where it paralleled
the tracks of the Memphis & Charleston. A bend of the Tennessee River
brought it back into view on the column's left near the little trackside town
of Shellmound, so called for the large bar of shells on which it sat. The highway continued upstream along the left bank until near the mouth of Running Water Creek, where it veered southeastward into the gap where the
creek had its headwaters on the saddle between Raccoon Mountain on the
north and Sand Mountain on the south. High in the gap, near another pair
of trackside shanties at a place called Whiteside, the van of the column, the
XI Corps division of Adolph von Steinwehr, camped for the night. Bringing
up the rear, the XII Corps division of John W. Geary bedded down for the
night in the open field around Shellmound.[23]

At sunrise the next morning, October 28, the men were back on the road
again, striding down the east side of Running Water Gap and into Lookout
Valley. The scenery was awe-inspiring. The four-mile-wide valley lay between the towering rampart of Lookout Mountain, fourteen hundred feet
above the valley floor on the southeast, and Raccoon Mountain, nearly as

high on the northwest. But the soldiers' appreciation of the grandeur of the scene was cramped by the rush of adrenaline that accompanied the threat of battle.

Near the hamlet of Wauhatchie, three miles from Brown's Ferry and the north end of the valley, the rattle of rifle fire challenged the head of the column. The small hills that framed the landing at Brown's Ferry were part of a chain of low hills, about two hundred feet high, that ran along the middle of the valley all the way up to Wauhatchie. To the southeast of the hills, Lookout Creek flowed down to meet the Tennessee just above Brown's Ferry. On the hills' northwest side, the railroad and highway passed toward Brown's Ferry and Chattanooga. On a couple of the hills nearest Wauhatchie, Law had deployed some of his men as skirmishers, and these were the Confederates who challenged Hooker's march. They were too few, however, to do much more than bid defiance. And when von Steinwehr shook out a couple regiments and sent them forward in line of battle, the audacious Rebels had to beat a hasty retreat.[24]

Once again, the blue-clad column swung into march step along the highway toward Brown's Ferry, but the Confederates were not finished. At the point of Lookout Mountain were the batteries that had tried unsuccessfully to make Chattanooga untenable for the Army of the Cumberland. Now the guns were swung around to bear into Lookout Valley and strike at the approaching eastern Federals. The range was extreme, and the low hills between Lookout and the highway provided some cover, but whenever they could, the Confederate artillerists got in some long-range target practice against the long blue column as it crawled across the valley floor. Though it produced only one casualty, the experience of being the target of lethal projectiles was anything but a sporting event for the sweating bluecoats down on the highway. A flash and a puff of smoke near the point of Lookout would be followed three or four seconds later by a distant boom, immediately followed in turn by the screech of a shell in flight or, worse, the sight of one of the low-velocity projectiles sailing through the air or bounding along the ground. One of them skipped under the belly of Hooker's horse as the general rode nonchalantly along at the head of the column. The general was in his element. "Gen. Hooker rode right out, in plain sight of the rebels," an XI Corps soldier wrote in his diary that night. "He seemed to [show] but little [concern] for the shells."

For the common soldier, who, unlike Hooker, could not be certain of a large and admiring audience for his feats of courage, every additional motivation to steadiness was welcome as the column tramped steadily along un-

der the vexing threat of momentary death and dismemberment. Conceal-
ment was out of the question, and no reply could be made to the cannon on
the distant mountaintop. The men would just have to take it, and some enterprising officer started casting about for a way to make it easier for them.
The regimental bands were not with the column today, but the drummers
were. Hitching their drums around from back to hip and drawing out their
sticks, these young musicians struck up an invigorating rolling and stutter-
ing of sound as the men stepped out with a jauntier stride and the color ser-
geants unfurled the flags at the head of each regiment. The XI and XII
Corps were marching to Chattanooga in the best Army of the Potomac style,
giving notice to the Rebels watching from the heights that, as an XI Corps
soldier put it, "we had come to stay."[25]

Two spectators to the stirring scene of rattling drum, waving flag, and
booming gun had a prime vantage point overlooking the picturesque valley
but were not enjoying the show. From Sunset Rock, a prominent crag on the
western crest of Lookout Mountain, James Longstreet and Braxton Bragg
viewed the spectacle with surprise and dismay.

Longstreet had been hopelessly befuddled by the recent Union operations. When the Federals had seized Brown's Ferry despite Law's warnings
about the need to occupy Lookout Valley in greater force, Longstreet had
avoided embarrassment by neglecting to inform Bragg. Bragg found out
later that morning and was understandably furious. He fired off a note to the
corps commander: "The loss of our position on the left is almost vital; it in-
volves the very existence of the enemy in Chattanooga." What, Bragg
wanted to know, did Longstreet plan to do about it?

Precisely nothing. The landing was a matter of no importance, he assured the astonished Bragg, and they had best ignore it. True, the enemy
appeared to be working at "shortening his line of communications," but
that was a minor consideration, he maintained. Perhaps this was just another of Longstreet's attempts to cover his embarrassment over the fiasco in
the valley. Otherwise he would have had to have been the only man in either
army who had not yet figured out what the Confederates had been trying to
accomplish by encamping in the vicinity of Chattanooga the past month. In
any case, he had already decided where the real threat lay; Hooker's command at Bridgeport was going to move southeast, not northeast, and get behind him by way of a pass called Johnson's Crook. Therefore, the affair at
Brown's Ferry could only be a diversion.

This response was so inane that Bragg was temporarily buffaloed, apparently assuming that Longstreet must know what he was talking about since

it was unreasonable to think that a general officer could concoct anything half so farfetched out of the resource of his own fancy. That, of course, was exactly what Longstreet had done, but Bragg actually allowed the eastern commander to draw him into a long and ludicrous discussion on the evening of the twenty-seventh regarding just how many men should be shifted southward to meet the imaginary threat via Johnson's Crook. The Army of Tennessee commander had not completely lost touch with reality, however, for when he left Longstreet at 11:00 P.M., he directed him to attack and re-take Brown's Ferry if the threat from the south should fail to materialize.[26]

Back at headquarters, Bragg continued to entertain doubts about Longstreet's strategic perspicacity, and the following morning, October 28, he sent orders for Longstreet to meet him at the point of Lookout Mountain to view and discuss the situation further. Bragg duly arrived on the mountaintop shortly before 9:00 A.M., but Longstreet was nowhere to be seen. Nothing seemed to be happening down toward Johnson's Crook. Certainly nothing was happening around Brown's Ferry, and Bragg's orders had definitely called for action at one place or the other. Presently a staff officer managed to locate Longstreet, eating breakfast at his headquarters halfway down the mountain. There was nothing for Bragg to do but wait for the corps commander to make his way to the summit. Eventually Longstreet showed up, and a rather unpleasant colloquy got under way. Bragg had recently learned that Longstreet had boasted to Davis that he could whip the whole Army of the Cumberland with his corps alone, but now the vaunted Virginia general was showing a marked disinclination to try his hand at whipping anybody.[27]

The tense exchange was interrupted by a courier who arrived to report Union activity in Lookout Valley. Bragg was incredulous. Had he not three days earlier ordered Longstreet to reconnoiter in that direction? If Longstreet had obeyed the order, they would have known exactly what the Federals were about. The courier was insistent and suggested that the officers follow him over to Sunset Rock, on the western crest, to see for themselves. They did and thus gained their prime vantage point for the dramatic display of Hooker's long column marching down the valley under artillery fire with waving flags and beating drums. So much for Johnson's Crook.

Bragg ordered Longstreet to attack as soon as possible and clear the valley, then returned to his headquarters while the corps commander presumably made his preparations for the assault. Longstreet did nothing of the sort. Indeed, to all appearances he had little intention of attacking until very late in the day. When the Federals in the valley made camp, however, with about one-fifth of their number separated from the main body by a gap of three miles, Longstreet changed his mind and decided to attack after all. He would not make the all-out assault to throw the Yankees into the river that Bragg expected and had ordered, but he would make a small-scale raid on what looked to him to be several hundred men and a wagon train camped near Wauhatchie. He sent a note to Bragg informing him of his intention to strike the enemy with a single brigade. Repeatedly Bragg wrote to urge Longstreet to use more force. "Since 11 P.M. last night your whole corps was placed at your disposal. . . . The movement should be prompt and decisive." In case Longstreet's three divisions were not enough, Bragg also informed him that a division of Breckinridge's neighboring corps was standing by, awaiting his summons.[28]

Nevertheless, Longstreet chose to use a single division, Jenkins's, and one of its four brigades was to be held in reserve and never used at all. His reasons for doing so remain obscure. In his memoirs, written many years later, he claimed that Bragg would let him have the use of no more troops, but that was an obvious falsehood. He may have thought the troops could not make it from their east-slope positions, around the shoulders of Lookout Mountain, and down into Lookout Valley because of Union artillery on Moccasin Bend that played on the northern end of the mountain. Yet the Federal officer who commanded those guns admitted at the time that he could do no more than harass such movements by the Confederates. In his report, Longstreet claimed that he dared not begin the movement until after dark and had to finish it before morning, despite the fact that Confederate troops had been marching around the slopes of the mountain with little hindrance for the past two days.[29]

The most likely explanation for Longstreet's strange behavior is a combination of his own inability to comprehend the military situation and his scheming designs to discredit Law and establish his own favorite, Jenkins, firmly in command of Hood's old division. Even now Longstreet was incapable of grasping the significance of the Union seizure of Lookout Valley. In his report, written the following March, he wrote, "That the point was not essential to the enemy at Chattanooga is established by the fact that he supplied his army at that place some six weeks without it." Such impenetrable obtuseness set Longstreet up for all manner of blunders. Since "the point was not essential," the enemy would probably not hold it in much force, and since Longstreet had taken not the least pains to gather information about Hooker's force, he was able to misjudge its numbers grossly in keeping with his own confused strategic ideas.

That miscalculation led him into his next blunder. Since Federal forces in the valley were few, one division should suffice to get a brief advantage over them. This was particularly desirable since Longstreet was anxious to make his protégé, Jenkins, look good to the officers of the division, who decidedly preferred Law. Longstreet's plan called for Law, with two brigades, to take up a position on the hills just east of the road through the valley, ready, in theory at least, to block the entire force at Brown's Ferry. In the meantime, Jenkins, with another brigade, would strike the isolated Union force at Wauhatchie. Law would undoubtedly have to give way sooner or later, causing him to look bad. Still, if he held out any length of time at all, Jenkins should have sufficient opportunity to gobble up the Union detachment and win the laurels for himself. Of course, nothing about this plan was remotely likely to remove the Union presence from the left bank of the Tennessee or to close the recently opened cracker line, but then such matters were, to Longstreet, "not essential."[30]

Longstreet neglected to brief Jenkins fully on the plan, and the young South Carolinian knew only that he was being sent to take one of his brigades to seize a Union wagon train and a few hundred guards. The operation was to be conducted during the night of October 28–29, and Jenkins got his brigades moving shortly after 8:00 P.M. Longstreet seems to have stopped them for several hours. Then, according to his own account, he decided not to attack after all and went back to his quarters and went to bed without telling a soul. It apparently did not occur to him that Jenkins might proceed as ordered, but the young Citadel graduate was a good soldier and did just that sometime around midnight. With cheerful thoughts in expectation of grabbing a rich Yankee supply train, the troops marched off toward one of the most confused actions of the war.[31]

The force they were about to hit was Geary's division, last in Hooker's column, which the latter general had ordered to camp at Wauhatchie while the two XI Corps divisions marched on to link up with Baldy Smith's troops at Brown's Ferry. Smith, Hazen, and Turchin were considerably alarmed at Hooker's cavalier disposition, reasoning that the Federal position in Lookout Valley was so essential that the Confederates were bound to hit it heavily and soon. Hooker was deaf to their entreaties. He wanted to cover the road back to Bridgeport by way of Running Water Gap, as well as the cracker line to Kelly's Ferry by way of Cummings Gap, and he anticipated no trouble from the Confederates. The troops stayed where they were. Geary's division, like the others of the XI and XII Corps, was badly depleted, and by this time substantial elements of it had been detached to cover Federal communications. The result was that his isolated command at Wauhatchie mustered hardly the numbers of a good-sized brigade, about fifteen hundred men. Geary was no professional, but he had become a proficient citizen-soldier. Sensing the possible vulnerability of his position this night, he took every possible precaution to guard against surprise. The men were to sleep in line of battle, their accouterments on and their weapons stacked close by. One of his brigade commanders went one better and had his men keep their boots on too. Around 10:30 P.M. a sharp flare-up in picket firing stirred the camp into life, and the troops waited tensely under arms for some time until continued quiet convinced the officers that it had been a false alarm and the order came to stand down.

Then between midnight and 1:00 A.M., the rattle of firing rose from the picket lines again, and this time no one needed to wonder whether it was the real thing. The Rebels hit the perimeter as if they intended to go straight through the camp from one end to the other. Geary's men were ready for them and stood their ground. The shocked Confederates, South Carolinians to a man, recovered quickly and hammered away at the Union position. The opposing forces were roughly equal, and each side gave about as good as it got.

At the height of the battle, a bit of comedy touched an otherwise grim scene. The Union teamsters became frightened and ran for cover; the unattended mules, falling into a similar state, broke loose and simply ran. Providentially, the majority of them seem to have run in the direction of the enemy, "with heads down and tails up, with trace-chains rattling and whiffletrees snapping over the stumps of trees." Their mad stampede temporarily broke up a Confederate regiment that had gained an advantageous position and might have done considerable damage if not distracted until the Federals could take countermeasures. Several days later, the quartermaster in charge of the beasts, in recognition of their service and in a jibe at the army's practice of granting honorary, or brevet, promotions to officers for meritorious service, requested that "the mules, for their gallantry in this action, may have conferred upon them the brevet rank of horses." It would be funny then; right now Geary's hard-pressed men were just thankful for whatever remarkable providences might help them in their nip-and-tuck struggle to prevent their camp from being overrun.[32]

Meanwhile, back at Brown's Ferry, the sound of the firing at Wauhatchie had brought practically everyone out of his blankets and into his boots, and the camp was all activity. Most active of all, perhaps because of an awareness that he should have foreseen this, was Hooker himself. He fired off orders both to XI Corps commander Oliver O. Howard and to the commander of one of Howard's divisions, Carl Schurz, to march at once to the relief of Geary, double-timing the whole three miles. The duplication of orders, the haste, and the weird, shadowy, dreamlike visual conditions produced as a chilly wind drove a broken rack of clouds across a bright moon, still almost full, all contributed to make the Union response about as confused as the Confederate attack.

As Howard's men marched up the road toward Wauhatchie, Law's Confederates on the hills just east of the road took them under fire. The Federals responded by charging the hills. Law's men, who comfortably outnumbered the first Union brigades to come up the road, beat them off. Hooker grew alarmed and threw additional units into the conflict, apparently either forgetting or not realizing that they were the same brigades he had ordered to double-time to Wauhatchie. A small but fierce battle raged on the slopes of the roadside hills, separate from the fight Geary's men were waging against Jenkins at Wauhatchie. Law's position was a strong one and his men some of the Army of Northern Virginia's best. Despite considerable bravery and a sobering casualty rate, the Federals had little chance of moving him. By three o'clock, however, Law received a correct report that the attack on Wauhatchie had failed and that Jenkins's other brigade was retiring across Lookout Creek. The cessation of firing from that direction confirmed the truth of the report, and in that case, no reason remained for Law to go on asking his men to die for a couple of rocky, tree-covered knobs in the middle of the valley floor. At his order, the two brigades fell back, pursued by the exultant Federals. The battle of Wauhatchie was over.[33]

The postmortems, of course, were just beginning. Hooker, embarrassed that his carelessness had nearly resulted in disaster for Geary's hard-pressed division, sought a scapegoat and settled on Schurz. The German-born division commander was exonerated by a court of inquiry called at his request in response to a harsh—and undeserved—condemnation in Hooker's report. The fact was that Hooker himself, in his confusion, had assigned Schurz's brigades two different missions at the same time.[34]

Longstreet tried to salvage what he could from the incredibly bungled operation by falsifying his report to state that the brigade attacking Wauhatchie had been enjoying complete success until Law's retreat compelled its withdrawal—the reverse of the truth. Such behavior by a corps commander was hardly calculated to raise the morale of his officers, and the personnel problems in Longstreet's command were only beginning.[35]

The results of the battlefield encounters were about 408 casualties for Jenkins and Law, 416 for Hooker, not counting mules. As Bragg and Hardee had to admit in disgust during an October 31 visit to the summit of Lookout, no further practical chance remained of dislodging the Federals in Lookout Valley and shutting off their recently opened conduit of supplies.[36]

"General Thomas' plan for securing the river and south side road hence to Bridgeport has proven eminently successful," Grant wired Halleck on the evening before the battle of Wauhatchie. "The question of supplies may now be regarded as settled. If the rebels give us one week more time I think all danger of losing territory now held by us will have passed away, and preparations may commence for offensive operations." Now, it seemed, the Rebels had done their worst and failed to choke off the flow of supplies or regain the leverage they had once held over the Federals in Chattanooga. Grant had the initiative, and he meant to keep it.[37]

CHAPTER EIGHT

I Have Never Felt Such Restlessness

The offensive operation Grant so eagerly anticipated once the cracker line was open had to await the arrival of his most trusted lieutenant, Sherman, leading four divisions, about twenty thousand men, of his most reliable troops, the sturdy and resourceful veterans of the Army of the Tennessee. Sherman had already started and was moving as rapidly as he could, but many obstacles stood in the way. His men were good marchers, but they were now being called on to make an epic journey. To Grant's frustration, the bright moon of Wauhatchie would wane and a new one come and wax full before his plans could be set in motion.

Halleck had sought troops from the Department of the Tennessee even before the battle of Chickamauga, when Washington was worried that a massive Confederate concentration might crush Rosecrans. Grant had no sooner started a division on its way than word arrived of Rosecrans's defeat, followed by even more frantic demands for troops. Grant had thereupon decided to send Sherman with three more divisions. Sherman moved promptly but was delayed by orders from Halleck that he repair the Memphis & Charleston Railroad as he came, using it as a line of supply and advancing no farther or faster than his track crews could get the trains running and his patrols and garrisons keep the guerrillas at bay. In an area that was and had been for over a year infested with guerrillas, this was a tall order, and it greatly impeded Sherman's march. Halleck had been anxious that Sherman have a separate supply line to Memphis so as not to burden further the already overtaxed Army of the Cumberland system stretching back to Nashville, but the trouble was that the task of keeping those 330 miles of track operating was wellnigh impossible, and the attempting of it was likely to keep Sherman and his valuable troops occupied for a good deal longer than the United States could afford to spare them.[1]

When Grant had gotten to Chattanooga in late October, the desperate situation there—and especially the movement of a substantial body of Confederate troops from Bragg's army up the Tennessee Valley toward Knoxville—convinced him that Sherman had better forget the railroad. "Drop all work on Memphis & Charleston Railroad," read the note a daring messenger carried down the Tennessee in a canoe, "cross the Tennessee, and hurry eastward with all possible dispatch toward Bridgeport." Grant was concerned lest those Confederates in the upper Tennessee Valley swing west to threaten his supply line with Nashville and he wanted Sherman in position to block such a move.

With what Grant called "characteristic promptness," Sherman obeyed. He had received Grant's message at Iuka, Mississippi, west of the lower Tennessee River and well over two hundred miles from Bridgeport by the route he would have to travel, though some of his troops had already reached the mid-valley of the Tennessee in northern Alabama. Sherman pushed ahead rapidly to the head of the column, crossing the Tennessee on November 1. Skirmishing frequently with Confederate cavalry, the lead units reached the Elk River on November 4. The Elk was wide and deep here at its mouth, and the only provision for crossing was a small ferry that would be far too slow in moving a small army from one bank of the river to the other. So Sherman set his men marching again, this time angling northeastward, up the valley of the Elk. By November 8 he was in Fayetteville, Tennessee, still more than one hundred miles from Grant.

Meanwhile, Grant was not ignoring the problem of supply that Halleck had attempted to solve by ordering Sherman to restore the railroad all the way from Memphis; he simply had a better idea for accomplishing the same goal. Just before setting out from Iuka, Sherman had ordered Maj. Gen. Grenville Dodge to take a reinforced division of the XVI Corps, about eight thousand men, and follow him eastward. Grant now had a stroke of genius. Dodge was not only a tough and skillful general but also, in civilian life, an efficient manager of the building of railroads. Grant detailed him to rebuild and maintain not the hopeless Memphis & Charleston but the much more practical Nashville & Decatur Railroad—and then the Memphis & Charleston only from the point of its junction with the former road. This was a realistic assignment, and Dodge was just the man to do it. With energy and resourcefulness, he got the lines running and kept them that way, opening up an important additional supply line for Grant and contributing significantly to the Federal effort around Chattanooga without ever appearing on the battlefield.[2]

Sherman's men marched along the foot of the Cumberlands near Winchester, where Rosecrans's Tullahoma campaign had halted the previous summer, crossed the Elk, and plunged into the forbidding mountain country toward Bridgeport along the line of the Nashville & Chattanooga Railroad. Though the tail end of his column was still in Winchester, Sherman himself reached Bridgeport on November 13, reported to Grant by telegraph, and, at the latter's behest, hurried on into Chattanooga by steamboat, for which the Tennessee was now usable.[3]

Grant was delighted to see Sherman and greeted him with a conviviality that surprised the officers of the Army of the Cumberland. General Hazen noted that Grant and Sherman "were new, and different from the commanders we had known before. They wore vests and coats unbuttoned" and displayed "a sort of outspoken frankness upon military matters."[4]

Grant was particularly happy to have Sherman present because his other top subordinates in Chattanooga, Thomas and Hooker, did not seem to have the hard-driving, can-do attitude that had made the Army of the Tennessee successful in clearing the Mississippi of major Rebel forces. Grant had encountered this lack in detail over the past couple of weeks. Those Confederates marching up the Tennessee Valley had not been aiming for Grant's supply line but rather for Burnside up in East Tennessee. Now that general wanted help. The War Department, sparked by the president's well-known and long-standing sensitivity about the region, had become agitated and begun plying Grant with dispatches imploring him to do something. To make matters worse, Halleck and Stanton had begun to wonder if Bragg might not be contemplating an end run clear around Grant's army, opening up the possibility of who could say how much mischief in East or Middle Tennessee. Grant was concerned about that too, the more so because the recent starving times had left the Army of the Cumberland all but destitute of usable draft animals and thus planted in the Chattanooga area almost as permanently as the mountains and the river. If Bragg did get into Middle Tennessee, there would be precious little Thomas's troops could do about it.

Indeed, there seemed to be precious little they could do about anything else either. Grant discovered just how bad things had gotten on November 7. Learning that day that Bragg had detached an even larger force toward East Tennessee, this one commanded by Longstreet, Grant gave Thomas a direct order to attack the Confederate right flank at Chattanooga and thus relieve the pressure on Burnside. Thomas did not want to make the attack

and informed Grant it could not be done. Grant told him to use mules, officers' horses, anything he could find to pull the needed guns—have the men
carry four days' rations in their haversacks and dispense with supply wagons
altogether. Still Thomas insisted the thing was impossible, and Grant finally
had to give it up. With considerable vexation, he had to answer the War Department's missives with assurances that he was doing all that could be
done, which, for the moment, was nothing.[5]

Thus Grant was all the more glad for the arrival of Sherman, a subordinate whom he trusted and who trusted him, a man who found ways to get
things done rather than reasons why they could not be done. Grant, Sherman, Thomas, and Smith rode out to view the terrain and the positions of
the armies the next day. Together they agreed on a plan of battle. Sherman
would follow the route of Hooker's march, fake toward the southern reaches
of Lookout Mountain with a single division, then cross the Tennessee at
Brown's Ferry and duck into the hills on the north bank of the river opposite
Chattanooga. Out of Bragg's sight he would work his divisions around until
they were opposite the north end of Missionary Ridge, cross the river on another set of pontoons Baldy Smith was building, and roll up Bragg's line
from the north. That was especially desirable because both of Bragg's key
railroads, the East Tennessee & Georgia, leading to Knoxville, and the
Western & Atlantic, leading to Atlanta, ran off to the east of Chattanooga
and would be vulnerable to a blow at the Confederate right flank. Thomas's
troops, about whose morale Grant had his doubts, would threaten the Confederate center along Missionary Ridge directly in front of Chattanooga.
Despite protests from Thomas, who wanted Hooker to attack Lookout
Mountain, Grant decided he had no need for that towering mass of earth
and rock and would just as soon have Hooker follow Sherman across the
bridge at Brown's Ferry and then back across the one at Chattanooga, thus
circumventing Chattanooga Creek and getting into a position to join
Thomas in threatening the main Confederate lines.[6]

As Grant had expected, Sherman shared his intense impatience to set the
plan in motion and hurried off to try to catch the steamboat back to
Bridgeport that night. He missed it. Very well then, he would take another
boat, and since the only available vessel seemed to be a five-man rowboat, he
took that and, with a detail of four soldiers at the oars, set out down the
river. They rowed all night, Sherman taking turns at an oar to spell the soldiers. At Shellmound he picked up a fresh crew of oarsmen and reached
Bridgeport by daylight. To his dismay, however, he found that even the

most relentless drive was not sufficient to overcome some obstacles—at least to overcome them speedily.[7]

Crossing the Cumberlands with an army was a difficult enough undertaking even in the best of weather, and by November the weather in southern Tennessee was anything but the best. Laboring through the mountains, over muddy roads and through countryside that provided no opportunity to eat by means of the foraging at which they were already adept, Sherman's men experienced many of the hardships suffered by the troops of the Army of the Cumberland detailed to move wagon trains across Walden's Ridge. To complete their misery, cold, hard rains poured out of leaden skies day after dreary day. After his lead divisions got past Bridgeport, Sherman decided that his troops had been on short rations long enough and directed that the supply wagons for each division should follow immediately in its rear, rather than having all the combat troops push on to the front and the wagons follow as best they could through the mud. That arrangement at least assured the men moderate supplies of hardtack and salt pork, but it impeded the march beyond all imagination as the wagons mired down and entangled the combat units with them.

In East Tennessee, the crisis appeared to grow worse. In Washington, Halleck fretted and sent fretful telegrams to Grant. In Chattanooga, Grant fumed. Thomas had been forced to borrow horses from Sherman just to move a few of his cannon, his own horses being either dead or too weak to pull anything. Sherman's command was the only real maneuver force Grant had, and now it was stuck in the mud. "I have never felt such restlessness before as I have at the fixed and immovable condition of the Army of the Cumberland," Grant wired Halleck. November 21 had been set as Grant's original target date for opening the attack, but because Sherman could not get into position in time, the operation had to be postponed to the twenty-second and then to the twenty-third. Still Grant had to admit that "Sherman has used almost superhuman effort to get up," and a correspondent of the *London Spectator* referred to the entire six-hundred-mile odyssey of Sherman's men from their camps east of Vicksburg as an "extraordinary march." So it was, but for Grant—and Halleck—that was small consolation. They wanted action now.[8]

It would have been some comfort to Bragg could he have known how much vexation his Tennessee Valley operations were causing the Federals. After the battle of Wauhatchie, he had known that the flow of supplies to the Union army in Chattanooga could no longer be seriously impeded. The siege of Chattanooga, with its promise of destroying a Union army at a fraction of the cost the Confederates had paid at Chickamauga, was over. The question was what to do next. In answering that question, Bragg had to bear in mind that a Federal force of several divisions was advancing eastward from Mississippi. Confederate cavalry in northern Mississippi and Alabama kept him well informed of the progress Sherman was making along the Memphis & Ohio. He had to consider the possibility that this force was on its way to Chattanooga, even though Longstreet maintained that Knoxville was the probable destination. Whichever it was, Bragg's chances would obviously be better if he could do whatever he was going to do before this additional Union force got within striking distance.[9]

His options were few. Retreat would be a disaster for Confederate morale both inside and outside the army, concede defeat in the campaign, allow the Union undisputed possession of a position of enormous strategic importance, and, in all probability, end his career as a general. A direct assault against the fortified Union lines at Chattanooga would have had the same result and cost five or ten thousand Confederate casualties in the bargain. Bragg had admitted the suicidal nature of that option weeks ago, shortly after taking up his position outside the town. It would be almost equally absurd for Bragg to concentrate his forces on the high ground around Chattanooga and wait for Grant to attack him. With the way open for the kind of supplies and reinforcements the North could afford, Grant could choose the time and place of attack, and Bragg could be sure that in that case the arrangement would definitely not be to his liking.[10]

He could not go back, he could not go forward, and he could not stand still. The only possible alternatives, then, were moves by either flank. A move by the left flank, to the west, would take him directly into the path of Sherman's advancing force. It would also involve passing through or within a dangerous proximity of Hooker's force in Lookout Valley, which Bragg and his generals had already decided they had no hope of removing. It would uncover Bragg's only meager line of supply, the Western & Atlantic Railroad running back toward Atlanta, and shift the scene of action toward an area in which his foe's supply problems would be greatly eased.[11]

And that left just one option: a move by the right flank in the direction of East Tennessee. Happily for Bragg, such a move was promising in several ways. Whereas a move to the west would expose his supply line, a move to the east would more effectively cover it. Better still, the East Tennessee & Georgia Railroad, connecting with Knoxville, one hundred miles up into East Tennessee, continued on into southwestern Virginia, and it was a po-

tential additional outlet for supplies. Plugging into it would give Bragg a secure supply line for a possible lunge to the west against Grant's communications. As an additional bonus, a Confederate force of about ten thousand
men was operating in southwestern Virginia under the command of Maj.
Gen. Samuel Jones, and the potential, at least, existed for a combination of
forces that would render Bragg even more formidable. The drawbacks of
this option—rough country, inadequate supply and transportation within
the Confederate army, and the possibility of effective countermeasures by
Grant—applied equally or more to about anything else Bragg could have
done.[12]

All that stood between Bragg and the realization of these promising prospects was Ambrose Burnside and the twenty thousand men of the Army of
the Ohio. Besides seizing Knoxville and occupying East Tennessee, Burnside had severed the direct rail link between Virginia and the western Confederacy. He then had begun to spread out a bit and had started crowding
Jones's southwestern Virginia command. Jones and the Richmond authorities had appealed to Bragg to do what he could, and Bragg had. On October
17, he dispatched Maj. Gen. Carter L. Stevenson with his division and two
cavalry brigades to East Tennessee "to press vigorously toward Knoxville,
to press the enemy's rear and develop him, driving him back as far as their
commands will allow," at the same time assuring Richmond that he would
"try to relieve General Jones by a move on the enemy's rear." Five days later
Bragg upped the ante by sending the division of Brig. Gen. John K. Jackson
to join Stevenson's force, bringing its total effective strength up to about
eleven thousand men. This was the movement that had prompted Grant to
order Sherman's rapid march to the Chattanooga area.

More to the point, Burnside was, by the end of October, reacting precisely according to Bragg's script and withdrawing his forces into an enclave
around Knoxville. The Federal general's supply situation in East Tennessee
had never been very good, and he felt compelled to maintain a large garrison
at Cumberland Gap, leaving him an effective field force of only about fourteen thousand men, two thousand of which were recent local levies.[13]

Thus by the time of the debacle at Wauhatchie, Bragg already had an unqualified, if small, success to his credit in East Tennessee. With hopes of
success at Chattanooga lost along with Lookout Valley, Bragg would naturally turn to the only attractive option left him and try to parlay his success
in East Tennessee into something that would break the current deadlock
and take the initiative away from the dangerous Ulysses Grant. He could
not, however, take the entire Army of Tennessee up the river to deal with

Burnside, not yet anyway. To release his grip on the Western & Atlantic Railroad before the East Tennessee line was firmly in his grasp would be courting the starvation of his already not overly well-supplied army. He would have to deal with Burnside first, destroying his force or expelling it from East Tennessee. For this purpose he made plans to reinforce Stevenson's command and to send Stevenson's corps commander, John C. Breckinridge, to take over the operation.[14]

At this point, forces outside Bragg's army intervened to influence his decision. Ever since Longstreet's departure from Virginia, Robert E. Lee, in nearly his every communication with President Davis, had been bemoaning the loss of troops. To be sure, Lee was the Confederacy's finest general, but he was a department commander, and was subject to the myopia that almost always afflicted such officers. Each tended to believe his own department was the most important, the most intensely threatened, and the most in need of troops. Lee may also have thought, with some justification, that he would have to win the war decisively in Virginia if it was to be won at all. At any rate, he consistently opposed any transfer of troops out of his command and constantly agitated for their return. Most of the time he was successful in winning Davis over to his views.[15]

Davis had thus come to think that Longstreet's command should get back to Lee as soon as possible. With a politician's knack for splitting the difference, he wrote Bragg in late October to suggest sending Longstreet up into East Tennessee to deal with Burnside, thus accomplishing that long-desired Confederate goal and, more important, placing Longstreet halfway back the road to Virginia, whence he could go either way as necessity might demand.[16]

The idea had several points to commend it. The exchange of Longstreet's two Army of Northern Virginia divisions for the divisions of Stevenson and Jackson, along with adding three more cavalry brigades to the two already there, would boost the East Tennessee force from eleven thousand to eighteen thousand effectives, about the increase that was needed and probably the best Bragg could afford. One command or another would have to go to East Tennessee, and sending Longstreet's would keep Davis and Lee happy.[17]

Finally, and perhaps best of all, such a move would rid Bragg's army of James Longstreet, whose incapacity and near-mutinous attitude had already cost Bragg and his army severely. Even today it is hard to sort out how much of Longstreet's appalling record in the West was the result of his incompetence and how much was caused by his mulish desire to thwart and spite Bragg at every opportunity. Certainly no one in Bragg's place could have made such a judgment. Longstreet came from the highly successful Army of Northern Virginia with an enviable reputation gained when he had carried out Lee's orders. He exuded self-confidence, not to say self-satisfaction, and had a way of convincing others to accept him at his own high estimate, often despite observable evidence to the contrary. The natural assumption for Bragg to have made, then, was that Longstreet was a moderately capable, if much overrated, general, who had been ineffective in the West because of a personality clash with his superior. Giving him a tactically independent command still under Bragg's strategic direction might be the way to get some use out of him. Thus, as Bragg commented to another of his officers, they would "see what [Longstreet] could do on his own resources."[18]

If any additional inducement had been needed to persuade Bragg to part with Longstreet, Davis promised to reinforce him with two brigades then stationed in Demopolis, Alabama. Johnston had promised him two more brigades from his force, and these four brigades would nearly make good the reduction in manpower at Chattanooga that Bragg would suffer as a result of swapping Longstreet for Stevenson. At any rate, even the flat loss of the number of good soldiers in Longstreet's divisions would have been a gain to the army in ridding it of their general's feuding and blundering.[19]

And so on November 4 Bragg gave orders for Longstreet to proceed to East Tennessee, "to drive Burnside out. . . , or better, to capture or destroy him." Bragg hoped that Longstreet might then be able to swing west into Middle Tennessee, and for that purpose he sent along an officer familiar with that region. He cautioned Longstreet that "it may become necessary in an emergency to recall you temporarily" and emphasized that "the success of the plan depends on rapid movements and sudden blows."[20]

Longstreet began complaining the very day he received the assignment. He wanted more troops; specifically, he wanted to keep Stevenson's division. He was dissatisfied with the harnesses and wagons available with the Army of Tennessee and groused about that too. Next he fell to quibbling over details of Bragg's instructions and then to more complaining, this time that he could not possibly be expected to maintain the railroad in his rear. Patiently Bragg explained his intentions and assured Longstreet that he need not concern himself with the railroad; Bragg would see to that. But Longstreet was not to be satisfied. Next he wanted more artillery; then it was the wagons again, and then the artillery. After that he claimed the railroad was not working right, and on and on the litany went.[21]

While he offered complaints at a distressing rate, Longstreet did not move his troops very rapidly. His command covered the first sixty miles or so to Sweetwater, Tennessee, in eight days, whereas the previous month Stevenson had covered the same ground in five even while approaching and skirmishing with the enemy. Indeed, at about the same time Longstreet was taking eight days to cover the distance northbound, Stevenson was making the southbound trip, by rail, in one. The slow pace of Longstreet's movement coupled with the rapid pace of his complaints disturbed Bragg. "Your several dispatches of today astonish me," he wrote to Longstreet. "Transportation in abundance was on the road and subject to your orders. I regret it has not been energetically used. The means being furnished, you were expected to handle your own troops, and I cannot understand your constant applications for me to furnish them." Longstreet replied to insist it was not his fault, and the slow movement went on.[22]

On November 13, as Sherman was arriving in Bridgeport ahead of his troops, Longstreet's columns marched northward from Sweetwater. Burnside's command fell back skirmishing, but some of Longstreet's subordinates began to doubt their commander when it appeared that he missed a chance to capture or destroy most of the Union force. The Confederates slogged on through the same rain that was impeding the march of Sherman's troops through the Cumberlands and around the hills back of Chattanooga. By November 17, while Grant still waited in frustration to begin executing his plans at Chattanooga, Longstreet had his army in line confronting the fortifications of Knoxville, in which Burnside had taken refuge.[23]

Yet he felt unable to do more. On the twentieth he wrote to tell Bragg that Burnside, whom he estimated had twenty thousand men, could not get out and he could not get in. The next day he wrote, "I think that my force is hardly strong enough to warrant my taking his works by assault," and "Can't you spare me another division? It will shorten the work here very much."[24]

At this point Longstreet had upward of 17,000 effectives, with another 3,000 or so daily expected from Jones, against Burnside's true effective strength of 12,000. In and around Chattanooga, Grant could put 60,000 men into line of battle, including the forces of Hooker and Sherman, while Bragg could muster only about 42,000, with about another 3,000 still on the way from Mississippi. Detaching more troops to Longstreet would entail a considerable risk, for Grant's offensive plans had to be nearing completion. Bragg had known as early as November 8 that Sherman had cut loose of the railroad and was moving fast. Now he knew that Sherman's men were in the Chattanooga area. Most of them had crossed the bridge at Brown's Ferry several days before and disappeared into the hills on the north side of the river across from the town. If they reached their jumping-off point and Grant's big push began with Bragg's army made even weaker by further detachments to Longstreet, the result could be disastrous. Yet defeat might be just as likely from continuing the status quo and waiting to receive Grant's attack with even his present force. Only quick and decisive action from Longstreet would release Bragg from his dilemma, and Longstreet seemed unable to do that without large reinforcements. At the same time, Bragg also had to consider the possibility that the reason nothing had been heard of Sherman's force since it had disappeared into the hills several days before was that it was on its way to relieve Burnside, as Longstreet still claimed. Bragg decided to risk everything on the hope of taking the initiative back away from Grant. On November 22, he gave orders for the divisions of Cleburne and Buckner, the latter now commanded by Bushrod Johnson, to pull out of line, march to nearby Chickamauga Station, and board the train for Knoxville.[25]

Pat Cleburne, commanding the two-division detachment, had his troops on the march at daybreak the next morning, and soon they were at the station, where trains came and went hour after hour, hauling off their loads of soldiers. At midmorning, however, the operation came to an abrupt halt. A dispatch had come from Bragg. Something, possibly movements sighted in the Union camps, had made the commander uneasy, and he directed that those troops that had not already boarded the trains stand by for possible recall. One brigade of Johnson's division and all of Cleburne's were still at the depot. There they waited until early afternoon, when another dispatch put them into vigorous motion. "We are heavily engaged," Bragg wrote. "Move up rapidly to these headquarters." Cleburne put the five brigades left at the station into a brisk march toward where the sound of firing was already rising beyond Missionary Ridge.[26]

CHAPTER NINE

Fix Bayonets and Go Ahead

By November 23, Sherman still was not ready, but having received information that Bragg might be withdrawing from his positions around Chattanooga, Grant decided some action was necessary, partially as a demonstration to keep Bragg's attention off the intended points of attack and partially to find out if Bragg really was retreating. The obvious place for such a demonstration was the Confederate center in front of Missionary Ridge since a move against either of Bragg's flanks at this point would draw Confederate attention to the sectors Grant wanted him to ignore. The obvious force to use in any such demonstration against the Confederate center was Thomas's Army of the Cumberland. So Grant issued orders for Thomas to advance a division or two and seize a knobby hundred-foot hill that stood almost alone in the plain between Chattanooga and Missionary Ridge. The hill, known locally as Orchard Knob, was part of the Confederates' advance line and would provide a handy vantage point and artillery position for any operations that circumstances might dictate.[1]

Thomas liked to do things first class or not at all, and for the movement against Orchard Knob he massed no less than four divisions, twenty-three thousand men, in parade-ground order out in front of the Union breastworks. Long lines, tight ranks, bright flags snapping in the November breeze all made a picture of war as the thousands of watching veterans had always imagined it before enlisting and never seen it since. So foreign did the panorama seem from the grim reality of combat that the watching Confederates thought it simply a grand review and were taken very much by surprise when Thomas's solid ranks kept on marching steadily toward their lines. A brief and by no means picture-book fight flared up around the knob itself, but the thin Confederate forces here were no match for the Army of the Cumberland's massed columns. Within less than half of a late autumn afternoon, Thomas had Orchard Knob and also had the information that Bragg's army was still present in force.[2]

The movements Grant had taken for the beginnings of a Confederate withdrawal were in fact those of Cleburne's and Buckner's divisions toward the railroad depot at Chickamauga Station, whence they were to entrain for transport to Longstreet in East Tennessee. If the attack on Orchard Knob had told Grant that this did not signal a general withdrawal by the Army of Tennessee, it also told Bragg a thing or two. Clearly Grant's attack plans were almost if not altogether ready. A day or two at most remained before the grand Union offensive at Chattanooga got under way. That in turn meant the failure of Bragg's daring gamble at scoring decisive success at Knoxville so as to change the strategic venue before Grant could marshal his potentially overwhelming strength and use it at Chattanooga. The basic plan might still have some chance of success, but only if Bragg could fight and win a defensive battle at Chattanooga first. That was something new for the Army of Tennessee. Bragg never voluntarily accepted battle at the time and place of the enemy's choosing, preferring to take the initiative by taking the offensive. Now, it seemed, he had no choice. The army's position around Chattanooga looked strong, but Bragg was realistic enough to believe that if Grant felt ready to attack, the Confederates would need all the manpower they could muster to deal with him. He sent orders recalling Cleburne's and Buckner's divisions. It was too late for most of Buckner's, but all of Cleburne's and one brigade of Buckner's division immediately started back toward Chattanooga. Since the threat on November 23 had seemed to come against his center or right-center in the Missionary Ridge sector, Bragg also gave orders that the Confederates for the first time should begin entrenching a line along the crest of Missionary Ridge as a possible defensive replacement or supplement for their present line of rifle pits at the base of the ridge. It was undeniably very late in the day to be starting such works, but supply problems would have made it very difficult to maintain large numbers of troops atop the ridge over long periods of time. It was more practical to move them up there when battle seemed to be in the offing.[3]

Across the Tennessee River and behind a chain of small hills that provided cover against prying Confederate eyes on Lookout Mountain and Missionary Ridge, the Army of the Tennessee's camps were stirring before midnight, November 23, and at 2:00 on the morning of the twenty-fourth, under Sherman's personal supervision, Brig. Gen. Giles A. Smith's brigade piled into the pontoon boats that had been secretly constructed some distance up a north bank inlet and shoved off into the Tennessee. They were to be the assault party that would secure Sherman a foothold on the left (i.e., Confederate) bank of the Tennessee River. Proceeding down the river as quietly as they could, rifles loaded but not capped so as to avoid a noisy mishap that would give them away, they approached their landing area on the south bank on either side of the mouth of Chickamauga Creek. It was about 2:30 when they splashed ashore, taking the Confederate pickets by surprise and capturing all but one of them. The oarsmen now rowed the pontoons back to the right bank—the boats were empty save for the Confederate prisoners and their guards—and began the laborious process of ferrying over the rest of the division. That, too, went off without a hitch, and the second of Sherman's divisions began to embark. By the time the sun rose, two full divisions, amounting to some eight thousand men, were entrenching their new beachhead on the left bank. With satisfaction, Sherman noted that the weather was gloomy and lowering, with a misting rain. The surrounding heights where the Confederates had their observation posts, particularly Lookout Mountain, were swathed in fog, making it much more difficult for the Confederates to learn exactly what he was up to.[4]

With the coming of daylight Baldy Smith arrived as well, in charge of engineering arrangements. Under his supervision and the still watchful eye of Sherman, the engineers took over the pontoons and began assembling a bridge. Sherman was impressed. "I have never beheld any work done so quietly [and] so well," he reported, "and I doubt if the history of war can show a bridge of that extent (viz., 1,350 feet) laid down so noiselessly and well in so short a time." He thought Smith's work was nothing short of genius.[5]

While the engineers worked and the troops entrenched on the far shore, the little steamboat *Dunbar* came chuffing up the river from Chattanooga to join the operation, ferrying Sherman's third division across the river during the course of the morning. The Confederate counterattack that Sherman and his men had half expected never materialized, and the morning's combat was confined to sparse picket firing and desultory exchanges of long-range artillery. Around noon, Howard arrived by way of the left bank, having moved directly north from Federal lines around Chattanooga. He brought along a brigade of his corps. Twenty minutes later the pontoon bridge was completed and Jefferson C. Davis's division of the Army of the Cumberland—on loan to Sherman for this operation—began to cross. Thus by early afternoon the landing on the left bank of the Tennessee had been transformed from a precarious foothold to a solid bridgehead held by a dozen brigades of infantry and as many batteries of artillery and connected to the other Union armies at Chattanooga both by the bridge and directly overland into Chattanooga along the left bank.[6]

All Sherman needed to do now was march over and seize the north end of Missionary Ridge, then move right along the crest of that height, rolling up Bragg's army as he went. Looking southwestward, Sherman could see the near end of the ridge about a mile and a half away across relatively flat, open, undulating ground, with nothing to impede his advance but a few hundred Confederate skirmishers and perhaps a marsh or two.[7]

At 1:00 P.M., the Federals stepped off and, with only light skirmishing, reached the nearest high ground and scrambled up the slope. On reaching the summit, however, Sherman's skirmishers found that instead of looking along the spine of a continuous ridge, they were gazing down into a deep, steep-sided ravine; the ridge proper was on the far side. Plunging through the ravine, they got astride the ridge and encountered a line of Rebel skirmishers coming their way. These they handily beat off, retaining their hold on the north end of Missionary Ridge.[8]

By this time it was 3:30 on a short, late autumn afternoon that had rarely been bright anyway, smothered as it was under a gray woolen blanket of clouds, another bank of which was just then rolling in over Lookout Mountain to the west, promising to make things even gloomier very shortly. With not much more than an hour of anything like daylight remaining at best, Sherman had to decide quickly what to do next. The day had been one of unbroken success. His men now held the northern end of Missionary Ridge and, he assumed, could sweep along it at will whenever they were ready, rolling up Bragg's army in the process. The short remains of a late November afternoon would not suffice for that task, and as Sherman saw it, the real danger now was that Bragg would launch a counterattack to throw the Federals off the ridge and save his position. Indeed, Giles Smith's brigade, skirting Chickamauga Creek on the far left of Sherman's line, had just had a brush with a Confederate formation of unknown strength on the opposite bank. Casualties had been few, though Smith had been one of them. The incident, and the confusion it generated, would naturally have fueled the seemingly logical conclusion that Bragg was bound to do something to counter Sherman's movement. Best, then, to use what little daylight remained to select and entrench a good position from which to fight off the expected onslaught.[9]

Bragg did not like the Federals' presence there, but he was in no position to take immediate major action against Sherman's lodgment and could have done little to prevent the Union general's advance. If Sherman could have known the situation in Confederate lines that afternoon—and how it would change before morning—he would never have issued his 3:30 P.M. halt order, clouds and darkness notwithstanding.[10]

Bragg had learned of Sherman's river crossing that morning and had ridden up to the north end of the ridge to have a look at it. He had been suspecting that Grant would try to cut off his communication with Longstreet, but this movement had other possible ramifications as well. Within striking distance of this newly landed Union force—by means of a movement around the north end of Missionary Ridge—were Bragg's railroad connections not only with Longstreet in East Tennessee but also with Atlanta to the south: his supply conduit, such as it was. That was too serious a threat to ignore, but Bragg had precious few troops available with which to counter it, having audaciously reduced his force to a minimum so as to maximize Longstreet's chances of decisive results at Knoxville. He decided to use two brigades to cover the threat to his railroad connections, one of Cleburne's now on its way back from Chickamauga Station pursuant to his recall orders of the day before and the other from Cheatham's division, then stationed near the other end of the Confederate line, in Chattanooga Valley, between Missionary Ridge and Lookout Mountain. It was the latter of these that brushed with Giles Smith's brigade and added to Sherman's confusion. With Cleburne's other three brigades, Bragg hoped to seize and hold the high ground at the north end of Missionary Ridge.[11]

The Irish general arrived none too soon. Having galloped ahead of his troops, Cleburne was surveying the position in company with an officer from Hardee's staff when a signalman brought them word that Sherman's troops were even then moving onto the ridge. Cleburne quickly brought up his lead brigade, three regiments of Texans under Brig. Gen. James A. Smith, and sent it charging along the ridge crest to try to dislodge the Yankees before they got too firm a grip. It was already too late, and Smith's advance was the feeble Confederate attack that was brushed aside by Sherman's skirmishers just before the advance halted on the afternoon of the twenty-fourth.

Theoretically, Sherman's position astride the ridge should have canceled out every advantage of the ridge for the defenders, but Missionary Ridge was a lot bigger and more rugged than the gentle swells of earth for which the theories were made. Its long, sloping sides were creased with deep ravines, and its crest undulated in dips and knolls. Cleburne quickly grasped the potential of the position. He pulled Smith's Texans out of their conventional line of rifle pits, facing down the ridge's long northwestern slope, and drew them several hundred yards farther back, wrapping their line around one of the many humps of the ridgeback in a sort of hilltop position, prepared for defense in three directions. The hilltop he chose was the highest knoll on that end of the ridge, Tunnel Hill, so called because the railroad there pierced the ridge in that manner. In the last fading light of the short November day, the former corporal in the British army who was now the Army of Tennessee's best division commander quickly and skillfully positioned his remaining brigades.[12]

Grant had meant Sherman's operation to be the main event of this first day of all-out offensive against Bragg, but most attention on both sides of the lines was instead turned toward what became one of the most dramatic events of the battle and the war.

High water in the Tennessee River had finally broken the pontoon bridge at Brown's Ferry before the last of Sherman's divisions, that of Brig. Gen. Peter J. Osterhaus, could follow the rest of Army of the Tennessee toward its position on the far left. Grant had hitherto resisted the urgings of both Thomas and Hooker that the latter be allowed to assault Lookout Mountain. Though an impressive pile of earth and rock, the mountain offered Grant relatively little militarily. Bragg's lines of supply and retreat were at the other end of his position, behind Tunnel Hill at the north end of Missionary Ridge. Taking Lookout Mountain would bring Grant no closer to bagging Bragg's army. Still, with Osterhaus temporarily stranded west of the mountain on the very eve of battle and thus added to Hooker's force there, the eastern general would have three divisions, and that was more than Grant cared to have sitting idle at such a time. Reluctantly he gave in and allowed that Hooker could attack the mountain. Perhaps it would draw attention away from Sherman's front, where Grant expected the truly decisive results to be produced.

Hooker was delighted. The broken pontoon bridge that had stranded Osterhaus's division west of Lookout had given him a chance to redeem the reputation tarnished six months earlier at Chancellorsville. In taking the mountain, he would perform a feat of arms that would be legendary because it was generally considered impossible. His force, oddly enough, consisted of a division of each of the three Union armies present at Chattanooga. Besides Osterhaus's command from the Army of the Tennessee, Hooker had Brig. Gen. Charles Cruft's division of the Army of the Cumberland and Geary's of his own Army of the Potomac contingent. One of Geary's soldiers recalled that the men were called into line of battle without breakfast that morning, and the announcement of what Hooker wanted them to do took their appetites away. "What!" gasped one of the veteran soldiers, "Does the General expect us to fly?"[13]

The prospect did indeed appear daunting. The Confederate lines on Lookout curved around the shoulders of the mountain, about halfway up between the river and the rocky summit, where the slope moderated enough to permit an occasional house and even a farm or two whose fantastic views compensated for the stony soil. That was the proper location for the defenses, rather than on the impressive crest of the mountain, since the steep upper slopes would render defenders there unable to fire on attackers scaling the mountainsides. The Confederate lines, bolstered by log breastworks, curved from the east slope of the mountain, around the point or nose of the mountain on the north end and several hundred yards down the west side. They faced downhill, and however natural that orientation may have seemed, it was just the feature of which Hooker planned to take advantage.

He sent Osterhaus straight ahead, west to east, against the Confederate picket lines along the east bank of Lookout Creek. Geary he sent marching southward, up the valley. After a couple of miles the column swung eastward, crossed the creek, and swung still further around and up the slope until the entire division faced northward along the side of the mountain. The men on the far right flank found themselves advancing along the base of the vertical rock face—the palisades—that led to the summit, and from there the line ran downhill until the left flank nearly touched the banks of Lookout Creek. In this fashion, Hooker's men moved along the mountainside, scrambling over and around boulders, tree trunks, and deadfalls until they ran right into the flank of the Confederate line. Many of the Rebels, focused on the approach of Osterhaus's division, were not aware of Geary's presence until the bluecoats had advanced to point-blank range. Many became prisoners; others fought as best they could and then fled desperately along the rugged mountainside. Now and then a Confederate officer would manage to get a few companies or a regiment swung back to face Geary's men head-on, but each time the Federals out on Geary's right, along the base of the palisades, came crashing down on the Confederates' exposed uphill flank and the position collapsed like those before. The combat became a running fight, along the west slope of the mountain and then around the curving north slope. As the Rebels fled Geary's flank attack, Osterhaus advanced and moved in on Geary's left as the line, now a two-division front, swung around the point of the mountain.

On the northern end of Lookout Mountain the shoulder broadened into a bench where a man named Cravens had built a house and cultivated a small farm. There the Rebels rallied for a major stand. By this time one entire Confederate brigade had been wrecked and another was in bad shape. Few additional reserves were available on this end of Bragg's long line, and division commander John K. Jackson was, at least according to one of his subordinates, unduly slow in bringing up what was available. The Yankees' fighting blood was up. They had for some hours now been driving their foes out of a position many had believed impregnable, and they were beginning to feel a sense of invincibility that, other things being equal, was almost a self-fulfilling prophecy. For Geary's men, members of one of the hard-luck corps of the hard-luck Army of the Potomac, it was a new sensation, and by all accounts they seemed to revel in it, throwing themselves at the Confederate lines with reckless abandon. For Osterhaus's Army of the Tennessee troops, such confidence had become a matter of course. Federal aggressiveness, numbers, and powerful artillery support from the batteries on Moccasin Bend combined with Confederate exhaustion to send the Cravens house line the way of the smaller and shorter-lived stands before it. Around the east shoulder of the mountain and back along the east side swept Hooker's elated bluecoats, pivoting on the right flank at the base of the palisades while the downslope brigades swept up hundreds of prisoners.

Then, as if on cue, the low-hanging clouds that had kept the mountain socked in with fog all day suddenly lifted, revealing a great natural amphitheater—the mountain, the plain and river below, the town of Chattanooga, and on the far side, Missionary Ridge, stretching out like a long, straight fold of the earth toward far-off Tunnel Hill, which Sherman's men were even then approaching. Down in Chattanooga and in the Army of the Cumberland's lines around it, ears had been cocked and eyes occasionally turned toward the mountain for most of the day, as soldiers listened to the rattle and crash of their comrades' battle and watched the flickering line of flashes pierce the fog as the combat rounded the point of the mountain. As the clouds moved aside and for the first time that day the sun broke through to light up the mountainside, the watchers below were awestruck by the sight of a battle spread out before them as if on canvas. The fleeing Confederates and the swarming ranks of blue-uniformed soldiers in pursuit, visible through the leafless treetops, brought resounding cheers from the men of the Army of the Cumberland.[14]

About four hundred yards beyond the Cravens house, well onto the mountain's eastern flank, the Confederates had erected a cross-slope line of breastworks, and there, with the aid of a fresh brigade just coming up to join the defense, they were able to halt the Union advance. A few companies of Rebels managed to scramble up to the base of the palisades themselves, countering the Federals there. Some of Hooker's units had by this time expended their ammunition, and most were understandably exhausted, if nevertheless highly elated. Another bank of clouds had quickly lowered the curtain that the sunburst had briefly raised for the spectators in Chattanooga and plunged the slopes into such a murky darkness as to make further offensive operations impractical. When Palmer, commanding the neighboring XIV Corps in the valley below, sent to find out if he needed assistance, Hooker replied, "Can hold the line I am now on; can't advance. Some of my troops out of ammunition; can't replenish." Hooker was now on the Chattanooga side of the mountain, however, so getting more of whatever he needed was no longer the problem it might have been. Within a couple of hours of the time darkness had brought a close to the Lookout Mountain fighting, Hooker was reinforced by a brigade of the XIV Corps and arrangements were under way for direct resupply via Chattanooga.[15]

For the Confederates the battle had been a sorry affair. When Bragg had sent Hardee over to the right the evening before, Stevenson had succeeded to the overall command of the Lookout Mountain defenses, including Jackson's division. Stevenson was unfamiliar with the deployments and the lay of the land on the slopes of Lookout, and since he took over command after nightfall on the twenty-third, he had no chance to inspect the sector by daylight before the battle was joined. The Confederate troops that did most of the fighting belonged to Jackson's division. His performance that day was criticized by several of his subordinates, and the controversy nearly led to several duels. In the end, the matter was dropped. From the evidence that remains, Jackson's performance that day appears to have been nothing special but probably about as good as could be expected under the circumstances. Aside from command issues, the shift of Walker's division from Chattanooga Valley up to the north-central segment of Missionary Ridge the evening before had removed a potential source of ready reinforcements for the Rebels fighting on the mountain.[16]

Bragg placed a relatively low estimate on the importance of Lookout Mountain. He was displeased at the poor showing the Confederates had made there, but he had no inclination to up the ante in the contest to hold the height. Indeed, ever since coming to the realization that he was going to have to fight on the defensive at Chattanooga, Bragg had been distinctly unwilling to wager very much of his scant available force on the impressive but now not particularly useful mountain. Since the cracker line had been opened a month before, Lookout had been of no use in denying the Federals their hardtack nor was it necessary in order to secure Bragg's own. The summit was of some use as a signal and observation point—when the weather was clear—but the artillery posted there had come to have little more than nuisance value against the Union forces around Chattanooga. Such thin benefits came at a high price when they required Bragg to keep his line stretched considerably farther than his now reduced manpower warranted. That the mountain's sheer bulk—particularly its prodigious length—made it, ironically, an asset of questionable value as a defensive bulwark had been manifestly demonstrated by 2:30 P.M. on the twenty-fourth, when Bragg dispatched orders for his troops to disengage from Hooker's up on the east slopes of the mountain, evacuate Chattanooga Valley, and withdraw all Confederate forces back to Missionary Ridge. If, as is not unlikely, he regretted not having given that order twenty-four hours earlier, his assessment would probably have been correct.[17]

That evening Grant wired news of the day's success to Washington. In response came dispatches from both Lincoln and Halleck, received by Grant the next morning, congratulating him but expressing concern for the condition of Burnside and the Army of the Ohio, besieged in Knoxville. "Remember Burnside" was all the president added. Halleck was more explicit. He feared "that any further delay may prove fatal" and concluded with the pointed assurance, "I know that you will do all in your power to relieve him." Grant could be assured that Washington would brook no dawdling about dispensing with Bragg and going to the aid of Burnside.[18]

Grant was not, in any case, a man to dawdle. He knew what he wanted to happen the next day, and by midnight, once things had quieted down around headquarters, he began writing out his orders to make those things happen. Hooker was to advance at dawn, making sure Lookout Mountain was clear of Rebels, then cross Chattanooga Creek and head toward Rossville Gap in Missionary Ridge, on the far left of Bragg's line. Once there, he would get astride the ridge and proceed along it rolling up the Confederate line there the way he had on Lookout Mountain the day before. Thomas would stand by and hold his army in readiness to launch an attack on the Confederate center and "carry the rifle-pits and ridge directly in front of them," simultaneously and in cooperation with the other Union attacks. Sherman would make the main Union effort, advancing from the ridge-top position he had gained the day before to crush Bragg's army. Grant sent him orders to begin at daybreak.[19]

All of that was, of course, contingent on Bragg's still being there when day broke, and Grant and his fellow officers were not at all sure he would be. Some of them were inclined to think that Bragg would leave at once while he still had the opportunity to avoid a further drubbing. Nor were Union officers the only ones who thought so. Cleburne, for one, tended to doubt that the Army of Tennessee would stay and risk another day's battle. In that, however, both he and those of like opinion across the lines were mistaken. At nine o'clock that evening, Bragg and his corps commanders, now just Hardee and Breckinridge, met in council. Hardee was for retreating, fearing that the rising waters of Chickamauga Creek would leave the army hopelessly cut off if anything should happen to the bridges. Better to retreat to the other side of the creek at once. Bragg disagreed. While their present position might have distinct drawbacks, he thought that trying to get out now might be more dangerous than staying and fighting. Breckinridge agreed and went further. He was eager to fight and opined that if the Army of Tennessee could not beat the Yankees in the position they now held, they probably could never beat them. Bragg may have had his doubts about the soundness of Breckinridge's judgment—he later claimed that the Kentuckian was just then halfway through a four-day drunk—but his own opinion was against retreating and he agreed with Breckinridge's high opinion of towering six-hundred-foot-high Missionary Ridge as an all-but-impregnable defensive position. Besides, to retreat now would be to abandon all hope of reaping any substantial gain from the entire late summer and fall campaign, a campaign from which the Confederacy desperately needed to profit. Judging too from reaction in the press and public on other occasions when Bragg had retreated on the advice of his generals, it would probably be the end of his career as well—there might be limits even to Jefferson Davis's stubborn support. The final decision was ultimately obvious for Bragg, whichever of these considerations weighed heaviest with him. The Army of Tennessee would stay and fight. Breckinridge, at least, was enthusiastic about the decision. To a subordinate officer he quipped grimly that night, "I never felt more like fighting than when I saw those people shelling my troops off of Lookout today, and I mean to get even with them." It seemed probable he would get the chance at least to try.

In preparation for the next day's fighting, then, the Confederate troops that were even then pulling out of Chattanooga Valley and up onto Missionary Ridge would continue along the crest of the ridge all the way up to the north end, almost to Cleburne's position, and there would be added to Hardee's command. Breckinridge with three divisions would defend about two-thirds of the army's front, all of it now on Missionary Ridge. With just over

half his force invested in holding the other third of his front, Hardee's sector, Bragg showed a clear perception of where Grant was preparing to strike
his main blow as well as an awareness of where the enemy could do him the
most damage: the north end of Missionary Ridge was the closest to his supply lines.[20]

The morning of November 25 dawned clear, bright, and cold. By first
light, enterprising Federals on Lookout made the scramble to the top of the
palisades and unfurled the Stars and Stripes from the point of the mountain,
drawing thunderous cheers from the Army of the Cumberland around Chattanooga and their own comrades on the slopes below. For the 140,000 men of
the four armies encamped in Chattanooga and on the heights around, this
would be the decisive day. For many, it would be the last day. Much had
been started the previous two days; the three Union armies had taken up
their vantage points of attack, and few in the assembled hosts could have
doubted that matters would soon be decided one way or another.

Having ascertained, as per his orders from Grant, that the Rebels had, as
expected, evacuated Lookout Mountain, Hooker moved his men out from
their positions on Lookout Mountain around 10:00 A.M., November 25, his
column swinging briskly down the road into the Chattanooga Valley and toward their Rossville Gap objective beyond. Thomas's men, as ordered,
stayed where they were.[21]

On Sherman's front, however, nothing seemed to be that simple. He was
uncertain of the enemy's position after Cleburne's withdrawal of the evening
before so he started the day by pushing skirmishers out in front to find out
where the Rebels were. The skirmish firing began at daylight. The woods
soon resounded to a more or less continuous rattle of musketry while clouds
of sulfurous white powder smoke drifted up through the leafless trees. Finally, around 10:30, Sherman launched his assault, right along the spine of
the ridge as planned. Only a single brigade went forward—the ridge top was
hardly wide enough even for it—and quickly ran into trouble. Brig. Gen.
John M. Corse's Illinoisans, Iowans, Michiganders, and Ohioans drove to
within feet of the Confederate breastworks and at places even got to close
quarters and engaged in hand-to-hand combat with the defenders. Yet they
could not dislodge the Southerners. Corse fell wounded, and his men pulled
back a few yards to the lower section of the crest.

Cleburne was in fine form today, deftly shifting troops around his hilltop
position and skillfully judging when and where to launch limited counterattacks—often leading them himself. In the strong position they occupied,
only very limited numbers of Federals could come at them at one time. Still

the bluecoats came back again and again, "like they were going to walk right over us," recalled one of the defenders. Fighting raged around the guns of a Confederate battery, but though all its officers were shot down and command devolved on a corporal, the guns remained in Confederate hands. One of the defenders counted six separate charges, and then the stubborn mid-westerners hung on among the dried leaves, rocks, and tree trunks of the sloping crest line and the steeper side slopes and began picking off any Confederate who showed himself on the crest. It was about noon now, and the Texas and Arkansas troops of Cleburne's division still had their hilltop.

Frustrated by the complicated terrain that seemed to offer no avenue of attack, Sherman rode forward to the Union-held end of the ridge to study the situation. As he sat his horse and pensively tugged at his red beard, the nearby soldiers, hugging the ground for shelter from Rebel rifle and artillery fire, noticed his presence. "This is no place for you, General," blurted one of them. "The enemy's batteries sweep this ground with canister." It was indeed an advanced position for an army commander, but Sherman stayed until he had seen all he felt there was to see from this vantage point before riding off unscathed.

After a lull of an hour or so, Sherman sent his men forward again, this time hitting the Tunnel Hill position from the northwest, the forward slope of the ridge. His personal reconnaissance may have convinced him that the ridgeback was too difficult. To be sure, it was no picnic, but the west face, toward which he now directed his main attacks, proved little better. Throughout the afternoon, additional brigades of Sherman's midwesterners, joined by Pennsylvanians from Howard's XI Corps, charged repeatedly up the steep slopes, only to be beaten back by Cleburne's skillful defense, as thousands watched and listened in Chattanooga. Within his compact position on Tunnel Hill, the Confederate general could shift units to reinforce threatened points much more rapidly than the Federals could position themselves for new attacks, struggling over rough terrain and going the long way around the base of the hill. Again Cleburne made use of local counterattacks, his men dashing downhill onto the Federals to roll back threatening advances and shift momentum when necessary. Fighting surged back and forth around a group of farm buildings near the mouth of the tunnel until one of the Confederate sorties succeeded in setting fire to them. In midafternoon a fierce series of Confederate charges finally succeeded in dislodging Union troops who had for an hour or more been clinging tenaciously to the slopes.

With superior grasp of the terrain, careful planning, a commanding position, and a good deal of up-front leadership, Cleburne had bested Sherman, at least for this day. Probably the only way Sherman could have overcome Cleburne's defense would have been to pull clear of the tangle of ravines that chopped up the terrain at the foot of the ridge, draw back onto clear ground, and form his numerically superior forces for a concerted simultaneous straight-on attack. Even then the skillful Cleburne might have stopped him, and in any case, the efficacy of such a system of attack against Missionary Ridge was only just about to be discovered, in another sector and by accident. As for Tunnel Hill, Grant and those watching with him from his new command post on Orchard Knob could have had no doubt, as they watched Sherman's men tumbling, scrambling, and sliding back down the hillside, that Cleburne's Confederates were not going to be dislodged from that ridge today by any number of troops the government of the United States might care to throw at them.[22]

So far this was shaping up to be an extremely frustrating day for the Union commander. With the authorities in Washington breathing down his neck to do something about Burnside's situation by finishing things quickly in Chattanooga, he had been spending the day watching his plans for offensive action miscarry one after the other. Sherman's attack had gone nowhere. Then there was Hooker. At 12:30 that afternoon his lead division, Osterhaus's, had reached Chattanooga Creek, three-fourths of the way to Rossville Gap. There the lead regiment, the Twenty-seventh Missouri, discovered that the Rebels had burned the bridge during their retreat the night before. This close to its mouth on the Tennessee River and in the rainy autumn season, the creek presented a significant obstacle. In short, Hooker was stuck. Osterhaus set his seventy-man pioneer detachment to work rebuilding the bridge, while the resourceful Missourians rigged up a precarious one-man-at-a-time footbridge and began crossing. Hooker determined to push all his infantry across first and leave the guns and wagons for later, but even at that rate his column did not move forward to cover the last mile of the march to Rossville Gap until 3:30, after a three-hour delay.[23]

On Orchard Knob, Grant pondered the situation and what to do about it. He could see troops marching northward along the crest of Missionary Ridge and thought these represented heavy Confederate reinforcements against Sherman. In fact, they were only Jackson's and Stevenson's divisions, shifting around from their previous day's positions on Lookout Mountain. Cleburne used not more than a brigade or so of these troops and only for skirmishing. He had no need for more. Not knowing this, of course, Grant sent Sherman another division of the Army of the Cumberland, but Sherman sent it back, explaining that he already had more troops than he knew how to employ to any advantage in the strange broken terrain at the end of the ridge. Yet the fighting there seemed to make no dent in the Confederate position, and still nothing was heard from Hooker, while only a few hours of daylight remained.

In this predicament, Grant began to contemplate proceeding to the next phase of his attack anyway, sending the Army of the Cumberland straight ahead to seize the line of Confederate rifle pits at the base of Missionary Ridge and then, perhaps after pausing to regroup, charging on to the top of the ridge. The original idea of Grant's order to Thomas the night before—"carry the rifle-pits and ridge directly in front of them"—had obviously been that the assault would be "simultaneous" with Sherman's triumphant advance along the crest of the ridge, but that plainly was not working out. It was time to think of something else. Grant approached Thomas, who was standing on Orchard Knob a dozen or so yards off, surveying Missionary Ridge through field glasses. Relations between Grant and Thomas were not good. Thomas envied Grant's position and resented being subordinate to him. He also seemed incapable of grasping the concept of Grant's aggressive style of warfare, and it scared him. Grant, in his personal dealings with Thomas, tried his best to avoid irritating the Virginian, treating him with kid gloves. So it was that when Grant decided to see if the Army of the Cumberland could make some contribution to the battle, he sidled up rather diffidently and in a mild tone of voice asked what Thomas thought about the matter. "Don't you think it's about time to order your troops to advance against the enemy's first line of rifle pits?" The staff officers who stood nearby did not hear what, if anything, Thomas said in response, but they did notice that he never once lowered his field glasses from scanning the ridge. Pretty much everyone on the hilltop knew that Thomas was adamantly opposed to any advance by his troops until Bragg's army was crumbling with both its flanks stove in. Rebuffed by Thomas's rudeness, Grant quietly walked back over to his side of the hilltop and went back to thinking.[24]

Grant was in some ways a very pragmatic man. He would take success whatever way he could get it. He had figured Sherman's attack for his best chance, but when that failed to pan out, Grant was willing to improvise and seek success in other ways. Here was perhaps his greatest strength as a general and his greatest difference from the likes of Rosecrans and Thomas—his ability to improvise, to find the best of several imperfect solutions, to look at a problem in a new light and conceive of other ways to get the job done. He could be flexible about means without losing his bulldog grip on the end he meant to achieve. Such superiority of mind appeared most clearly in times of stress and confusion, when carefully prearranged plans went to pieces—that is, in war. A contemporary European general would later point out that no plan survives contact with the enemy. Grant's style of war was one of constant contact with the enemy, and it was precisely there that he was at his best.[25]

And so Grant thought and came to the conclusion that Bragg's center must be weak and that Thomas must strike it. If it broke, well; if not, perhaps it would divert Bragg's strength and soften things up for Sherman. Grant was not particular; he would take it either way. Meanwhile, Gordon Granger, now commanding the Army of the Cumberland's IV Corps, was irritating Grant and most of the others on the knob by personally directing the fire of one of the nearby batteries currently hotly engaged with Confederate guns on the ridge. In all likelihood, Granger was nervous and sought relief by pretending to be the captain of an artillery battery. Still, that was not his job, and watching him do it made other people nervous. Grant wished he would stop but said nothing because Granger was Thomas's subordinate. Finally, at 3:00 P.M., about half an hour after having approached Thomas the first time, Grant decided it was time to start being department commander whether that hurt Thomas's feelings or not.

In a voice loud enough for everyone on the hilltop to hear above the ongoing artillery firing—and that left no doubt that he was giving an order— Grant barked, "General Thomas, order Granger to turn that battery over to its proper commander and take command of his own corps. And now order your troops to advance and take the enemy's first line of rifle pits." Grant apparently meant that it was time for Thomas to initiate compliance with Grant's order of the previous evening regarding that day's operations: Thomas's attack would be "simultaneous" and "in co-operation" with Sherman's, and it would consist of "carry[ing] the rifle pits and ridge directly in front." The rifle pits, at the base of the ridge, naturally came first, but there was no point in stopping there any longer than necessary for the troops to catch their breath and reform their ranks. Grant probably intended this as an order to go all the way to the top.[26]

Thomas did not want to advance at all, but orders were orders, and he went off to give the necessary directions. More time passed, and nothing happened. Thomas returned. Still nothing happened. When Grant turned from watching the front to find Thomas and learn about the delay, he was surprised to see Thomas J. Wood, whose division was supposed to be part of the attack, standing near Thomas. Wood and Grant were old West Point acquaintances and on friendly terms, so Grant asked Wood why his division was not on the move. Wood replied that he had received no orders. Grant turned to Thomas for an explanation, and he averred that he had given the necessary orders to Granger. And where was Granger? Grant looked around and saw that the IV Corps commander had once again taken over a nearby battery and was indulging his penchant for playing artillerist. Grant approached him and asked why he did not have his troops in motion. Because, Granger explained, he had no orders. Two things, at least, were clear: first, somebody was lying, and second, between Grant and his troops at Chattanooga there was at least one too many layers of command. At the moment, Grant had no time for such considerations. He wanted Granger's troops to advance—now.

"If you will leave that battery to its captain," he growled at Granger, "and take command of your corps, it will be better for all of us."

That seemed to do the trick, and Granger hurried off to his command. Very quickly thereafter the troops moved out. It was 3:40 P.M. Grant and the others on Orchard Knob could not see them at first because of intervening trees, but the start of the charge could be perceived by the roar of cheers from the Cumberlanders as they surged out over their own fortifications and onto the mile-wide cleared plain that separated them from the line of Confederate rifle pits at the base of the ridge.[27]

Once again, as two days earlier when it had taken Orchard Knob, the Army of the Cumberland put on a grand show. Ranged in neat ranks, parade-ground style, some 23,000 men in four divisions strode forward under waving flags. From the crest of Missionary Ridge thousands of Confederates watched in awe at the storybook panoply of war spread out before them. This was the sort of war they had dreamed of when they enlisted but had not seen in more than two years of death and squalor. Now their enemy was making it real. The very solidity of the Union formation and the steadiness in the rhythmic alternating tread of 46,000 boots across the cotton stubble made the blue-clad line seem unstoppable.

Those who would first have the duty of trying to stop the Cumberlanders were the approximately nine thousand Confederates deployed in the rifle pits at the bottom of the ridge. They should not have been there. For some reason, when Bragg had ordered the construction of a line of fortifications along the crest after the loss of Orchard Knob, commanders in some sectors of the Confederate front specified that half their troops be kept in the rifle pits at the base and the other half moved back to the ridge. In other sectors the plan was modified to provide for yet another line of defense, halfway up the ridge. The idea cropped up occasionally in the thinking of one or another Civil War general of deploying some portion of his troops out in front of the main line of resistance to break up incoming attacks. Much later, near the end of World War I, the basic idea would be developed properly into the concept of defense in depth. The Confederate arrangement at Chattanooga was not, however, the proper development of it, and no one else during the Civil War seemed to use the idea correctly either. At its worst, as here at Chattanooga, the system meant that neither line of troops was strong enough to stop the enemy, neither could truly support the other, and the troops in the second position were prevented from firing on the advancing enemy because their fleeing comrades from the first set of defenses were in their line of fire.[28]

Now as the Army of the Cumberland marched across the plain, the men in the rifle pits blazed away, supported at least by the more than fifty pieces of artillery along the crest. Men began to fall in the blue ranks, but the others closed the gaps and came on. As the advancing line bore down irresistibly upon them, most of the Rebels in the rifle pits fled back up the ridge. Indeed, Breckinridge had given some of them orders to fire a single volley before retiring. Others were ignorant of any such orders and suffered a serious shock to their morale when neighboring regiments appeared to stampede at almost the first fire. Those who tried to stick it out in the line at the base of the ridge were overrun.

Now it was the Federals' turn to become confused about their orders. In Baird's and Johnson's divisions of Palmer's XIV Corps, everyone seemed to be clear that the order was to go to the top of the ridge, and that was what the XIV Corps units set out to do as soon as they caught their breath in the rifle pits. In Granger's IV Corps, however, matters were different, perhaps because Granger had missed something while playing artillerist. At any rate, most IV Corps officers either thought the orders called for them to halt in the rifle pits or had no idea what the objective of their charge was to be.[29]

One of the latter was Phil Sheridan, a feisty customer who did not need any particular objective for fighting. Still, this being the military and all, it would probably be just as well to have such a thing, and so as the troops were forming up for the attack he sent a staff officer to find Granger and get the information. Before the officer could return, the signal for the charge came, and Sheridan led his division off not knowing where he was supposed to stop. Wood, Granger's other division commander, seemed convinced that they were to halt at the rifle pits. Such an order would have made absolutely no sense, of course, since the rifle pits were right under the guns of the Confederates on the crest and would offer no protection against them, but then Wood had experience carrying out nonsensical orders. His men seem to have had more sense; those of his second line urged him to allow them to continue, and he readily consented. The first line had already gone on. Both Wood and Granger later insisted in their reports that the troops went up the ridge without orders. This may have been true in some cases, but far more often it was alert—or misinformed—regimental or brigade officers who ordered the men on up. In some outfits the belief was simply that they were to conform to the movements of neighboring units; when the neighbors went up, so did they. In Sheridan's division the situation was especially frustrating. Many of his men had made it nearly halfway to the top when Sheridan's staff officer returned with word from Granger that everyone was to stop at the rifle pits. Dutifully, one of Sheridan's brigadiers recalled his troops, who struggled down the hill under fire, taking casualties, and then huddled in the rifle pits under fire, taking more casualties. Finally, a message arrived from Granger that if Sheridan thought he could take the ridge top he should go ahead and try. That was all the invitation the Irishman needed. Back up the hill went his panting troops, still under fire and, of course, taking still more casualties. One way and another, on somebody's orders or no one's at all, the various units of the four assaulting divisions all began their climb up the six-hundred-foot slope of Missionary Ridge.[30]

By all odds, it seemed, they ought to have been slaughtered. Some of their officers thought that was just what would happen to them. For a strange combination of reasons, it did not. One reason was the shape of the ridge itself. The folds and creases of the hillside often provided sheltered avenues of approach for at least part of the way up. The very steepness of the slope worked for the Federals by frequently providing "dead ground," sheltered from Rebel fire, where attackers could rest and catch their breath before making another rush, and for most areas of the face of the ridge, the Cumberlanders enjoyed substantial immunity from artillery fire because the Rebel cannoneers could not depress the muzzles of their guns adequately. Confederate riflemen trying to get shots at the Union soldiers who hugged the steep hillside often had to rise up well above their own parapets, exposing themselves as silhouetted targets.

Some of the Confederate disadvantages were self-inflicted, the result of poor planning by Confederate officers. The most obvious of these was the division of troops between upper and lower defensive lines. In some places of the ridge, fleeing Rebels from the first line of rifle pits were as little as fifty yards in front of their Union pursuers, effectively blocking their comrades' fire. Even when the defenders of the lower line arrived with a bit more of a lead, they were usually no help in defending the ridge-top line. Sprinting up a six-hundred-foot slope under the influence of a great deal of adrenaline left most of them gasping and retching on the ground. Another self-inflicted Confederate disadvantage was the specific placement of the upper defensive line. It ran along the geographical crest of the ridge—the highest point— rather than the military crest—the highest point from which all points on the ridge below are visible, usually some distance down the front slope. The most direct result of that error was to provide an especially ample zone of dead ground just below the crest, where Federals could rest within yards of Confederate lines and gather their strength and numbers for the final rush. While Cleburne skillfully made the terrain work for him at Tunnel Hill, Confederate dispositions along the central and southern portions of Missionary Ridge allowed the terrain to work for the attackers. The difference probably indicates that the specific tactical defensive arrangements originated below the level of army headquarters. Probably they had a good deal to do with the difference between the highly trained professional Hardee and the Army of Tennessee's other corps commander, the rank amateur Breckinridge. Ultimately, the responsibility still falls on Bragg, of course. Though it is impossible for a commanding general to see personally to every minute disposition of his troops, he remains responsible for them nevertheless. In the final analysis the strength of the seemingly impregnable Missionary Ridge position turned out to be mostly a bluff.[31]

None of that meant, however, that the attackers' lot would be easy or their success guaranteed. They enjoyed a numerical superiority of not quite two to one, not counting the Confederates in the first line—no overwhelming margin in Civil War attacks—and they were, after all, climbing a steep ridge to come at the enemy, whatever factors might have made that task less nearly impossible than it at first seemed. Color-bearers went down by the dozen, sometimes five or six in a single regiment. Indeed, casualties ran about 20 percent in the assaulting divisions. Getting up the ridge required intense courage and motivation and perhaps a bit of savvy as well. Tactical formations were abandoned as the Cumberlanders made use of every available bit of cover, spreading out and moving fast over exposed ground and crowding into sheltered ravines that led them steadily upward. A watching officer on Orchard Knob thought their constantly shifting alignment put him in mind of a large flock of migrating birds, as they wheeled and shifted and grouped first one way and then another. Often regiments advanced in a rough V formation, the colors at the apex along with the leaders and the strongest men and the flanks trailing back on either side.

Laboring up the slope near the center of the ridge was the brigade of August Willich, Cincinnati's "Red" newspaper editor and erstwhile Prussian army officer. Today he could only work his way along behind his men at the best pace his lungs and legs would afford. The men of his brigade, veterans who had driven the Rebels at Liberty Gap in the Tullahoma campaign and all the way into the Winfrey field on the first day at Chickamauga, had made up their minds to take that ridge. Beside them struggled the men of Hazen's brigade, which since the reorganization also included the regiments that Hans Heg had led across the La Fayette Road and into the Viniard field fighting on the first day at Chickamauga. They had also been the first brigade to try to plug the infamous gap on the second day and had been overrun by Longstreet's rampant Confederates. Now they toiled upward, bent on evening the score. Like Willich, the hard-driving Hazen had all he could do to keep up with his men. Just under the crest, men of both brigades, much intermingled, paused out of sight of the defenders, fixed bayonets, and then charged over the top. For a few minutes chaos broke loose, with point-blank firing and hand-to-hand fighting among the guns—artillerists swinging ramrods and handspikes against bayonets and clubbed rifles. Then it was over and the Rebels were fleeing down the back slope—those who did not surrender—leaving behind whole batteries of guns. Willich's and Hazen's men had scored one of the first breakthroughs along the ridge.

Who was the very first to break the Confederate line can never be known. Indeed, it seems to have broken simultaneously in at least half a dozen places and practically everywhere else not too long after that. The stories were much the same. Up toward the northern end of the attacking formation, in the XIV Corps sector, Van Derveer's brigade, the same that had rolled back the Rebel breakthrough in the Kelly field and then helped hold Horseshoe Ridge at Chickamauga, worked its way up to the base of a steep spur on which a Confederate battery was posted. The Second Minnesota led the bayonet charge this time, piling into the Confederate redoubt before the Southerners fairly realized they were being attacked. Fierce hand-to-hand fighting lasted only a few minutes, and the brigade took most of the batteries' guns. Turchin's brigade, charging next on the right, got the others. From there the Confederate line unraveled rapidly all the way up to within a mile of Cleburne's Tunnel Hill position, and Hardee had a horse shot out from under him as he desperately tried to cobble together a line that could prevent the collapse of that whole end of the army.

In the south-central portion of the ridge, the Confederates had gotten off to a better start. The sector in which Bragg's headquarters were located was held by Bate's division, and it appeared that Bate's men had hurled back the Federal attackers on their front. In fact, the Federals here belonged to Sheridan's division and were victims of the mixed-up orders that had called them back from nearly halfway up the ridge. Bragg was riding along Bate's line congratulating the men when he got the news that the line further right had gone to pieces. He had no sooner directed Bate to detach a brigade and restore the situation when it appeared that the left had disintegrated as well and the Federals—Sheridan's men, of course—were coming back up the hill at the front of Bate's line. After that it did not much matter which threat finally got the division, and no one could have said for sure anyway. Things just generally went to ruin in all directions at the same time.

Bragg did his best, riding a large horse and holding aloft the flag of the Third Florida in the midst of the disintegrating position. A mounted staff officer was shot down at his side, but, oblivious to danger, Bragg galloped one way and the other along the line imploring the men to rally. "I am here," he cried. "Stop, don't disgrace yourselves, fight for your country!" It was no use. The final disadvantage under which the men of the Army of Tennessee suffered was their own abysmal morale. A long train of failures and perceived failures, bickering and insubordination among the officers, and too many days on short rations had so sapped their confidence in their commander that even his appearance in their midst at the crisis of battle was insufficient to swing the moral momentum in their direction. Indeed, they sometimes responded with open ridicule. When Bragg rushed into a collapsing formation shouting, "Here's your commander," one of his men answered with the stock punch line of Civil War soldiers, "Here's your mule," before turning to flee down the back slope of the ridge.

Sheridan's exultant troops fought their way over the crest as had their comrades on either flank. The fiery Sheridan urged them on vigorously. Recognizing the Seventy-third Illinois, longtime members of his division, he called out, "I know you, fix bayonets and go ahead." Over in the Twenty-fourth Wisconsin, which had stood by its gallant and lamented brigadier William Lytle defending a nameless hilltop above the Dyer field at Chickamauga two months before, the regimental adjutant, eighteen-year-old Lieutenant Arthur MacArthur seized the flag, shouted, "On Wisconsin," and led his regiment over the top. A bit further down the ridge, men of Harker's brigade, defenders of Snodgrass Hill, overran a Confederate battery, and little Charley Harker was so exultant that he jumped astride the barrel of one of the guns, straddling it like a horse and flourishing his sword. He got off quickly enough though; the gun had been in action and was still red hot.

Examples of Confederate courage abounded as well, though to no avail. Around the fallen colors of the Twenty-fourth Tennessee Regiment lay the bodies of five of the color guard who fought to the last in its defense. Rebel artillerists were especially conspicuous in standing by their guns, often until all hope of escape was past and they fell or were captured when their positions were overrun.

Still further south on the ridge things were perhaps worst of all for the Southerners. Thomas's Federals pursuing southward along the crest of the ridge met up around nightfall with Hooker's men pressing north from Rossville Gap, where they had finally succeeded in rolling up the Confederate flank just as Grant had hoped. They had already demolished one Confederate division and were after more. The two converging Union forces made a nice haul of prisoners between them.

The sun had set while the Cumberlanders were toiling up the ridge, and the subsequent Confederate debacle had been played out in the gloaming. The onset of night, coupled with Federal exhaustion and disorganization—most of the units had gotten badly mixed up and intermingled in the various charges, climbs, and dashes after escaping artillery pieces—finally set a limit to the extent of Bragg's disaster. When the final volleys spluttered out in the moonlight around 6:00 P.M., the only live and uncaptured Confederates on Missionary Ridge were those of Hardee's command, including Cleburne, on Tunnel Hill and just to the south. In the darkness they pulled out and helped cover the flight of the broken army against such immediate pursuit as aggressive Federal officers like Sheridan still had the drive, energy, and manpower to carry out. By the pale glow of yet another full moon, the second since the one that had lighted Lincoln on his ride back from the Soldiers' Home to ponder a response to the defeat at Chickamauga, the final halting encounters of the battle of Chattanooga took place in the cold woods between Missionary Ridge and Chickamauga Creek, fought between exhausted soldiers who had experienced a lifetime in the last few hours.[32]

In many ways the battle of Chattanooga was a remarkably exact reversal of Chickamauga. In each case, the defending army's line of communication had run off toward one flank—Rosecrans's at Chickamauga to his left, Bragg's at Chattanooga to his right. The attacking general had wisely aimed his main effort at that flank, but in each case the defending general had reinforced the key flank heavily and outstanding leadership there—Thomas's at

Chickamauga and Cleburne's at Chattanooga—had held the position. Instead, in each case the center and opposite end of the defending line had collapsed, producing a rout, but a rout that had someplace to go. The defeated army was not trapped as the attacker had intended but was able to flee over its still intact line of communication back toward its base. Finally, at each battle the reinforced and brilliantly led troops that had defended the crucial flank became the rear guard that blocked such pursuit as the victorious attackers were able to make.

The next day was Thursday, November 26, and it was America's first official national Thanksgiving Day. Back at the beginning of October, Lincoln had issued a proclamation exhorting Americans to set aside this day to give thanks to Almighty God for the series of remarkable victories—Chickamauga notwithstanding—with which He had blessed the national cause. Across the broad, peaceful, and remarkably prosperous lands from New England to the Great Plains, many did so that day even as the news went out over the telegraph wires of the resounding Union victory at Chattanooga. The nation indeed had much for which to be thankful. In Washington, Lincoln received the news in bed, were he was confined by illness. It was good medicine, but always in the president's thoughts was the situation in East Tennessee, which he had promised to regard with as much solicitude as he would if his own family lived there. He would keep that promise, and an astute general would bear that fact in mind.[33]

Grant was nothing if not politically astute. His sensitivity to Lincoln's intense concern for East Tennessee—and thus for Burnside at Knoxville—influenced his military decisions over the next days and weeks and made them different than they would have been if this or any other war could be considered as a strategic chess match carried out in a political vacuum.[34]

Even before the battle of Chattanooga, Grant had earmarked Granger's IV Corps, about twenty thousand men, to go to the relief of Burnside as soon as Bragg should be dispensed with. That was still his plan on the evening of the twenty-fifth as he sat down to write a dispatch to Sherman, notifying him of the massive Union success on the central and southern portions of Missionary Ridge, but as he composed the note he reconsidered. It ran contrary to Grant's nature to let a beaten foe retire at leisure. "On second thought," he added in a postscript to his note to Sherman, "I think we will push Bragg with all our strength tomorrow, and try if we cannot cut off a good portion of his rear troops and trains." Burnside would have to wait another day or two; the present opportunity was simply too good to pass up.[35]

The next two days' operations are almost a case study in why Civil War

armies were all but indestructible (unless trapped) and why decisively successful pursuits were such a rarity. Grant was a dangerous man to whom to
lose a battle. No general in the entire conflict was to show himself more
ruthless and skillful in pursuing a beaten foe. Yet in this case even his leadership was insufficient to overcome the enormous odds in favor of the loser's
escape. First, there was the weather. In northwestern Georgia, Thanksgiving Day 1863 was one of fog and rain, and the troops groped and stumbled
and bogged down in the mud. Then there was the condition of the troops.
Most of them were bone weary to begin with; the few who were rested could
not hope to face even a beaten Confederate army alone. The men were also
hungry because resupply was exceedingly difficult with the army on the advance through axle-deep mud, and at the same time that Union supply lines
were growing longer as Federal troops advanced, Confederate supply lines
were growing correspondingly shorter as Southern troops retreated. Finally, there was what the enemy could do to make matters more difficult for
the pursuer. The fleeing Confederates found intact bridges over streams
such as Chickamauga and Pea Vine Creeks, but they very understandably
and wisely made sure that the Federals coming along behind them found
nothing but charred timbers.

Throughout November 26, Grant's men pursued as best they could, exacting a moderate additional price of Bragg in prisoners of war and captured
artillery pieces. Despite the disadvantages against which the pursuers had
to struggle, their chances still looked good for substantial additional results
the next day. That evening, Bragg confided to a fellow officer that the Army
of Tennessee's artillery and wagon trains were probably about as good as
lost. The Federals were nearby in force, and only Cleburne's division was fit
and available to try to hold them back until the wheeled vehicles could be
dragged to safety over the seemingly bottomless roads. The Union troops
would obviously advance the next morning, and Bragg was not optimistic of
the result.[36]

Cleburne surprised him. Throughout the retreat, the Irish Confederate's
performance—and that of his division—had been about the only bright
spot for the Army of Tennessee. At a time when, according to Bragg's testi-
mony, corps commander John C. Breckinridge was literally falling down
drunk, Cleburne's steadiness was a pillar of strength for the Confederate
commander. That in itself was a large part of the reason Cleburne's division
had drawn the duty of holding off this most serious of Union threats to the
retreating army. The former Helena druggist's performance this day would
demonstrate that his steadiness was accompanied by genius as well. It

helped that a good defensive position was available to him. Just south of Ringgold, Georgia, the Western & Atlantic Railroad, along which Bragg was retreating, climbed through a gap between Taylor's Ridge and White Oak Mountain. The passage was known as Ringgold Gap, and there Cleburne prepared to make his stand.[37]

The first pursuers to reach the scene on the morning of November 27 were under the command of Joseph Hooker. Though his artillery was not yet up and he had not had time to reconnoiter either the ground or the enemy's deployments, Hooker rightly decided to strike at once. If he was to have a chance of doing further damage to the retreating Confederates, he could not afford to take the time to fight set-piece battles, and so he sent his men directly into an assault on the gap, hoping to keep the momentum going. In this case, however, it proved to be impossible. Though Hooker outnumbered Cleburne slightly more than two to one, that was no surplus for an attacker moving against so formidable a position as Ringgold Gap. Cleburne's superior preparation and knowledge of the terrain—coupled with his customary brilliant battlefield leadership—then combined to give Hooker a very sound drubbing. Having held off the Federals for most of the day, Cleburne retired at his leisure, having saved the Confederate wagon trains and artillery. Realizing that further pursuit would yield no results unless continued far longer than he dared, Grant called off the operation and turned his attention to getting a relieving column on its way to Knoxville. "Had it not been for the imperative necessity of relieving Burnside," Grant reported, "I would have pursued the broken and demoralized retreating enemy as long as supplies could have been found in the country." As it was, though, Grant had word that Burnside's supplies would not last more than another six days, and so there was no time to be lost.[38]

CHAPTER TEN

I Was Never More Disgusted

While Union troops had pursued the defeated Confederates, Grant had left Thomas in Chattanooga along with Gordon Granger and a force of four divisions ready to march northeast for Knoxville as soon as Grant was sure he would not need them to finish off Bragg. With the chase given up and apparently very scant time remaining to relieve Burnside, Grant sent orders to Thomas to start Granger at once for Knoxville. Yet upon arriving back in Chattanooga himself on the evening of November 29, Grant was appalled to find Granger still there and complaining about the Knoxville movement. He thought it was a bad idea and did not want to go. Grant was not impressed. So he turned to Sherman, whom he knew he could trust to carry out an energetic movement, and ordered him to take Granger's and his own troops and get to Knoxville within the four days that Burnside's supplies were supposed to last. Sherman's men had left their camps five days earlier carrying two days' rations and not very much in the way of overcoats and blankets since they had expected to go into battle. Now, despite empty stomachs, muddy roads, and a bitterly chilling late November wind, they set out marching directly for Knoxville.[1]

Unbeknownst to any of them, the main crisis at Knoxville had been met and passed a few hours before. Longstreet, whose once admiring soldiers had of late (behind his back) altered his nickname from "Old Pete" to "Peter the Slow," had felt the pressure of Bragg's repeated prods. His actions, however, gave ominous signs that as on other occasions in the war when he had held independent command or been allowed too much discretion, he was at an almost complete loss to know what to do. His efforts to starve Burnside out of Knoxville were not very promising, especially because loyal East Tennesseeans were rafting foodstuffs down the Holston River to boost the stocks of the beleaguered Army of the Ohio. While Longstreet waited, Burnside's men improved their fortifications.[2]

In search of a quicker solution, he began casting about for a way to carry Burnside's lines by assault. The obvious place to do so was at a fort the Confederates had built and named Fort Loudon back when they held the city. Since then the Federals had renamed it Fort Sanders, after one of their fallen officers, and strengthened it, though to what degree the Confederates could only guess. Though it perched atop a 198-foot hill, it had glaring weaknesses as a defensive work. A steep slope provided an area of dead ground big enough to hold a division just 150 or 200 yards from the parapet. Approaching the fort by the shortest distance from that sheltered staging area, attackers would be heading directly toward a projecting angle of the fort, where the defenders would have the least firepower. Edward Porter Alexander considered the fort little short of an engraved invitation to assault. "It would have [been] impossible, I think, to find on the continent another earth work so advantageously situated for attack," wrote Longstreet's chief of artillery. "No military engineer could ask for an easier task."[3]

That might be the case, but then, Longstreet was no military engineer. His first solution, on November 21, was to ask Lafayette McLaws if he thought his division could carry the place in a night assault. Knowing what chaos night assaults invariably became, McLaws and his brigadiers were skeptical. The next day, however, a staff officer came in, full of excitement with the news that he had discovered a hill on the left bank of the Holston whence artillery could fire across the river and into Fort Sanders. Just the thing, proclaimed Longstreet, and ordered a skeptical Alexander to get some guns up there at once. That was no easy matter, as the artillery officer and his men had to haul the guns across the Holston in a makeshift ferryboat, then cut a road through the woods and drag the heavy Parrott guns up to the hilltop. Despite serious misgivings based on the poor quality of his long-range ammunition, Alexander nevertheless got started bright and early on Monday, November 23. All that day and all night without pause and most of the next day the artillerists toiled. Finally, late on Tuesday afternoon, November 24, as the battle of Lookout Mountain was coming to a close roughly one hundred miles to the southwest, Alexander reported to Longstreet that the guns were in position and ready to open fire at first light in the morning.[4]

Longstreet, however, announced that the attack had been postponed. He had just gotten word that Bragg was sending him reinforcements, Buckner's and, as originally planned, Cleburne's division. They were to arrive by

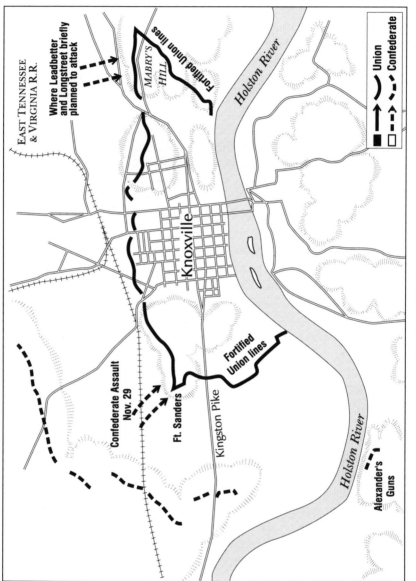

The Knoxville Campaign

Wednesday afternoon, and operations would be delayed so that they could be on hand for whatever came off. Cleburne's division, of course, and a brigade of Buckner's had been recalled by Bragg, but the remaining brigades arrived on time late on the afternoon of November 25, probably about the time the Army of the Cumberland was beginning its advance toward Missionary Ridge. With them arrived Brig. Gen. Danville Leadbetter. A Maine native who had graduated third in the West Point class of 1836, Leadbetter had been Bragg's chief engineer, and among his works of military engineering, interestingly enough, was the former Fort Loudon, now Fort Sanders. If anyone should know how the fort could be taken, Leadbetter should be the man.[5]

Not surprisingly, Leadbetter confided to Longstreet that Fort Sanders was much too strong and that they had better try to find a place to attack at the opposite end of the Union perimeter. Late that night Longstreet issued orders postponing the next morning's attack. The next day, while the North gave thanks and Bragg's army fled from the debacle at Chattanooga, Longstreet and Leadbetter rode to the north end of the Knoxville lines, where Leadbetter seemed to think a better opportunity was available. When they got back, Longstreet ordered Alexander to drag the guns back down off the hill, ferry them back over the Holston, and get them into position to support the newly planned attack. "I never was more disgusted in my life," observed Alexander in his memoirs, but Longstreet assured him that he had seen the place himself and it was very promising.

The next morning, Friday, November 27, while Cleburne was fighting off Hooker's pursuit at Ringgold Gap, Longstreet and Leadbetter took the division commanders and several of the brigade commanders out to look at this promising position. Somehow, though, with the other officers there to ask questions and point out potential problems, it seemed to promise nothing so much as a general slaughter of any troops sent to attack there. That was it, then; they would attack Fort Sanders. Naturally, this decision brought orders for Alexander and his men to work all night and get the artillery back across the Holston and up to the top of the hill. For the third time that week they wrestled the iron monsters into the boat, and after another marathon work session in a cold, driving rain, Alexander was able to report his guns ready for action by noon on Saturday, November 28.[6]

That had not been quick enough for Longstreet, who during the night had issued orders to McLaws to have his division ready to attack at daybreak, then canceled them till the weather broke. The weather still had not broken by noon, and a dense fog blanketed the landscape so that Fort

Sanders was not visible from Confederate lines. Longstreet ordered the attack put off until Sunday morning, November 29. That afternoon, McLaws and Alexander worked out a carefully planned timetable for coordinating the artillery bombardment with the infantry advance. All, it seemed, was finally in readiness for the grand assault.

That night, however, Longstreet sent out a change of orders. Instead of a daylight attack supported by artillery, he now wanted a night attack, just before dawn, that would take advantage of the element of surprise. Incongruously, the 6:00 A.M. surprise attack was to be preceded by a 10:00 P.M. advance to drive in the Union picket lines, a sure tip-off to the Yankees that something was afoot. In fact, the Federals in the Knoxville lines had been fully alerted since they had observed McLaws's troops forming up for the attack about 3:00 that afternoon. Throughout the night Union artillery pounded away toward Confederate lines in an obvious indication of readiness to receive an attack. Meanwhile, Alexander's gunners glumly contemplated their new orders, calling for a grand total of three rounds to be fired as a signal for the advance.

The attack went in as planned and proceeded as planned until the troops reached the ditch just in front of the fort's parapet. The three assault brigades had not received adequate instructions and all bunched together into the ditch in complete disorder. Far worse, however, was the nature of the ditch itself. Longstreet had insisted that it was shallow and easily crossed. Thus no scaling ladders or similar equipment would be needed. Instead, it turned out that one of the changes the Yankee engineers had made was to deepen the ditch substantially and also raise the top of the parapet with rawhide-bound bales of cotton. The ditch itself was now six to eight feet deep with vertical sides. The earthen parapet, or scarp, rose at a forty-five-degree angle about that much higher starting from the very edge of the ditch, and the cotton bales rose vertically several more feet on top of that. An all-night misting rain in freezing conditions now guaranteed that such parts of the scarp as were not slick with wet clay were even slicker with ice. Climbing up that wall was all but impossible. Some of McLaws's men boosted each other on backs and shoulders and succeeded in reaching the top but in such small numbers that the defenders easily mowed them down. The Federals also tossed shells with lit fuses over the parapet and into the massed Confederates. Shortly after daylight the attack broke up and streamed back in defeat. "The slaughter was tremendous," wrote a Union soldier in his diary. "The blood run in a brook in the ditch, where the dead and dying were 2 and 3 deep." For Longstreet there could at least be the consolation that the butchery, if intense, was nevertheless limited in extent—a relatively large number of men had been killed in a small space, but the total number lost was small by the standards of Civil War battles. Longstreet's total casualties numbered 813 men. The Union had lost 13.[7]

Within an hour of the failure of the attack, Longstreet received a dispatch from Richmond, notifying him of Bragg's defeat at Chattanooga four days earlier. That did it as far as any further assault on Knoxville was concerned. Despite the protests of such younger officers as Alexander and Jenkins, Longstreet quashed all plans for a further attack. Though the message from Richmond, and another that arrived some time later from Bragg, directed him to rejoin the Army of Tennessee somewhere in the vicinity of Dalton, Georgia, Longstreet decided that it was impractical to attempt any such movement. Instead, he would keep his Army of Northern Virginia detachment—along with several brigades of cavalry and most of a division of infantry belonging to Bragg's army—in the vicinity of Knoxville and wait for something to turn up.

What turned up, in fact, was the advance guard of Sherman's relief force. Longstreet's scouts detected the Federals' approach, and he entertained no thought of staying to fight it out. Instead, he prepared to pull his force further back into East Tennessee when Sherman's troops drew near. That same evening, December 3, Sherman's cavalry rode into Knoxville. After all the frustrating delays of the battle for Chattanooga, Sherman had finally managed to carry out a movement with all of his accustomed drive and speed. His leading elements had indeed reached Knoxville in the four days Grant had directed, and the rest of his force marched in the next day. What Sherman found in Knoxville surprised him. On coming into town he observed large herds of fat beef cattle. This "did not look much like starvation," Sherman later noted. After conferring with Burnside about the situation, he then accompanied the general to his quarters, where a repast was laid on the like of which Sherman had not seen for some time. "There was a regular dining-table, with clean table-cloth, dishes, knives, forks, spoons, etc.," he recalled. The food was also of interest, and Sherman could not help exclaiming that he and his men had thought the Army of Ohio was starving. Not so, Burnside explained; with the food sent by the East Tennessee Unionists things had never been that bad, and Sherman reflected ruefully on the hardships his footsore Army of the Tennessee had endured as it raced northward in the belief that Burnside's men were at the point of boiling and eating their cartridge-box hinges. Burnside's timidity and Washington's undue agitation about his supposed plight had added to the trials and diminished the extent of the successes of Grant and his soldiers.

Sherman offered to stay and help Burnside chase Longstreet back to Virginia where he belonged, but Burnside assured him that two of Granger's divisions, about ten thousand men, added to his own Army of the Ohio, would be ample to accomplish that chore. Granger groused so bitterly at the assignment as to raise serious questions in Sherman's mind about his fitness for a significant command. Indeed, having convinced the two rising generals of the army that he was a simpleton and a whiner, Granger had pretty well destroyed the bright hopes for his future career that his one afternoon of greatness at Chickamauga had kindled eleven weeks before.[8]

While the Army of the Tennessee marched back to Chattanooga at a more reasonable pace, Longstreet's Army of Northern Virginia contingent, with the Army of Tennessee elements it had absorbed, trudged northeastward, along roads paralleling the railroad that would eventually take them back into Virginia. Though Longstreet would lurk about far northeastern Tennessee until spring and toy with various schemes for offensive action, his western adventure was, for practical purposes, at an end. Around sundown on the fourth, just as the Confederates passed out of sight of Knoxville, a cold, drenching downpour gushed out from the low-hanging clouds and kept up all night. Through the long, cold night Longstreet's soaked and shivering men stumbled ahead through inky blackness and deep mud and had plenty of opportunity to reflect on the nature of their defeat in the campaign that had now very obviously come to an end.[9]

CHAPTER ELEVEN

The Death Knell of the Confederacy

Despite mistakes that limited the scope of the Federal victory, the five-and-a-half-month-long campaign for control of Middle and East Tennessee had ended decisively in favor of the Union. Never again would any substantial part of the state of Tennessee be considered Confederate territory in a military sense, and though Confederate forces would make several minor and one major foray into the state before the conflict ended, Tennessee was now firmly in Union control. Except for Virginia and North Carolina, the Confederacy had lost the states of the Upper South. The Deep South now lay exposed to the advancing armies of the Union. Most of East Tennessee was free at last, much to Lincoln's relief, and with Chattanooga as a forward base, the same Union armies that had won the climactic struggle for Tennessee in 1863 would open the struggle for Georgia the following spring, their target: Atlanta. The Army of Tennessee, licking its wounds in Dalton, Georgia, thirty miles or so south of Chattanooga, could only hope to stop them. The Confederate offensive hopes of the previous summer had faded, and few Southerners were inclined to continue speaking of them.[1]

For many of the individual officers who took part in it, the six-month struggle for Tennessee was decisive. For Grant it was the final proof necessary to show that his earlier successes were no flukes. The victor of Donelson, Vicksburg, and Chattanooga was clearly the leading Northern general of the war. He made war Lincoln's way, or at least close enough to it to keep the president satisfied, and he never plied the president or the secretary of war with complaints that he did not have enough of this or that or that he knew better than Lincoln how the war ought to be waged—even when he did. For him, the contest for Tennessee became the launching pad to overall Union command and the full rank of lieutenant general, previously held only by George Washington.

Despite the setbacks and disappointments dealt him as a result of the weather, the terrain, and sudden immersion into an unfamiliar theater of combat operations, Sherman retained Grant's full confidence. The commanding general was close enough to appreciate the difficulties he faced, and in any case, Grant seemed to prefer officers who fell short when attempting the impossible to those who feared to attempt the possible lest they should fall short. In that comparison, Thomas appeared to disadvantage alongside Sherman, despite his much greater success in the Chattanooga campaign. A competent, skillful general, he had nevertheless shown himself unable or unwilling to approach war according to Grant's formula of getting at the enemy as soon as possible, hitting him as hard as possible, and always moving on. That simply was not Thomas's way, and though he was in some respects an excellent general, Grant would have but limited use for him. Of course, Thomas's rudeness to Grant had done nothing to help the Virginian's cause.

While Gordon Granger's star sank rapidly at Chattanooga after its meteoric rise at Chickamauga, Philip Sheridan's career took an opposite course. Chickamauga was not one of Sheridan's more inspiring performances, but the assault on Missionary Ridge definitely was. Grant witnessed the latter and was much taken with Sheridan. Here was an officer who waged war Grant's way. When Grant went east to overall command the following spring, Sheridan would go along, eventually to become the general in chief's most trusted subordinate in Virginia and, in after years, commanding general of the army, following Grant and Sherman.

The last six months of 1863 in Tennessee understandably had a far more negative effect on the careers of Confederate generals. Bragg, of course, was finished as an army commander. Once the army was safely back in Dalton, the failed commander submitted his resignation and Jefferson Davis accepted it. Given Bragg's negative reputation by that time with many of the officers and men of the Army of Tennessee as well as the Confederate public, that was probably just as well. He had made mistakes during the campaign. The most glaring of them was overlooking his subordinates' poor tactical deployments on Missionary Ridge on November 25, yet Bragg had never intended to fight there and had taken steps that might have produced a different outcome in a different place. Indeed, an entire category of Bragg's errors can be classed as his naïve persistent confidence in his subordinates. Polk and Hardee failed him during the Tullahoma campaign, Polk, Hindman, and Hill during the maneuvering before Chickamauga. Then Polk failed dismally once again at the battle of Chickamauga itself. Longstreet blundered at Wauhatchie, allowing Grant to open the cracker line, and when Bragg tried to remedy that situation with a right-flank turning strategy, Longstreet made a mess of the necessary preliminary movement of opening a supply line through East Tennessee. Again and again Bragg's reliance on such generals as Polk or Longstreet brought him disaster, but then a commanding general can hardly function without entrusting important tasks to subordinates. Bragg's worst problem, spawned long before Rosecrans advanced on Tullahoma and growing more hideous ever since, was that he had few capable generals who trusted him and whom he could trust to carry out his commands.[2]

Hill was effectively demoted from lieutenant general to major general for his role in agitating against Bragg. He received no further assignments of high responsibility. Hindman served in the Atlanta campaign until he was incapacitated by a wound.

Longstreet continued to be Lee's "Old Warhorse" until his wounding in May 1864 and again after his recovery. Yet there was no further talk on his part or anyone else's, once he got back to Lee's army, about his assuming an independent command. His stock with the Davis administration had been lowered by his behavior toward Bragg and his subsequent treatment of his own subordinates. After his withdrawal from the environs of Knoxville, the embittered Longstreet had relieved his old friend Lafayette McLaws of command for, of all things, "exhibit[ing] a want of confidence in the efforts and plans which the commanding General has thought proper to adopt." Longstreet said he was afraid such an attitude might spread within the army and have bad results. There can be no denying that Longstreet had, by rights, some claim to be an expert on such matters. The move got him into trouble with Richmond, especially when he deliberately prevented the holding of court-martial proceedings at which McLaws had hoped to vindicate himself. Longstreet's vendetta against Evander Law also ran him afoul of Jefferson Davis, whose direct orders he twice set aside in the matter.

Yet the blackest mark on Longstreet's record after the Tennessee campaign was the result of his own failure as a general. Though his abilities were considerable within their limits, they did not extend beyond carrying out the instructions of a wise commander. When Longstreet lacked an immediate, direct battlefield commander, or when he refused to obey the orders of the one he had, the results were uniformly dismal for the Confederacy. The Knoxville campaign made that fact painfully obvious—to the Confederate

soldiers, probably to Longstreet himself, and definitely to the Davis administration. Richmond diarist Mary Chesnut, whose husband was a confidant
of the president, wrote, "Detached from General Lee, what a horrible failure. What a slow old humbug is Longstreet."[3]

Neither Hardee nor, more surprisingly, Polk suffered for their performances in the struggle for Tennessee. Despite habitual disobedience and
chronic incompetence, Polk continued to serve in highly responsible positions as a lieutenant general, first in Mississippi and then, beginning in May
1864, with the Army of Tennessee again, now under the command of Joseph
E. Johnston. As Johnston's army fell back before the advance of Sherman's
three armies in Georgia that year, Polk was killed instantly by artillery fire
on Pine Mountain, Georgia, on June 14, 1864. He was mourned by his
troops, his fellow officers, and the Confederate president.[4]

Almost alone among Confederate generals, Pat Cleburne had turned in a
sterling performance through the entire campaign from Tullahoma to Chattanooga, excepting only the second day's fight at Chickamauga, when he had
been handicapped by factors beyond his control. Yet he remained in his position as major general for the remaining one year before he fell in battle at
Franklin, Tennessee, even though during that year other, less capable men
with poorer records were promoted over his head. Perhaps this was because
of a controversial proposal he broached to the army's officers while in winter
camp at Dalton that year, suggesting that the Confederacy solve its manpower troubles by arming and freeing its slaves. That certainly won him no
favor in the eyes of some of his fellow generals. More likely, however, he was
held back because he was not a professional soldier, and Jefferson Davis
doubted his abilities to rise above division command.[5]

For the Union and Confederate causes, the moral impact of the campaign
in some ways exceeded even the strictly military and economic importance
of the vast area and large population that had changed hands. Both sides had
invested enormously in the struggle for Tennessee. The North had com-
mitted all or part of the nation's three major field armies, those of the Tennessee, the Cumberland, and the Potomac, plus a fourth field army, the
smaller Army of the Ohio. The South, with its scant resources of manpower,
had probably risked even more by sending a large detachment from the
Army of Northern Virginia to join the Army of Tennessee in an all-out effort
not only to save the parts of Tennessee the Confederacy still held but also to
reverse and restore the losses of more than a year and a half of defeat in the
western theater of the war. The Union victory in this contest of six armies,
coming on the heels of Gettysburg and Vicksburg, resounded with corre-

sponding force throughout the nation. Northerners, on November 26, could give thanks to the God who had blessed their arms with victory and feel confirmed in His blessing when news followed within days of another great victory. Although the stunning successes of 1863 contributed to a dangerous sense of overconfidence when the 1864 campaign opened the following spring, they were nevertheless vital to the cause of the Union—and emancipation—by laying in a bountiful harvest of public goodwill and political capital to carry Lincoln's administration through the long lean months of long casualty lists and apparent military stalemate before the next autumn's harvest of victories.

The moral impact was great for the men of the four Federal armies that helped to win the struggle in Tennessee. They had succeeded in doing what had seemed militarily impossible in driving Bragg out of his mountain fastnesses. They had breached the barrier of the Appalachians, and the land of cotton lay before them with few such awe-inspiring natural ramparts against an advancing army. Somewhere along the way to that victory, the Army of the Cumberland—shaken by its defeat at Chickamauga and more so by the loss of its beloved Rosecrans—the hard-luck XI and XII Corps of the Army of the Potomac, and the hitherto timidly led Army of the Ohio had learned to exhibit some of the Army of the Tennessee's can-do spirit. The following spring, all four of these armies would advance together against their now familiar foes (the Army of the Potomac contingent by then formally incorporated into the Army of the Cumberland). When they did, they expected to labor, suffer, fight hard, and sometimes bleed, but they never showed a doubt that final victory would be theirs. They had come out to do a job, and they were going to finish it.

Southerners, by contrast, were impelled to wonder how, if ever, they could succeed in this war. This feeling was voiced most clearly where it was no doubt felt most clearly, by some of the beaten soldiers of the Army of Tennessee. As that army had struggled southward in its weary retreat after Missionary Ridge, one lieutenant had blurted his doubts to his company commander, "Captain, this is the death knell of the Confederacy. If we cannot cope with those fellows with the advantages we had on this line, there is not a line between here and the Atlantic Ocean where we can stop them." The captain could not deny the truth of the statement but was not ready to admit it either. "Hush, Lieutenant," he replied, "that is treason you are talking." The long-suffering Army of Tennessee would go on fighting, bravely, fiercely, under good or bad commanders as Richmond might ordain, but after Missionary Ridge, they knew they would lose in the end.[6]

Notes

PREFACE

1. Thomas Lawrence Connelly, *Army of the Heartland: The Army of Tennessee, 1861–1862* (Baton Rouge: Louisiana State University Press, 1967), and *Autumn of Glory: The Army of Tennessee, 1863–1865* (Baton Rouge: Louisiana State University Press, 1971); Edward Carr Franks, "The Detachment of Longstreet Considered: Braxton Bragg, James Longstreet, and the Chattanooga Campaign," in *Leadership and Command in the American Civil War*, ed. Steven E. Woodworth (Campbell CA: Savas Woodbury, 1995).

1. THE ARMY BEGINS TO MOVE

1. U.S. War Department, *The War of the Rebellion: A Compilation of the Official Records of the Union and Confederate Armies*, 128 vols. (Washington DC: Government Printing Office, 1880–1901), vol. 23, pt. 1, 457–58 (hereafter OR; except as otherwise noted, all volumes cited are from Series 1); Benjamin T. Smith, *Private Smith's Journal: Recollections of the Late War*, ed. Clyde C. Walton (Chicago: Lakeside Press, 1963), 76; James A. Connolly, *Three Years in the Army of the Cumberland: The Letters and Diary of Major James A. Connolly*, ed. Paul M. Angle (Bloomington: Indiana University Press, 1959), 89–90.

2. William M. Lamers, *The Edge of Glory: A Biography of General William S. Rosecrans, U.S.A.* (New York: Harcourt, Brace, & World, 1961).

3. James Lee McDonough, *Stones River: Bloody Winter in Tennessee* (Knoxville: University of Tennessee Press, 1980); Peter Cozzens, *No Better Place to Die: The Battle of Stones River* (Urbana: University of Illinois Press, 1989).

4. Francis F. McKinney, *Education in Violence: The Life of George H. Thomas and the History of the Army of the Cumberland* (Detroit: Wayne State University Press, 1961); Freeman Cleaves, *Rock of Chickamauga: The Life of General George H. Thomas* (Norman: University of Oklahoma Press, 1948), 1–137; Donn Piatt, *General George H. Thomas: A Critical Biography* (Cincinnati: Robert Clarke, 1893).

5. Roy P. Basler et al., eds., *The Collected Works of Abraham Lincoln*, 9 vols. (New Brunswick NJ: Rutgers University Press, 1953–55), 6:424–25.

6. OR 20, pt. 2, 306, 23, pt. 2, 255–56; Cleaves, *Rock of Chickamauga*, 138–39.

7. Ulysses S. Grant, *Personal Memoirs of U. S. Grant*, 2 vols. (New York: Charles L. Webster, 1885).

8. OR 23, pt. 2, 111, 171; Cleaves, *Rock of Chickamauga*, 139.

9. OR 23, pt. 1, 9, 403–4, pt. 2, 383.

10. Grady McWhiney, *Braxton Bragg and Confederate Defeat*, vol. 1 (Tuscaloosa: University of Alabama Press, 1991; originally published 1969).

11. McWhiney, *Braxton Bragg*, 150–336; Steven E. Woodworth, *Jefferson Davis and His Generals: The Failure of Confederate Command in the West* (Lawrence: University Press of Kansas, 1990), 93–108, 125–61.

12. Joseph H. Parks, *General Leonidas Polk, C.S.A.: The Fighting Bishop* (Baton Rouge: Louisiana State University Press, 1962); Woodworth, *Jefferson Davis and His Generals*, 25–45, 135; OR 17, pt. 2, 627–28, 654–55, 658, 667–68, 673; Steven E. Woodworth, "'The Indeterminate Quantities': Jefferson Davis, Leonidas Polk, and the End of Kentucky Neutrality, September 1861," *Civil War History* 38 (December 1992): 289–97.

13. James Lee McDonough, *War in Kentucky: From Shiloh to Perryville* (Knoxville: University of Tennessee Press, 1994), 304–8; Woodworth, *Jefferson Davis and His Generals*, 147–61.

14. Woodworth, *Jefferson Davis and His Generals*, 162–68.

15. Nathaniel C. Hughes, *General William J. Hardee: Old Reliable* (Baton Rouge: Louisiana State University Press, 1965), 3–85; Thomas Lawrence Connelly, *Autumn of Glory: The Army of Tennessee, 1862–1865* (Baton Rouge: Louisiana State University Press, 1971), 20–21, 90.

16. Christopher Losson, "Major General Benjamin Franklin Cheatham and the Battle of Stone's River," *Tennessee Historical Quarterly* (fall 1982): 280–83, 286; Irving A. Buck, *Cleburne and His Command* (Jackson TN: McCowat-Mercer, 1958), 119–20; McDonough, *Stones River*, 97–100, 104, 193, 227; Herman Hattaway and Archer Jones, *How the North Won: A Military History of the Civil War* (Urbana: University of Illinois Press, 1983), 320–21; Connelly, *Autumn of Glory*, 55, 64–65, 84–85; OR 20, pt. 1, 662–72, 700; pt. 2, 492; William C. Davis, *Breckinridge: Statesman, Soldier, Symbol* (Baton Rouge: Louisiana State University Press, 1974), 343–46, 356; Stanley Horn, *The Army of Tennessee: A Military History* (Indianapolis: Bobbs-Merrill, 1941), 208.

17. OR 20, pt. 1, 682–84, 698–99, 701–2; pt. 2, 484; Connelly, *Autumn of Glory*, 74–75; Davis, *Breckinridge*, 350; McWhiney, *Braxton Bragg*, 376–78; Dunbar Rowland, ed., *Jefferson Davis, Constitutionalist: His Letters, Papers and Speeches*, 10 vols. (Jackson: Mississippi Department of Archives and History, 1923), 5:418, 420–21; Woodworth, *Jefferson Davis and His Generals*, 194–96.

18. McWhiney, *Braxton Bragg*, 375; Davis, *Breckinridge*, 331–33; OR 17, pt. 2, 813,

816–17, 822, vol. 20, pt. 1, 674, 684–85, 698–99, 708, 745–46, pt. 2, 476, vol. 24, pt. 1, 215, pt. 3, 870; Rowland, ed., *Jefferson Davis*, 5:433–35, 448, 452, 468–69; McDonough, *Stones River*, 220; Woodworth, *Jefferson Davis and His Generals*, 197–98.

19. Connelly, *Autumn of Glory*, 114; Timothy H. Donovan Jr., Roy K. Flint, Arthur V. Grant Jr., and Gerald P. Stadler, *The American Civil War* (Wayne, NJ: Avery Publishing Group, 1987), 169.

20. Connelly, *Autumn of Glory*, 114–15; George R. Stewart, ed., *Synopsis of the Military Career of General Joseph Wheeler* (Birmingham: Birmingham Public Library, 1988); OR 23, pt. 1, 465.

21. Connelly, *Autumn of Glory*, 117–19; OR 23, pt. 1, 588.

22. OR 23, pt. 1, 404.

23. Hattaway and Jones, *How the North Won*, 385–87.

24. OR 23, pt. 1, 404.

25. William B. Feis, "The Deception of Braxton Bragg: The Tullahoma Campaign," *Blue and Gray* (October 1992): 10–21, 46–53.

26. Basler, ed. *Collected Works of Lincoln*, 6:236; OR 23, pt. 2, 395, 413–15, 423, vol. 24, pt. 3, 376; Cleaves, *Rock of Chickamauga*, 142–43; Peter Cozzens, *This Terrible Sound: The Battle of Chickamauga* (Urbana: University of Illinois Press, 1992).

27. OR 23, pt. 1, 10.

2. A NINE DAYS' CAMPAIGN

1. OR 23, pt. 1, 405.

2. OR 23, pt. 1, 405; Ezra J. Warner, *Generals in Blue: Lives of the Union Commanders* (Baton Rouge: Louisiana State University Press, 1964), 294.

3. Warner, *Generals in Blue*, 100; Stewart Sifakis, *Who Was Who in the Civil War* (New York: Facts on File, 1988), 152, 409.

4. OR 23, pt. 1, 405.

5. McDonough, *War in Kentucky*, 159–81; Cozzens, *This Terrible Sound*, 14–15; Connolly, *Three Years in the Army of the Cumberland*, 56, 83.

6. OR 23, pt. 1, 405.

7. OR 23, pt. 1, 405; Donovan et al., *American Civil War*, 172.

8. OR 23, pt. 1, 457–58; Connolly, *Three Years in the Army of the Cumberland*, 89–90.

9. OR 23, pt. 1, 458, 602–3, 611–14; Cleaves, *Rock of Chickamauga*, 144; Connelly, *Autumn of Glory*, 126–27; Connolly, *Three Years in the Army of the Cumberland*, 89–90.

10. OR 23, pt. 1, 458.

11. Marshall Wingfield, *General A. P. Stewart: His Life and Letters* (Memphis: West Tennessee Historical Society, 1954), 9–95, 152–61.

12. Warner, *Generals in Gray*, 19; Sifakis, *Who Was Who in the Civil War*, 38; OR 23, pt. 1, 602–3, 611–14.

13. OR 23, pt. 1, 430, 454–55, 458–59, 611–14; Connolly, *Three Years in the Army of the Cumberland*, 89–93.

14. OR 23, pt. 1, 601–3.

15. OR 23, pt. 1, 465–66, 483.

16. Warner, *Generals in Blue*, 565; Sifakis, *Who Was Who in the Civil War*, 720.

17. OR 23, pt. 1, 465, 483–84, 486–87, 588–89; Adam S. Bright and Michael S. Bright, *"Respects to All": Letters of Two Pennsylvania Boys in the War of the Rebellion*, ed. Aida Craig Truxall (Pittsburgh: University of Pittsburgh Press, 1962), 92.

18. OR 23, pt. 1, 406, 430. On the shortcomings of the Pioneer Brigade, an exception to Rosecrans's otherwise extremely successful record on matters of engineering, see Philip L. Shiman, "General William S. Rosecrans and the Application of Engineering to War," in *The Art of Command: Facets of Civil War Generalship*, ed. Steven E. Woodworth (Lincoln: University of Nebraska Press, forthcoming).

19. Donovan et al., *American Civil War*, 170–71.

20. Woodworth, *Jefferson Davis and His Generals*, 112–14, 130–34, 224–25; Brian Steel Wills, *A Battle from the Start: The Life of Nathan Bedford Forrest* (New York: Harper Collins, 1992), 121–27; Robert Selph Henry, *"First with the Most": Forrest* (Indianapolis: Bobbs-Merrill, 1944), 142–44, 160–64; Robert G. Hartje, *Van Dorn: The Life and Times of a Confederate General* (Nashville: Vanderbilt University Press, 1967), 308–17; James A. Ramage, *Rebel Raider: The Life of General John Hunt Morgan* (Lexington: University Press of Kentucky, 1986), 146–67; Connelly, *Autumn of Glory*, 26–28, 123–29.

21. OR 23, pt. 2, 703–4, 715, 784–85, pt. 1, 267–70; John P. Dyer, *From Shiloh to San Juan: The Life of "Fightin' Joe" Wheeler* (Baton Rouge: Louisiana State University Press, 1941), 83.

22. OR 23, pt. 1, 466, 484, 487, 490–91, 493–97, 589–92; Bright and Bright, *"Respects to All,"* 92.

23. OR 23, pt. 1, 406, 430–31, 459.

24. OR 23, pt. 1, 618; Connelly, *Autumn of Glory*, 117.

25. OR 23, pt. 1, 618. For the potential marching abilities of Polk's corps, evidence is available in the amount of time needed to prepare to march and the actual average speed of march on June 27 in response to Bragg's orders to fall back on Tullahoma, over similar terrain and in the same weather conditions and impeded by far more baggage as well as the need to share the few adequate roads with other retreating units. OR 23, pt. 1, 619–20, 796.

26. OR 23, pt. 1, 466.

27. OR 23, pt. 1, 466, 471, 618. For the numerical strengths of Polk's and Davis's commands, see 410–11, 585–86.

28. Connelly, *Autumn of Glory*, 116–17.

29. Connelly, *Autumn of Glory*, 116–17; Hughes, *General William J. Hardee*, 156; OR 23, pt. 2, 741.

30. OR 23, pt. 1, 884.

31. OR 23, pt. 1, 419–24, 604–5.

32. OR 23, pt. 1, 618–20, 888; Connolly, *Three Years in the Army of the Cumberland*, 94–95.

33. OR 23, pt. 1, 425, 431, 459.

34. OR 23, pt. 1, 535–41, 620; Sifakis, *Who Was Who in the Civil War*, 451; Dyer, *From Shiloh to San Juan*, 83; Stewart, *Synopsis of the Military Career of General Joseph Wheeler*, 12; T. C. De Leon, *Joseph Wheeler: The Man, the Statesman, the Soldier* (Kennesaw, GA: Continental Book Co., 1960), 101; Wills, *A Battle from the Start*, 127–29.

35. John Beatty, *Memoirs of a Volunteer, 1861–1863* (New York: Norton, 1946), 213; Smith, *Private Smith's Journal*, 78–79.

36. OR 23, pt. 1, 402, 406, 426, 460–61; Connolly, *Three Years in the Army of the Cumberland*, 95–98.

37. OR 23, pt. 1, 402, 407, 426–28; Smith, *Private Smith's Journal*, 79.

38. OR 23, pt. 1, 621–23; Lamers (*Edge of Glory*, 284) surmises that Rosecrans's advance toward Tullahoma was a feint and that Rosecrans had no intention of mounting an actual attack against powerful fortifications and over rough terrain.

39. OR 23, pt. 1, 623–24, 889; Connolly, *Autumn of Glory*, 108.

40. OR 23, pt. 1, 624–27.

41. OR 23, pt. 1, 402–8, 514–17.

42. OR 23, pt. 1, 408.

43. Connelly (*Autumn of Glory*, 24) asserts that Bragg should have taken up this position the previous fall, instead of the one he then selected at Murfreesboro.

44. OR 23, pt. 1, 425, 610.

45. Cozzens, *This Terrible Sound*, 21.

3. WE MUST FORCE HIM TO FIGHT

1. Cozzens, *This Terrible Sound*, 21–26; Lamers, *Edge of Glory*, 295; Piatt, *General George H. Thomas*, 370–71; Basler, ed., *Collected Works of Lincoln*, 6:373.

2. Piatt, *General George H. Thomas*, 370–71; OR 30, pt. 1, 50; Glenn Tucker, *Chickamauga: Bloody Battle in the West* (Indianapolis: Bobbs-Merrill, 1961), 401.

3. Cozzens, *This Terrible Sound*, 25.

4. Cozzens, *This Terrible Sound*, 25–26; Warner, *Generals in Blue*, 166–67.

5. Cozzens, *This Terrible Sound*, 26.

6. Hattaway and Jones, *How the North Won*, 442; Thomas Lawrence Connelly and Archer Jones, *The Politics of Command: Factions and Ideas in Confederate Strategy* (Baton Rouge: Louisiana State University Press, 1973), 44–45.

7. OR 23, pt. 2, 948.

8. Connelly, *Autumn of Glory*, 147; Woodworth, *Jefferson Davis and His Generals*, 216–19.

9. OR 23, pt. 2, 948, 950, 952–53; John B. Jones, *A Rebel War Clerk's Diary*, ed. Earl Schenck Miers (New York: Sagamore Press, 1958), 252, 260–61; Stanley Horn, *The Army of Tennessee: A Military History* (Indianapolis: Bobbs-Merrill, 1941), 237.

10. OR 23, pt. 1, 235, pt. 2, 954.

11. Jeffry D. Wert, *General James Longstreet: The Confederacy's Most Controversial Soldier—A Biography* (New York: Simon & Schuster, 1993), 1–55, 300; Steven E. Woodworth, "Confederate Command at Williamsburg," in *The Peninsula Campaign of 1862: Yorktown to the Seven Days,* ed. William J. Miller, 3 vols. to date (Campbell, CA.: Savas Woodbury, 1995), vol. 3; Steven E. Woodworth, *Davis and Lee at War* (Lawrence: University Press of Kansas, 1995); William Garrett Piston, "Cross Purposes: Longstreet, Lee, and Confederate Attack Plans for July 3 at Gettysburg," in *The Third Day at Gettysburg and Beyond,* ed. Gary W. Gallagher (Chapel Hill: University of North Carolina Press, 1994), 31–55; Connelly, *Autumn of Glory,* 151; Judith Lee Hallock, *Braxton Bragg and Confederate Defeat,* vol. 2 (Tuscaloosa: University of Alabama Press, 1991), 78–79.

12. Connelly, *Autumn of Glory,* 138–46; Tucker, *Chickamauga,* 25–26.

13. Hallock, *Braxton Bragg,* 44–45.

14. OR 30, pt. 1, 51, 601, 760–61.

15. OR 30, pt. 1, 445–46, 760–61; Connolly, *Three Years in the Army of the Cumberland,* 116–17; McKinney, *Education in Violence,* 220.

16. Cozzens, *This Terrible Sound,* 36–37; Tucker, *Chickamauga,* 25–26; Connelly, *Autumn of Glory,* 166–67.

17. OR 30, pt. 2, 26–27; Connelly, *Autumn of Glory,* 166–68; Hallock, *Braxton Bragg,* 47–49; Cozzens, *This Terrible Sound,* 37.

18. OR 30, pt. 1, 50–51.

19. OR 30, pt. 1, 51–52; Beatty, *Memoirs of a Volunteer,* 239–40.

20. OR 30, pt. 1, 52.

21. OR 30, pt. 1, 52, 398, 439; McKinney, *Education in Violence,* 221.

22. OR 30, pt. 1, 52, 602; Cozzens, *This Terrible Sound,* 45.

23. OR 30, pt. 1, 52–53.

24. Connolly, *Three Years in the Army of the Cumberland,* 98, 100, 107–8; Smith, *Private Smith's Journal,* 86–87.

25. OR 30, pt. 1, 445; Cozzens, *This Terrible Sound,* 46; Connolly, *Three Years in the Army of the Cumberland,* 114.

26. Cozzens, *This Terrible Sound,* 46.

27. Beatty, *Memoirs of a Volunteer,* 243–44.

28. OR 30, pt. 1, 53, 246–47, 486, 603, pt. 3, 479, 482–84.

29. Tucker, *Chickamauga,* 29, 62; Cozzens, *This Terrible Sound,* 63; McKinney, *Education in Violence,* 224–27; Alfred Lacey Hough, *Soldier in the West: The Civil War Letters of Alfred Lacey Hough,* ed. Robert G. Athearn (Philadelphia: University of Pennsylvania Press, 1957), 129.

30. OR 30, pt. 1, 247, 326, pt. 2, 27; W. J. Wood, *Civil War Generalship: The Art of Command* (Westport, Conn.: Praeger, 1997), 107.

31. OR 30, pt. 2, 27; Hallock, *Braxton Bragg,* 48–50; Connelly, *Autumn of Glory,* 166–72.

32. Hallock, *Braxton Bragg*, 49–50; Connelly, *Autumn of Glory*, 149.

33. James Longstreet, *From Manassas to Appomattox: Memoirs of the Civil War in America*, ed. James I. Robertson Jr. (Bloomington: Indiana University Press, 1960), 434–36; Hattaway and Jones, *How the North Won*, 443; Clifford Dowdey and Louis H. Manarin, eds., *The Wartime Papers of R. E. Lee* (New York: Bramhall House, 1961), 596; Rowland, ed., *Jefferson Davis*, 5:26; Connelly, *Autumn of Glory*, 152, 160–62.

34. Longstreet, *From Manassas to Appomattox*, 436–37.

35. Connelly, *Autumn of Glory*, 168–73; Hallock, *Braxton Bragg*, 53–54; OR 30, pt. 2, 27.

36. Hallock, *Braxton Bragg*, 54; Connelly, *Autumn of Glory*, 174–75.

37. OR 30, pt. 2, 28; Connelly, *Autumn of Glory*, 174–75.

38. Connelly, *Autumn of Glory*, 175.

39. OR 30, pt. 2, 27–28.

40. OR 30, pt. 2, 28–29.

41. Warner, *Generals in Gray*, 136–37; Hal Bridges, *Lee's Maverick General: Daniel Harvey Hill* (Lincoln: University of Nebraska Press, 1991); Woodworth, *Davis and Lee at War*, 178.

42. OR 30, pt. 2, 28; Tucker, *Chickamauga*, 67–68; Cozzens, *This Terrible Sound*, 65–66; Connelly, *Autumn of Glory*, 177–78; Hallock, *Braxton Bragg*, 56.

43. OR 30, pt. 2, 28–29.

44. Hallock, *Braxton Bragg*, 56–57; Connelly, *Autumn of Glory*, 178–79; Tucker, *Chickamauga*, 67–68.

45. OR 30, pt. 2, 294, 301.

46. OR 30, pt. 2, 294.

47. OR 30, pt. 2, 28–29; Connelly, *Autumn of Glory*, 182–83.

48. OR 30, pt. 2, 29; Hallock, *Braxton Bragg*, 57.

49. Tucker, *Chickamauga*, 69; OR 30, pt. 2, 138.

50. OR 30, pt. 2, 29, pt. 4, 634; Tucker, *Chickamauga*, 67–69.

51. Connelly, *Autumn of Glory*, 180–84; Beatty, *Memoirs of a Volunteer*, 243–44.

52. OR 30, pt. 4, 636; Connelly, *Autumn of Glory*, 183–84.

53. Connelly, *Autumn of Glory*, 182–86. Connelly argues that Bragg was at fault. He was, Connelly asserts, hesitant and therefore did not do all that he could have done to force Hindman to advance. This idea is unreasonable. Bragg had given the plainest possible orders, both orally and in writing. The commanding general of an army cannot be expected to be everywhere in order to have his orders carried out. That is a human impossibility. If the officers of an army cannot be relied on to carry out their commander's orders—most of the time, at least, and more or less in the way he intends—that army ceases to be an effective fighting force. The Army of Tennessee verged on that state.

54. Cozzens, *This Terrible Sound*, 69–79; OR 30, pt. 3, 564–65.

55. Cozzens, *This Terrible Sound*, 76–79.

56. OR 30, pt. 3, 545, 570, 574–76, 598–99.

57. OR 30, pt. 1, 711–12, 802, pt. 2, 30; Cozzens, *This Terrible Sound*, 81–82; Connelly, *Autumn of Glory*, 186–87.

58. Cozzens, *This Terrible Sound*, 82–83; OR 30, pt. 2, 30.

59. OR 30, pt. 2, 44–45.

60. Cozzens, *This Terrible Sound*, 84.

61. Connelly, *Autumn of Glory*, 189–91; Cozzens, *This Terrible Sound*, 86–87; OR 30, pt. 4, 643.

4. SAVAGERY AND CONFUSION

1. OR 30, pt. 4, 645, 652–53; Cozzens, *This Terrible Sound*, 89.

2. Carl von Clausewitz, *On War*, ed. Anatol Rapoport (New York: Penguin, 1983; originally published 1832), 164; OR 30, pt. 2, 31, pt. 4, 657; Cozzens, *This Terrible Sound*, 89–92; Connelly, *Autumn of Glory*, 191–97.

3. OR 30, pt. 2, 31, 451; Connelly, *Autumn of Glory*, 197.

4. OR 30, pt. 2, 31, 451.

5. OR 30, pt. 2, 31, 451.

6. OR 30, pt. 1, 922–23, pt. 2, 451–52; Cozzens, *This Terrible Sound*, 105.

7. OR 30, pt. 1, 447, pt. 2, 32, 239.

8. OR 30, pt. 1, 605–6.

9. Cozzens, *This Terrible Sound*, 113–14.

10. OR 30, pt. 2, 32, 357.

11. OR 30, pt. 4, 725.

12. OR 30, pt. 1, 55, 115, 248–49, pt. 4, 724; Cozzens, *This Terrible Sound*, 115–17; McKinney, *Education in Violence*, 230–31.

13. OR 30, pt. 1, 248–49, 274–75, 400, 440; McKinney, *Education in Violence*, 231–32; Cozzens, *This Terrible Sound*, 123.

14. OR 30, pt. 1, 56, 124, 249, 854, 860, 871; Cozzens, *This Terrible Sound*, 121–25; Tucker, *Chickamauga*, 126–28.

15. OR 30, pt. 1, 56, 249, 400, 407; Cozzens, *This Terrible Sound*, 124–28.

16. OR 30, pt. 2, 32, 240.

17. OR 30, pt. 1, 250, 275–76, 401, pt. 2, 240, 252; Cozzens, *This Terrible Sound*, 139–51.

18. OR 30, pt. 1, 251; Warner, *Generals in Blue*, 254.

19. OR 30, pt. 1, 535.

20. Cozzens, *This Terrible Sound*, 139–40.

21. OR 30, pt. 1, 250, 535, 712.

22. OR 30, pt. 2, 32.

23. Timothy D. Johnson, "Benjamin Franklin Cheatham: The Early Years," *Tennessee Historical Quarterly* (fall 1983): 275–78; Losson, "Major General Benjamin Franklin Cheatham and the Battle of Stone's River," 281–82, 286; McDonough,

Stones River, 97–100, 227; Connelly, *Autumn of Glory*, 55, 84–85; OR 20, pt. 1, 663–72.

24. OR 30, pt. 1, 713.

25. OR 30, pt. 1, 535, 538–39, 543, 713, 761–62, 780–81, pt. 2, 78–79, 83–84, 94–96, 106–7, 117–19, 130–31; Tucker, *Chickamauga*, 141–46; Cozzens, *This Terrible Sound*, 152–56.

26. OR 30, pt. 1, 250, 440, 803, pt. 2, 32, 361–62.

27. Cozzens, *This Terrible Sound*, 196–99.

28. OR 30, pt. 1, 496–99, 515–17, 528–30, pt. 2, 453–56, 471–75; Cozzens, *This Terrible Sound*, 196–200.

29. OR 30, pt. 2, 453–56, 471–75; Cozzens, *This Terrible Sound*, 198–200.

30. OR 30, pt. 1, 498–99, 515–16, 529, 631–32, 838–39; Cozzens, *This Terrible Sound*, 200–205.

31. OR 30, pt. 1, 608, pt. 2, 357.

32. OR 30, pt. 2, 32, 140, 197–98, 302–3.

33. OR 30, pt. 2, 32. Connelly (*Autumn of Glory*, 202–5) judges Bragg by an unrealistic standard in indicting him for not attacking decisively in the Viniard field sector earlier in the day. He asserts that Bragg might have cut off and captured much of Rosecrans's army by attacking with Hood and Buckner in midmorning rather than midafternoon. This is true in part. Depending on exactly when such an attack had been launched, it would have missed cutting off only the divisions of Brannan, Baird, and possibly Reynolds, Johnson, and Palmer. Somewhere between five and eight (out of a total of ten) Federal infantry divisions would have been south of the Viniard field at that time. Yet most of those five to eight divisions would have been very nearby, and Rosecrans obviously would have fought desperately to avoid being cut off. Bragg would have needed to use most of his army, not just Hood and Buckner. Asserting that Bragg should have done this assumes that Bragg somehow could have had the information on which such an attack would have been based. The truth is that Bragg could not possibly have known the location of all those Federal units until he engaged them, nor could he have known the strength of the Federal force that assailed his right rear to open the battle and whether he dared ignore it.

34. OR 30, pt. 1, 498–99, 516, 529, 608–9, 632–33; Cozzens, *This Terrible Sound*, 200–210.

35. OR 30, pt. 1, 447–48, 498–99, 516, 529–30, 607–9, 632–34, pt. 2, 430–31, 510–11, 517–18; Cozzens, *This Terrible Sound*, 221–29.

36. Cozzens, *This Terrible Sound*, 230–45; OR 30, pt. 1, 440; Tucker, *Chickamauga*, 152–58.

37. OR 30, pt. 1, 440.

38. OR 30, pt. 1, 250, 329, 401, pt. 2, 362, 371, 383, 402.

39. OR 30, pt. 1, 441, 762, 799, pt. 2, 384.

40. Cozzens, *This Terrible Sound*, 263–65; Connelly, *Autumn of Glory*, 207.

41. OR pt. 1, 250–51, 276–77, 535, pt. 2, 32, 154.

5. THEY FOUGHT LIKE TIGERS

1. OR 30, pt. 1, 57, 251, 488, 609.

2. Wert, *General James Longstreet*.

3. OR 30, pt. 2, 11–18, 33; Connelly, *Autumn of Glory*, 208–9. Connelly characterized Bragg's decision to reorganize the army as "inexplicable."

4. Connelly, though admitting that Bragg's battle plan might have been successful if adequate strength had been concentrated on the Confederate left, implied that Bragg was at fault in that "he did not plan to cut off the Federals by moving northward and seizing the pass [Rossville Gap] to Chattanooga" (*Autumn of Glory*, 209). The idea of moving north to seize Rossville Gap is another of the concepts that looks good at first glance but less so when examined closely. If Bragg had chosen to move toward the gap on the east bank of the Chickamauga, Rosecrans would have beat him there; if on the west bank, he would have been in much the same situation in which Rosecrans found himself—trying to move his army by the flank while in contact with the enemy. In short, to the commander of the Army of Tennessee on the evening of September 20, a move against Rossville Gap would have offered scant prospect of success and ominous chance of disaster. If decisive Confederate victory was to be obtained the next day, it would have to be done by driving the Federals south of the Dyer Road and its connection with McFarland's Gap and the Dry Valley Road.

5. OR 30, pt. 2, 33; Connelly, *Autumn of Glory*, 210.

6. OR 30, pt. 2, 33, 47, 140–41; Connelly, *Autumn of Glory*, 211–14.

7. OR 30, pt. 2, 47, 140–41, 197–98, 203, 209–11, 214, 216, 219, 231, 233, 236, 239; Connelly, *Autumn of Glory*, 215–16.

8. OR 30, pt. 2, 33, 47, 140–41, 193; Connelly, *Autumn of Glory*, 218–20; Cozzens, *This Terrible Sound*, 305–9; Davis, *Breckinridge*, 371–72; Hallock, *Braxton Bragg*, 71–73; Tucker, *Chickamauga*, 222–31; Parks, *General Leonidas Polk*, 334–36.

9. OR 30, pt. 2, 33, 47–48, 141, 216, 219, 231, 233, 236, 239; Connelly, *Autumn of Glory*, 219–21; Cozzens, *This Terrible Sound*, 308–10.

10. Cozzens, *This Terrible Sound*, 310–13; McKinney, *Education in Violence*, 235–40.

11. OR 30, pt. 1, 441, 535, 714, 763; Cozzens, *This Terrible Sound*, 338–56.

12. Cozzens, *This Terrible Sound*, 338–56; Connelly, *Autumn of Glory*, 209–21; Tucker, *Chickamauga*, 253–60.

13. OR 30, pt. 1, 251, 367–69, pt. 2, 198–99; McKinney, *Education in Violence*, 238–41; Cozzens, *This Terrible Sound*, 320–26; Connelly, *Autumn of Glory*, 221; Beatty, *Memoirs of a Volunteer*, 246.

14. OR 30, pt. 2, 198–99, 203–4; Cozzens, *This Terrible Sound*, 320–21.

15. OR 30, pt. 1, 251, 277–78, pt. 2, 199–200, 216–17, 231; Cozzens, *This Terrible Sound*, 329–32; Tucker, *Chickamauga*, 233–42.

16. OR 30, pt. 1, 278; Cozzens, *This Terrible Sound*, 332–33.

17. McKinney, *Education in Violence*, 238; Cozzens, *This Terrible Sound*, 232–34.

18. OR 30, pt. 1, 429–30; Cozzens, *This Terrible Sound*, 334–36.

19. OR 30, pt. 2, 200.

20. OR 30, pt. 1, 763, pt. 2, 154–58; Tucker, *Chickamauga*, 242–46; Cozzens, *This Terrible Sound*, 338–49.

21. OR 30, pt. 2, 245–46; Connelly, *Autumn of Glory*, 222–23; Cozzens, *This Terrible Sound*, 350–56.

22. McKinney, *Education in Violence*, 244.

23. Lamers, *Edge of Glory*, 342; Cozzens, *This Terrible Sound*, 359–61.

24. OR 30, pt. 1, 635; Cozzens, *This Terrible Sound*, 361.

25. Cozzens, *This Terrible Sound*, 360.

26. Warner, *Generals in Blue*, 569–70; Tucker, *Chickamauga*, 205–7; Beatty, *Memoirs of a Volunteer*, 191–92.

27. Cozzens, *This Terrible Sound*, 362–67; Tucker, *Chickamauga*, 255–59.

28. OR 30, pt. 2, 288, 457.

29. OR 30, pt. 1, 500.

30. OR 30, pt. 1, 457–58.

31. Cozzens, *This Terrible Sound*, 380.

32. OR 30, pt. 1, 448.

33. OR 30, pt. 1, 580–81, 583–84, 590, 595.

34. OR 30, pt. 1, 448–49.

35. OR 30, pt. 1, 414, 622–23, 678.

36. OR 30, pt. 2, 458–59; Connelly (*Autumn of Glory*, 224–25) argues that Longstreet could indeed have seized the Dry Valley Road, but this would have required his driving nearly a mile into the enemy position while ignoring the flanks of his own assault column. Such tactical ideas had to await World War II.

37. OR 30, pt. 1, 623, pt. 2, 458–59.

38. Wert, *General James Longstreet*, 313.

39. Cozzens, *This Terrible Sound*, 406–12.

40. Cozzens, *This Terrible Sound*, 412–16; OR 30, pt. 1, 637, 694–95, pt. 2, 503–4.

41. OR 30, pt. 1, 252, 637–38, 694–95; Cozzens, *This Terrible Sound*, 423; Beatty, *Memoirs of a Volunteer*, 250.

42. Wert, *General James Longstreet*, 315–16; Cozzens, *This Terrible Sound*, 454–55; Longstreet, *From Manassas to Appomattox*, 450–51.

43. OR 30, pt. 1, 854–55, 860, 862, 867, pt. 2, 525; Cozzens, *This Terrible Sound*, 438–44.

44. McKinney, *Education in Violence*, 249; Cozzens, *This Terrible Sound*, 443; Beatty, *Memoirs of a Volunteer*, 250–51.

45. OR 30, pt. 1, 252–53, 860; Cozzens, *This Terrible Sound*, 443–44.

46. OR 30, pt. 1, 253, 403, 388–89, 695, 860, 862–63, 865, 867, 869–70; Cozzens, *This Terrible Sound*, 444–46.

47. Wert, *General James Longstreet*, 315.

48. Wert, *General James Longstreet*, 315–17; Longstreet, *From Manassas to Appomattox*, 452.

49. Longstreet, *From Manassas to Appomattox*, 452; OR 30, pt. 2, 34; Hallock, *Braxton Bragg*, 80; Connelly (*Autumn of Glory*, 225) follows Longstreet in asserting that at this point Bragg left the battlefield and spent the rest of the day apparently sulking at his headquarters at Reed's Bridge. In fact, Bragg left Longstreet's sector to give much-needed personal oversight to Polk's.

50. OR 30, pt. 1, 253; Cozzens, *This Terrible Sound*, 487–502.

51. Cozzens, *This Terrible Sound*, 502–9.

6. LIKE A DUCK HIT ON THE HEAD

1. Wiley Sword, *Mountains Touched with Fire: Chattanooga Besieged, 1863* (New York: St. Martin's, 1995), 14–15; Lamers, *Edge of Glory*, 356–60; Hough, *Soldier in the West*, 150–51.

2. Sword, *Mountains Touched with Fire*, 17, 37–39; Cozzens, *This Terrible Sound*, 520; Chesley A. Mosman, *The Rough Side of War: The Civil War Journal of Chesley A. Mosman, First Lieutenant, Company D, Fifty-ninth Illinois Volunteer Infantry Regiment*, ed. Arnold Gates (Garden City NY: Basin, 1987), 88–89; Lamers, *Edge of Glory*, 360–61.

3. Sword, *Mountains Touched with Fire*, 15–17; David H. Donald, *Lincoln* (New York: Simon & Schuster, 1995), 457.

4. OR 30, pt. 3, 762; Sword, *Mountains Touched with Fire*, 38; Lamers, *Edge of Glory*, 365.

5. Sword, *Mountains Touched with Fire*, 38–39; Cozzens, *This Terrible Sound*, 520–21.

6. Connelly, *Autumn of Glory*, 228–29; Cozzens, *This Terrible Sound*, 517; Wert, *General James Longstreet*, 318–19. Parks (*General Leonidas Polk*, 340) asserts that Polk knew of the Union departure and so informed Bragg around midnight of the night after the battle, but this is based on an unreliable account given nearly twenty years after the battle and is contrary to other evidence.

7. Connelly, *Autumn of Glory*, 227–31; Cozzens, *This Terrible Sound*, 517–18; Wert, *General James Longstreet*, 318–19; Longstreet, *From Manassas to Appomattox*, 461–62.

8. Connelly, *Autumn of Glory*, 230–31.

9. Connelly, *Autumn of Glory*, 226–27; Hallock, *Braxton Bragg*, 83.

10. Sword, *Mountains Touched with Fire*, 19–20; Hallock, *Braxton Bragg*, 84; James Lee McDonough, *Chattanooga—A Death Grip on the Confederacy* (Knoxville: University of Tennessee Press, 1984), 20–24; Connelly, *Autumn of Glory*, 231–33; Wills, *Battle from the Start*, 141–42.

11. Wills, *Battle from the Start*, 141–42; Sword, *Mountains Touched with Fire*, 19–20.

12. Hallock, *Braxton Bragg*, 84; Connelly, *Autumn of Glory*, 231–33.

13. Lamers, *Edge of Glory*, 368; McKinney, *Education in Violence*, 268; Mosman, *Rough Side of War*, 87–89.

14. Mosman, *Rough Side of War*, 88–89.

15. OR 30, pt. 3, 808, 834–35; Sword, *Mountains Touched with Fire*, 41, 44; Lamers, *Edge of Glory*, 368–69; McKinney, *Education in Violence*, 267–68.

16. Sword, *Mountains Touched with Fire*, 38–39.

17. Sword, *Mountains Touched with Fire*, 39; Lamers, *Edge of Glory*, 365–66.

18. Sword, *Mountains Touched with Fire*, 40; Donald, *Lincoln*, 457; T. Harry Williams, *Lincoln and His Generals* (New York Vintage Books, 1953), 283; OR 30, pt. 3, 834–35.

19. Sword, *Mountains Touched with Fire*, 40–41.

20. On the rail movement of troops from the Army of the Potomac to Chattanooga in September 1863 see Roger Pickenpaugh's excellent *Rescue by Rail* (Lincoln: University of Nebraska Press, forthcoming).

21. Sword, *Mountains Touched with Fire*, 41.

22. Donald, *Lincoln*, 458.

23. Hallock, *Braxton Bragg*, 83–84.

24. Woodworth, *Jefferson Davis and His Generals*, 238; Horn, *Army of Tennessee*, 259; OR 30, pt. 2, 47, 54, 67–68; Hallock, *Braxton Bragg*, 89; Connelly, *Autumn of Glory*, 235–36; McDonough, *Chattanooga*, 28; Wert, *General James Longstreet*, 300–303; Parks, *General Leonidas Polk*, 342–43; Bridges, *Lee's Maverick General*, 228.

25. Woodworth, *Jefferson Davis and His Generals*, 238–39; Longstreet, *From Manassas to Appomattox*, 464; OR 30, pt. 2, 67–69, pt. 4, 705–6; McDonough, *Chattanooga*, 29–30; Connelly, *Autumn of Glory*, 51; Wert, *General James Longstreet*, 325–26; Parks, *General Leonidas Polk*, 342–44.

26. OR 30, pt. 2, 55–56, vol. 52, pt. 2, 534; Connelly, *Autumn of Glory*, 236.

27. OR 30, pt. 2, 55, 67–68, vol. 52, pt. 2, 533–34; McDonough, *Chattanooga*, 29–30; Connelly, *Autumn of Glory*, 236.

28. OR 30, pt. 2, 65–66; Longstreet, *From Manassas to Appomattox*, 465; Horn, *Army of Tennessee*, 286; McDonough, *Chattanooga*, 30; Arndt M. Stickles, *Simon Bolivar Buckner: Borderland Knight* (Chapel Hill: University of North Carolina Press, 1940), 234–38; Connelly, *Autumn of Glory*, 239–40; Davis, *Breckinridge*, 381–82.

29. OR 30, pt. 2, 54, 56, vol. 51, 772, vol. 52, pt. 2, 535, 540; Longstreet, *From Manassas to Appomattox*, 465; Jones, *Rebel War Clerk's Diary*, 289; McDonough, *Chattanooga*, 35; Rowland, ed., *Jefferson Davis*, 5:62–63; Connelly, *Autumn of Glory*, 241–42; Hallock, *Braxton Bragg*, 94; William C. Davis, *Jefferson Davis: The Man and His Hour* (New York: Harper Collins, 1991), 518–19.

30. Davis, *Jefferson Davis*, 519–21; Hudson Strode, *Jefferson Davis, Confederate President* (New York: Harcourt, Brace, 1959), 479–80; OR 30, pt. 4, 751; Connelly, *Autumn of Glory*, 241, 245; Longstreet, *From Manassas to Appomattox*, 465–66.

31. OR 30, pt. 2, 148–49, pt. 4, 751, vol. 52, pt. 2, 535; Connelly, *Autumn of Glory*, 240–41; Henry, *"First with the Most,"* 198–200; Wills, *Battle from the Start*, 145–49.

32. McDonough, *Chattanooga*, 39; OR 52, pt. 2, 557; Connelly, *Autumn of Glory*, 246, 250–51.

33. Sword, *Mountains Touched with Fire*, 41–43; Peter Cozzens, *The Shipwreck of Their Hopes: The Battles for Chattanooga* (Urbana: University of Illinois Press, 1994), 14–18.

34. Cozzens, *Shipwreck of Their Hopes*, 18–20; Sword, *Mountains Touched with Fire*, 43; McDonough, *Chattanooga*, 47–48; Lamers, *Edge of Glory*, 373–76; McKinney, *Education in Violence*, 269.

35. Mosman, *Rough Side of War*, 106–7; McDonough, *Chattanooga*, 48; Sword, *Mountains Touched with Fire*, 42–44; Cozzens, *Shipwreck of Their Hopes*, 20–22.

36. Mosman, *Rough Side of War*, 106–7; McDonough, *Chattanooga*, 48; Sword, *Mountains Touched with Fire*, 42–44; Cozzens, *Shipwreck of Their Hopes*, 20–22.

37. Sword, *Mountains Touched with Fire*, 44–45, 48–49, 103; Cozzens, *Shipwreck of Their Hopes*, 18–19.

38. Smith, *Private Smith's Journal*, 112; Cozzens, *Shipwreck of Their Hopes*, 11.

39. Sword, *Mountains Touched with Fire*, 107–11; Cozzens, *Shipwreck of Their Hopes*, 29–31; McDonough, *Chattanooga*, 63–64; Woodworth, *Jefferson Davis and His Generals*, 252.

40. Mosman, *Rough Side of War*, 90–91, 93; Sword, *Mountains Touched with Fire*, 90–91.

41. Mosman, *Rough Side of War*, 92–93; Sword, *Mountains Touched with Fire*, 91–95; Beatty, *Memoirs of a Volunteer*, 258.

42. Mosman, *Rough Side of War*, 92; Sword, *Mountains Touched with Fire*, 93.

43. Mosman, *Rough Side of War*, 104.

44. Sword, *Mountains Touched with Fire*, 39, 49–50; Lamers, *Edge of Glory*, 386–87; Warner, *Generals in Blue*, 100–101, 294–95.

45. McKinney, *Education in Violence*, 269–70; Cozzens, *Shipwreck of Their Hopes*, 4; Sword, *Mountains Touched with Fire*, 46–50.

46. McKinney, *Education in Violence*, 269.

47. Donald, *Lincoln*, 419–20, 455.

48. Lamers, *Edge of Glory*, 379.

49. Lamers, *Edge of Glory*, 379–80.

50. Sword, *Mountains Touched with Fire*, 51–52.

51. Grant, *Personal Memoirs*, 1:583–84, 2:17; Sword, *Mountains Touched with Fire*, 51–53.

7. THE CRACKER LINE

1. Grant, *Personal Memoirs*, 1:578–81.

2. Bruce Catton, *Grant Takes Command* (Boston: Little, Brown, 1968), 25–27; OR 30, pt. 4, 274.

3. Sword, *Mountains Touched with Fire*, 53; Catton, *Grant Takes Command*, 33–34; Grant, *Personal Memoirs*, 2:17–18.

4. Grant, *Personal Memoirs*, 2:18–19; Sword, *Mountains Touched with Fire*, 53–54; Catton, *Grant Takes Command*, 34.

5. Grant, *Personal Memoirs*, 2:19; Catton, *Grant Takes Command*, 34; McDonough, *Chattanooga*, 49; McKinney, *Education in Violence*, 272.

6. Grant, *Personal Memoirs*, 2:26; OR 30, pt. 4, 479; Lamers, *Edge of Glory*, 393; McKinney, *Education in Violence*, 272.

7. Catton, *Grant Takes Command*, 35; Lamers, *Edge of Glory*, 392; Grant, *Personal Memoirs*, 2:28; Mosman, *Rough Side of War*, 225.

8. Catton, *Grant Takes Command*, 37–41; McDonough, *Chattanooga*, 53–54; Grant, *Personal Memoirs*, 2:28–29; Horace Porter, *Campaigning with Grant*, ed. Wayne C. Temple (New York: Bonanza Books, 1961), 1.

9. Catton, *Grant Takes Command*, 40; McDonough, *Chattanooga*, 54; McKinney, *Education in Violence*, 273–74; Sword, *Mountains Touched with Fire*, 58.

10. Porter, *Campaigning with Grant*, 1–7; Grant, *Personal Memoirs*, 2:29–30; McDonough, *Chattanooga*, 54–55; Sword, *Mountains Touched with Fire*, 58–59.

11. McDonough, *Chattanooga*, 55–57; Sword, *Mountains Touched with Fire*, 59.

12. McDonough, *Chattanooga*, 57.

13. Grant, *Personal Memoirs*, 2:31; Porter, *Campaigning with Grant*, 8; Catton, *Grant Takes Command*, 42–43.

14. Sword, *Mountains Touched with Fire*, 112–15; McDonough, *Chattanooga*, 76–79; Catton, *Grant Takes Command*, 50; Cozzens, *Shipwreck of Their Hopes*, 52–53.

15. Connelly, *Autumn of Glory*, 25–56; Wert, *General James Longstreet*, 330–33.

16. Wert, *General James Longstreet*, 331.

17. Connelly, *Autumn of Glory*, 256–58; Wert, *General James Longstreet*, 333.

18. Richard M. McMurry, *John Bell Hood and the War for Southern Independence* (Lexington: University Press of Kentucky, 1982), 76; Guy R. Swanson and Timothy D. Johnson, "Conflict in East Tennessee: Generals Law, Jenkins, and Longstreet," *Civil War History* 31 (June 1985): 101–10; Wert, *General James Longstreet*, 333, 337.

19. Connelly, *Autumn of Glory*, 256; Wert, *General James Longstreet*, 334–35.

20. Sword, *Mountains Touched with Fire*, 119; Wert, *General James Longstreet*, 33; McDonough, *Chattanooga*, 81–83; Cozzens, *Shipwreck of Their Hopes*, 58–59.

21. OR 31, pt. 1, 40, 49–51, 77–92; Grant, *Personal Memoirs*, 2:36–37; Catton, *Grant Takes Command*, 51–53; Sword, *Mountains Touched with Fire*, 112–22; Porter, *Campaigning with Grant*, 8–9; Cozzens, *Shipwreck of Their Hopes*, 57–65.

22. Grant, *Personal Memoirs*, 2:36–37; Porter, *Campaigning with Grant*, 8–9.

23. OR 31, pt. 1, 43–49, 51–55, 92, 97, 101, 110, 112; Sword, *Mountains Touched with Fire*, 125–26; Catton, *Grant Takes Command*, 53; Cozzens, *Shipwreck of Their Hopes*, 69–70.

24. OR 31, pt. 1, 93, 97, 99, 101.

25. OR 31, pt. 1, 93, 97, 99, 101; Sword, *Mountains Touched with Fire*, 126–27; John T. McMahon, *John T. McMahon's Diary of the 136th New York, 1861–1864*, ed. John Michael Priest (Shippensburg PA: White Mane, 1993), 67; Cozzens, *Shipwreck of Their Hopes*, 71–72.

26. Connelly, *Autumn of Glory*, 257–59; McDonough, *Chattanooga*, 85; Cozzens, *Shipwreck of Their Hopes*, 66–69; Wert, *General James Longstreet*, 334–35.

27. Hallock, *Braxton Bragg*, 122–23; Wert, *General James Longstreet*, 35; Connelly, *Autumn of Glory*, 259.

28. Connelly, *Autumn of Glory*, 259–60; McDonough, *Chattanooga*, 88; Cozzens, *Shipwreck of Their Hopes*, 79; Sword, *Mountains Touched with Fire*, 129–30; Wert, *General James Longstreet*, 335–36; Hallock, *Braxton Bragg*, 123; Swanson and Johnson, "Conflict in East Tennessee," 101–10; Longstreet, *From Manassas to Appomattox*, 474–78.

29. OR 31, pt. 1, 52–54, 217–18; Longstreet, *From Manassas to Appomattox*, 475.

30. OR 31, pt. 1, 217–18; Swanson and Johnson, "Conflict in East Tennessee," 104–6.

31. Connelly, *Autumn of Glory*, 259–69; McDonough, *Chattanooga*, 88; Cozzens, *Shipwreck of Their Hopes*, 79; Sword, *Mountains Touched with Fire*, 129–30; Wert, *General James Longstreet*, 335–36; Hallock, *Braxton Bragg*, 123; Swanson and Johnson, "Conflict in East Tennessee," 101–10; Longstreet, *From Manassas to Appomattox*, .475–76.

32. Sword, *Mountains Touched with Fire*, 134–37; McDonough, *Chattanooga*, 89–93; Cozzens, *Shipwreck of Their Hopes*, 82–90; Porter, *Campaigning with Grant*, 9–10.

33. OR 31, pt. 1, 98–234; McDonough, *Chattanooga*, 91–94; Sword, *Mountains Touched with Fire*, 135–44; Cozzens, *Shipwreck of Their Hopes*, 97–100.

34. OR 31, pt. 1, 98–216.

35. OR 31, pt. 1, 218.

36. OR 31, pt. 1, 95, 218, 230, 233, 235.

37. OR 31, pt. 1, 56.

8. I HAVE NEVER FELT SUCH RESTLESSNESS

1. OR 31, pt. 1, 242–54; Grant, *Personal Memoirs*, 2:44–45; William T. Sherman, *Memoirs of General William T. Sherman*, 2 vols. (Bloomington: Indiana University Press, 1957), 1:347–57; John F. Marszalek, *Sherman: A Soldier's Passion for Order* (New York: Free Press, 1993), 238–40.

2. Sherman, *Memoirs*, 1:359; Grant, *Personal Memoirs*, 2:47–48.

3. Marszalek, *Sherman*, 241–42; Sherman, *Memoirs*, 1:357–62; Grant, *Personal Memoirs*, 2:45–46; OR 31, pt. 3, 39.

4. Marszalek, *Sherman*, 242.

5. Grant, *Personal Memoirs*, 2:49–50; Catton, *Grant Takes Command*, 59–61; McKinney, *Education in Violence*, 281; OR 31, pt. 2, 29.

6. Grant, *Personal Memoirs*, 2:58–60; Sherman, *Memoirs*, 1:361–63; OR 31, pt. 2, 31–32, 571; McKinney, *Education in Violence*, 281–82; Catton, *Grant Takes Command*, 67–71; Marszalek, *Sherman*, 242–43.

7. Sherman, *Memoirs*, 1:363.

8. Sword, *Mountains Touched with Fire*, 158–63; Catton, *Grant Takes Command*, 69; Sherman, *Memoirs*, 1:364; OR 31, pt. 2, 31, 572.

9. Edward Carr Franks, "The Detachment of Longstreet Considered: Braxton Bragg, James Longstreet, and the Chattanooga Campaign," in *Leadership and Command in the American Civil War*, ed. Steven E. Woodworth (Campbell CA: Savas Woodbury, 1995), 32–35; Connelly, *Autumn of Glory*, 232, 261–62; Horn, *Army of Tennessee*, 296.

10. Franks, "Detachment of Longstreet Considered," 49–50, 62.

11. Franks, "Detachment of Longstreet Considered," 50–52.

12. Franks, "Detachment of Longstreet Considered," 50–53.

13. Franks, "Detachment of Longstreet Considered," 41–45; Connelly, *Autumn of Glory*, 263; OR 30, pt. 2, 547, 551–52, 574, 639, pt. 4, 756, 760–61, vol. 31, pt. 1, 8, 267, 613, 680, 770, 778, pt. 3, 292, 607, vol. 34, pt. 2, 862, vol. 52, pt. 2, 555; Richard C. Drum, "The Opposing Forces at Knoxville," in Robert U. Johnson and Clarence C. Buel, eds., *Battles and Leaders of the Civil War*, 4 vols. (New York: Century, 1884), 3:752.

14. Franks, "Detachment of Longstreet Considered," 52–53.

15. See Woodworth, *Davis and Lee at War*.

16. Davis to Bragg, October 29, 1863, Philip H. and A. S. W. Rosenbach, Rosenbach Museum and Library, Philadelphia; OR 29, pt. 2, 742; Dowdey and Manarin, eds., *Wartime Papers of R. E. Lee*, 604–5.

17. Franks, "Detachment of Longstreet Considered," 53; OR 31, pt. 3, 634.

18. Connelly, *Autumn of Glory*, 263; Hallock, *Braxton Bragg*, 126.

19. Franks, "Detachment of Longstreet Considered," 36; Davis to Bragg, October 29, 1863, Philip H. and A. S. W. Rosenbach, Rosenbach Museum and Library, Philadelphia; Joseph E. Johnston, *Narrative of Military Operations Directed During the Late War Between the States* (New York: Appleton, 1874), 261; Hallock, *Braxton Bragg*, 126.

20. OR 31, pt. 3, 634–35. That Bragg intended an eventual movement into Middle Tennessee is also borne out by his assurance to Longstreet that he would be able to forage for food "until you strike the mountains." This would have had to have meant going somewhere besides Knoxville because it lay in the Tennessee Valley, up which Longstreet would be moving. The mountains Bragg had in mind were probably the Cumberlands, which an army would have to cross to reach Middle Tennessee from the upper Tennessee Valley.

21. OR 31, pt. 2, 635–37, 644–45, 670–71; Wert, *General James Longstreet*, 340–41.

22. Franks, "Detachment of Longstreet Considered," 59; Wert, *General James Longstreet*, 340–45; OR 31, pt. 3, 686–87.

23. Franks, "Detachment of Longstreet Considered," 59; Wert, *General James Longstreet*, 340–45.

24. OR 31, pt. 3, 721, 732–33.

25. Franks, "Detachment of Longstreet Considered," 53–57.

26. See Craig L. Symonds's excellent new biography of Cleburne, *Stonewall of the West* (Lawrence: University Press of Kansas, 1997).

9. FIX BAYONETS AND GO AHEAD

1. OR 31, pt. 2, 32; Ulysses S. Grant, "Chattanooga," in Johnson and Buel, eds., *Battles and Leaders*, 3:698; Grant, *Personal Memoirs*, 2:60–64; Cozzens, *Shipwreck of Their Hopes*, 126–28; McDonough, *Chattanooga*, 109–10; McKinney, *Education in Violence*, 280–86; Sword, *Mountains Touched with Fire*, 175–78; Catton, *Grant Takes Command*, 68–72.

2. OR 31, pt. 2, 32–33, 94–95, 128–30, 253–56, 263–65; Sword, *Mountains Touched with Fire*, 175–85.

3. OR 31, pt. 2, 745–46; Connelly, *Autumn of Glory*, 272; Hallock, *Braxton Bragg*, 131–32; Sword, *Mountains Touched with Fire*, 186–88.

4. OR 31, pt. 2, 572, 643, 646; Grant, *Personal Memoirs*, 2:66–68; Grant, "Chattanooga," 3:699–701; A Committee of the 55th Illinois, *The Story of the Fifty-Fifth Regiment Illinois Volunteer Infantry in the Civil War, 1861–1865* (Huntington WV: Blue Acorn Press, 1993), 282–83; S. H. M. Byers, "Sherman's Attack at the Tunnel," in Johnson and Buel, eds., *Battles and Leaders*, 3:712; Catton, *Grant Takes Command*, 76; McDonough, *Chattanooga*, 119–20; Sword, *Mountains Touched with Fire*, 192–96; Cozzens, *Shipwreck of Their Hopes*, 147–48.

5. OR 31, pt. 2, 572–73.

6. OR 31, pt. 2, 19–20, 22–24, 33, 490–94, 573, 643; Grant, *Personal Memoirs*, 2:67–68; Grant, "Chattanooga," 3:701; Committee of the Fifty-fifth Illinois, *Fifty-fifth Illinois*, 283–84.

7. Cozzens, *Shipwreck of Their Hopes*, 154–55.

8. OR 31, pt. 2, 573, 629, 636, 646; Grant, "Chattanooga," 3:701–2; Sword, *Mountains Touched with Fire*, 198–99.

9. OR 31, pt. 2, 24, 573; Committee of the Fifty-fifth Illinois, *Fifty-fifth Illinois*, 284–85; McDonough, *Chattanooga*, 122; Marszalek, *Sherman*, 243–44; Cozzens, *Shipwreck of Their Hopes*, 154–55. Historians, including the present writer, have for years criticized Sherman for supposedly being on the wrong height, a detached hill rather than the north end of the ridge, as he supposed and reported to Grant. Careful examination of the ground and the written evidence, however, reveals that the high ground Sherman's men took on the afternoon of November 24 was indeed part of Missionary Ridge. Sherman's mistake, like Bragg's next day, was in miscalculating the terrain effect the ridge would produce on combat operations. In fact, and to almost everyone's surprise, the ridge turned out to be a better defensive position end-on than it was broadside.

10. Sword, *Mountains Touched with Fire*, 199.

11. OR 31, pt. 2, 664, 678, 745–46; Hallock, *Braxton Bragg*, 131; McDonough, *Chattanooga*, 124–26; Cozzens, *Shipwreck of Their Hopes*, 149–53; Connelly, *Autumn of Glory*, 272; Hughes, *General William J. Hardee*, 170–71.

12. OR 31, pt. 2, 660, 746–47; McDonough, *Chattanooga*, 124–25; Cozzens, *Shipwreck of Their Hopes*, 151–53.

13. George K. Collins, *Memoirs of the 149th Regiment New York Volunteer Infantry* (Syracuse: Published by the author, 1891), 207.

14. Connolly, *Three Years in the Army of the Cumberland*, 153–54.

15. OR 31, pt. 2, 33, 154–56, 314–17, 390–99, 411–12, 599–600, 665, 677, 688–96; Grant, *Personal Memoirs*, 2:70–73; McDonough, *Chattanooga*, 130–40; Catton, *Grant Takes Command*, 73–76; Cozzens, *Shipwreck of Their Hopes*, 159–91; Sword, *Mountains Touched with Fire*, 202–21.

16. OR 31, pt. 2, 677, 688–96, 718–22; McDonough, *Chattanooga*, 137–40; Connelly, *Autumn of Glory*, 270–73; Hallock, *Braxton Bragg*, 130–34.

17. OR 31, pt. 2, 664; Hallock, *Braxton Bragg*, 132–34; Connelly, *Autumn of Glory*, 270–71; Robert D. Goforth, "Sherman and Cleburne at Tunnel Hill: The Myth of the Inevitability of Confederate Defeat at Chattanooga, November 23–25, 1863" (master's thesis, East Carolina University, 1992), 107–9.

18. OR 31, pt. 2, 24–25; Grant, "Chattanooga," 3:704.

19. Grant, *Personal Memoirs*, 2:75; OR 31, pt. 2, 43–44.

20. OR 31, pt. 2, 664, 721–22; Hallock, *Braxton Bragg*, 134–36; Connelly, *Autumn of Glory*, 273; Hughes, *General William J. Hardee*, 171–72; Davis, *Breckinridge*, 386–87; Sword, *Mountains Touched with Fire*, 235–37; Cozzens, *Shipwreck of Their Hopes*, 195–97; Goforth, "Sherman and Cleburne at Tunnel Hill," 108–9.

21. OR 31, pt. 2, 318, 600.

22. OR 31, pt. 2, 574–75, 631–32, 633–37, 643–44, 748–52; Grant, *Personal Memoirs*, 2:76–77; Byers, "Sherman's Attack at the Tunnel," 3:713; Committee of the Fifty-fifth Illinois, *Fifty-fifth Illinois*, 285–88; McDonough, *Chattanooga*, 143–60; Catton, *Grant Takes Command*, 77–78; Sword, *Mountains Touched with Fire*, 231–62; Cozzens, *Shipwreck of Their Hopes*, 204–43; Connelly, *Autumn of Glory*, 275; Marszalek, *Sherman*, 244; Hughes, *General William J. Hardee*, 174–75.

23. OR 31, pt. 2, 318, 600–601; Grant, *Personal Memoirs*, 2:78; McDonough, *Chattanooga*, 159–60; Catton, *Grant Takes Command*, 79; Sword, *Mountains Touched with Fire*, 306–7; Cozzens, *Shipwreck of Their Hopes*, 244–45.

24. OR 31, pt. 2, 44; McKinney, *Education in Violence*, 294.

25. Michael H. Fitch, *The Chattanooga Campaign* (Madison: Wisconsin History Commission, 1911), 219; Helmuth von Moltke quoted in Jay M. Shafritz, ed., *Words on War* (New York: Prentice Hall, 1990), 474.

26. OR 31, pt. 2, 44.

27. Grant, *Personal Memoirs*, 2:78–79; Cozzens, *Shipwreck of Their Hopes*, 245–48; McKinney, *Education in Violence*, 294–95; Catton, *Grant Takes Command*, 79.

28. Hughes, *General William J. Hardee*, 174.

29. OR 31, pt. 2, 132–33, 189–90, 200, 257–58, 264–65; Connolly, *Three Years in the Army of the Cumberland*, 156.

30. OR 31, pt. 2, 132–33, 189–90, 200, 257–58, 264–65; Joseph S. Fullerton, "The Army of the Cumberland at Chattanooga," in Johnson and Buel, eds., *Battles and Leaders*, 3:725–26; McDonough, *Chattanooga*, 163–80; Sword, *Mountains Touched with Fire*, 275–85; Cozzens, *Shipwreck of Their Hopes*, 259–81; Catton, *Grant Takes Command*, 80–83.

31. McDonough, *Chattanooga*, 181–86; Hughes, *General William J. Hardee*, 174; Goforth, "Sherman and Cleburne at Tunnel Hill," 124–25.

32. OR 31, pt. 2, 132–35, 189–93, 208, 230–32, 258–61, 264–65, 281–83, 318–20, 527–29, 600–602; Fullerton, "The Army of the Cumberland at Chattanooga," 3:725–26; Samuel Watkins, *"Co. Aytch," Maury Grays, First Tennessee Regiment; or A Side Show of the Big Show* (Jackson TN: McCowat-Mercer Press, 1952), 125; Sword, *Mountains Touched with Fire*, 282–325; McDonough, *Chattanooga*, 176–205; Hallock, *Braxton Bragg*, 138–42; Connolly, *Autumn of Glory*, 275–76; Cozzens, *Shipwreck of Their Hopes*, 282–360; Goforth, "Sherman and Cleburne at Tunnel Hill," 127–28; Connolly, *Three Years in the Army of the Cumberland*, 150; Smith, *Private Smith's Journal*, 121–22.

33. Cozzens, *Shipwreck of Their Hopes*, 361.

34. Grant's political astuteness is ably discussed by Brooks Simpson in *Let Us Have Peace: Ulysses S. Grant and the Politics of War and Peace, 1861–1864* (Chapel Hill: University of North Carolina Press, 1991).

35. Grant, *Personal Memoirs*, 2:84; Sherman, *Memoirs*, 364–65.

36. Sword, *Mountains Touched with Fire*, 326–35; Cozzens, *Shipwreck of Their Hopes*, 362–69.

37. Davis, *Breckinridge*, 394–96. Davis argues that Bragg's account is incorrect in its claim of Breckinridge's intoxication.

38. OR 31, pt. 2, 35; Sword, *Mountains Touched with Fire*, 335–51; Cozzens, *Shipwreck of Their Hopes*, 370–86.

10. I WAS NEVER MORE DISGUSTED

1. OR 31, pt. 2, 35–36, 47, 49–50, 577; Grant, *Personal Memoirs*, 2:92–94; Sherman, *Memoirs*, 1:366–67; Committee of the Fifty-fifth Regiment, *Fifty-fifth Regiment Illinois Volunteer Infantry*, 290–91.

2. Orlando M. Poe, "The Defense of Knoxville," in Johnson and Buel, eds., *Battles and Leaders*, 3:745; Mary Boykin Chesnut, *Mary Chesnut's Civil War*, ed. C. Vann Woodward (New York: Book of the Month Club, 1994; originally published 1981), 495.

3. Poe, "Defense of Knoxville," 3:742–43; Edward Porter Alexander, *Fighting for the Confederacy: The Personal Recollections of General Edward Porter Alexander*, ed. Gary W. Gallagher (Chapel Hill: University of North Carolina Press, 1989), 327;

Longstreet, *From Manassas to Appomattox*, 497–98; Wert, *General James Longstreet*, 344–47.

4. OR 31, pt. 1, 484; Alexander, *Fighting for the Confederacy*, 322–23.

5. Alexander, *Fighting for the Confederacy*, 323; Longstreet, *From Manassas to Appomattox*, 501–2; Warner, *Generals in Gray*; Douglas Southall Freeman, *Lee's Lieutenants: A Study in Command*, 3 vols. (New York: Charles Scribner's Sons, 1942–44), 1:388–90; Wert, *General James Longstreet*, 348–49.

6. Alexander, *Fighting for the Confederacy*, 323–25.

7. OR 31, pt. 1, 460–61, 486–88; Alexander, *Fighting for the Confederacy*, 324–39; Poe, "Defense of Knoxville," 3:742–45; Longstreet, *From Manassas to Appomattox*, 503–7; Freeman, *Lee's Lieutenants*, 3:292–96; Wert, *General James Longstreet*, 349–53; Ralph Ely, *With the Wandering Regiment: The Diary of Captain Ralph Ely of the Eighth Michigan Infantry*, ed. George M. Blackburn (Mount Pleasant: Central Michigan University Press, 1965), 67.

8. Sherman, *Memoirs*, 1:367–68.

9. Alexander, *Fighting for the Confederacy*, 330–31.

11. THE DEATH KNELL OF THE CONFEDERACY

1. Jefferson Davis was one of the exceptions, though his ideas were never on a very grandiose scale. See Woodworth, *Jefferson Davis and His Generals*, 270–74.

2. See Woodworth, *Jefferson Davis and His Generals*.

3. Freeman, *Lee's Lieutenants*, 3:299–314; Chesnut, *Mary Chesnut's Civil War*, 509.

4. Parks, *General Leonidas Polk*, 348–86.

5. Woodworth, *Jefferson Davis and His Generals*, 261–64.

6. Cozzens, *Shipwreck of Their Hopes*, 391.

Bibliographical Essay

Many fine books deal with various parts of the struggle for control of Tennessee during late 1863. Peter Cozzens's *This Terrible Sound: The Battle of Chickamauga* (Urbana: University of Illinois Press, 1992) and *The Shipwreck of Their Hopes: The Battles for Chattanooga* (Urbana: University of Illinois Press, 1994) provide highly detailed accounts of those two contests. Steven E. Woodworth's *A Deep Steady Thunder: The Battle of Chickamauga* (Fort Worth: Ryan Place, 1996) and *This Grand Spectacle: The Battle of Chattanooga* (Fort Worth: Ryan Place, forthcoming) provide brief, fast-paced overviews of the battles. Two other accounts are available of the battles of Chattanooga, both excellent: James Lee McDonough's *Chattanooga—A Death Grip on the Confederacy* (Knoxville: University of Tennessee Press, 1984) and Wiley Sword's *Mountains Touched with Fire: Chattanooga Besieged, 1863* (New York: St. Martin's, 1995).

The characters in the struggle have also been the subject of fine works. David Donald's *Lincoln* (New York: Simon & Schuster, 1996) now dominates the landscape of Lincoln literature. Bruce Catton's *Grant Takes Command* (Boston: Little, Brown, 1968) includes an insightful and highly readable account of the Chattanooga campaign. Brooks D. Simpson's *Let Us Have Peace: Ulysses S. Grant and the Politics of War and Peace, 1861–1864* (Chapel Hill: University of North Carolina Press, 1991) gives a good sense of Grant's astuteness in political matters. John Marszalek's *Sherman: A Soldier's Passion for Order* (New York: Free Press, 1993) is the best book from which to gain an understanding of Grant's most trusted lieutenant. The best and most recent biographies of both Rosecrans and Thomas are still rather old: William M. Lamers, *The Edge of Glory: A Biography of General William S. Rosecrans, U.S.A.* (New York: Harcourt, Brace, & World, 1961), and Francis F. McKinney, *Education in Violence: The Life of George H. Thomas and the History of the Army of the Cumberland* (Detroit: Wayne State University Press, 1961). Both these officers are probably due for a reexamination.

Confederate generals in the western theater and their relationship with their commander in chief is the subject of Steven E. Woodworth's *Jefferson Davis and His Generals: The Failure of Confederate Command in the West* (Lawrence: University Press of

Kansas, 1990). Individual Confederate generals' biographies include Grady McWhiney and Judith Lee Hallock's joint effort, *Braxton Bragg and Confederate Defeat*. The second volume, by Hallock (Tuscaloosa: University of Alabama Press, 1991), covers the period dealt with in this work. A recent and fairly positive biography of Longstreet is Jeffry D. Wert's *General James Longstreet: The Confederacy's Most Controversial Soldier—A Biography* (New York: Simon & Schuster, 1993). A different view of Longstreet, in connection with his western operations, is provided by Judith Lee Hallock in *General James Longstreet in the West: A Monumental Failure* (Fort Worth: Ryan Place, 1995). William C. Davis's *Breckinridge: Statesman, Soldier, Symbol* (Baton Rouge: Louisiana State University Press, 1974) is the best biography of that officer. Joseph H. Parks's *General Leonidas Polk, C.S.A.: The Fighting Bishop* (Baton Rouge: Louisiana State University Press, 1962) is an overly sympathetic account, while Nathaniel Cheairs Hughes's *General William J. Hardee: Old Reliable* (Baton Rouge: Louisiana State University Press, 1965) is an excellent biography.

On the Confederate side, the armies have had their biographers too. Thomas Lawrence Connelly's *Army of the Heartland: The Army of Tennessee, 1861–1862* (Baton Rouge: Louisiana State University Press, 1968) and *Autumn of Glory: The Army of Tennessee, 1862–1865* (Baton Rouge: Louisiana State University Press, 1971) are monumental works on that army, though perhaps a bit overcritical and over-analytical. Richard McMurry's fine *Two Great Rebel Armies: An Essay in Confederate Military History* (Chapel Hill: University of North Carolina Press, 1989) is a fascinating comparison of the Army of Tennessee with the Army of Northern Virginia. The Union's armies, the Army of the Cumberland and the Army of the Tennessee, have had no recent historians (as units) and are due for some.

Accounts by individual soldiers and company officers are numerous and worthwhile. Probably the best accounts for the Northern side are Chesley A. Mosman's *The Rough Side of War: The Civil War Journal of Chesley A. Mosman, First Lieutenant, Company D, Fifty-ninth Illinois Volunteer Infantry Regiment* (Garden City NY: Basin, 1987) and James A. Connolly's *Three Years in the Army of the Cumberland: The Letters and Diary of Major James A. Connolly* (Bloomington: Indiana University Press, 1959). For the Confederate side the best reading is Samuel Watkins' *"Co. Aytch," Maury Grays, First Tennessee Regiment; or A Side Show of the Big Show* (Jackson TN: McCowat-Mercer Press, 1952).

Index